THE ART OF WRITING FOR PUBLICATION

Kenneth T. Henson
Eastern Kentucky University

Allyn and Bacon

Boston • London • Toronto • Sydney • Tokyo • Singapore

Copyright © 1995 by Allyn & Bacon
A Simon & Schuster Company
Needham Heights, Massachusetts 02194

Library of Congress Cataloging-in-Publication Data

Henson, Kenneth T.
     The art of writing for publication / Kenneth T. Henson
         p.   cm.
     Includes bibliographical references and index.
     ISBN 0–205–15769–6
     1. Authorship.   I. Title.
PN151.H446   1995
808´.02--dc20   94-26187
                                                                     C I P

Printed in the United States of America

10   9   8   7   6   5   4   3   2   98   97   96   95

Throughout the world people are struggling under pressure to produce articles in refereed journals as a requirement to earn tenure, promotion, or merit pay. But writing is a creative act, and fear and pressure contribute little to our creative efforts. On the contrary, we are most creative when we do those things at which we feel competent, those things we do well, those things we enjoy. This book is dedicated to all those professors who feel pressure to write for publication, and it is aimed at simplifying the process and making it easier and more enjoyable.

Contents

Illustrations

Preface

There are many genres of writing, but all can be grouped into two types, fiction and nonfiction. People who read fiction insist on being entertained. Those who read nonfiction often enjoy some entertainment, but they demand to be informed. I know this because I have been speaking to and writing for nonfiction audiences for over a decade, and my audiences always arrive with a definite purpose—to learn how to write for publication. I have only one choice; I must either meet this expectation or get out of the business. As a nonfiction writer, I face the same choice—either make good on my promises or stop writing.

In my years of speaking and administering large organizations, I have learned that people are complex, and the ways of grouping and identifying them are unlimited. One possible segmentation would be to view all people either as successes or failures. But the truth is that in some ways we are all successes, and in other ways we are all failures. The trick is to experience more of the first than of the second. The purpose of this book is to help you do just that.

In this book you will find a system that has worked for thousands of people. Yet, to work for you it will require your trust in its ability to do just that. More importantly, it will require trust in your own ability to develop the skills needed to succeed at the level you wish to succeed. Oscar Wilde said, "We are all in the gutter but some of us are looking up at the stars."

The sad news is that most people are content to stay in the gutter; some even take comfort in knowing that as long as they stay at the bottom they are safe from falling. The good news is that, by using this book and the often overlooked resource of "yourself," you can raise yourself to the heights that you choose.

This book is prescriptive, and I make no apology for that. Furthermore, like this preface, it is written in first and second person. I chose this style because I find it the clearest and most direct way to communicate. Robert Louis Stevenson has said that, "The job of the writer is not just to write but to write what you mean; not to affect your reader but to affect your reader precisely as you wish." My goal is to help you set and reach your personal and professional goals through writing for publication.

Kenneth T. Henson

Acknowledgments

I want to express my appreciation to the staff at Phi Delta Kappa for the opportunities they have given me to expand and improve my own writing program. Starting in 1984, former *Kappan* Editor Bob Cole and current *Kappan* Editor Pauline Gough have published all of my biennial surveys of journal editors in PDK's premier journal, the *Kappan*. Thanks to Derek Burleson, Special Publications Editor, for publishing my *Kappan* fastback *Writing for Professional Journals*.

A special thanks to Phil Harris who has provided many opportunities for me to take my writing workshop to campuses from Miami to San Diego and for asking me to develop and teach week-long, advanced summer writing institutes at Indiana University. Phil, thanks to you; of all the workshops we've done, there's never been a snare. Anyone who has attended a PDK biennial conference understands the precision, quality, and integrity that permeate the staff at Phi Delta Kappa. I thank all of you.

As every writer knows, producing a book requires a lot of word processing. I have been fortunate to have the assistance of an excellent secretary whose word processing skills are matched only by her patience. I appreciate Jennifer Martin's contribution to this book.

For their advice on this manuscript, I want to thank Bonnie Lass, Lesley College, Cambridge, MA; Robert G. Meyer, University of Louisville; and James P. Raffini, University of Wisconsin.

Finally, I want to acknowledge Mylan Jaixen and Sue Hutchinson at Allyn & Bacon for their dedication to this project and to Rebecca Boyter for making it an enjoyable experience. Thanks.

About the Author

Kenneth Henson received his B.S. from Auburn University, M.Ed. from the University of Florida, and Ed.D from the University of Alabama. He is dean at the College of Education at Eastern Kentucky University. His numerous books were published by Allyn & Bacon, D.C. Heath, F.E. Peacock, Harper Collins, Longman, Macmillan, McGraw-Hill, Merrill, National Educational Service, Sycamore Press, and Teachers College Press, and he has written articles for more than two dozen nationally circulated journals and magazines. In addition, Henson has received over $2 million in grants. He presents writing workshops throughout the United States.

If you do not write for publication,
there is little point in writing at all.

George Bernard Shaw

1

Why Write?

The first trip to Nassau was all anyone could want and more, considerably more. The tall coconut palms that graced the beaches, the small Christmas palms of uniform height and distance that lined the sidewalks, and the poinsettias in full, red bloom in January clouded the memory of the immediate past filled with dark morning drives to work and old snow—black, carbon-coated snow—and grey skies.

But the shock of the change paled with the start brought by the flip of the motel room light. A two-foot iguana had also sought a room and had rested itself below the cool window air conditioner.

Dozens of memorable trips would follow, trips to Nassau on Paradise Island and trips to Freeport on the Grand Bahama Island. A few of these trips would be eventful enough to be remembered, such as the day of the iguana and the day we were deplaned at the Miami Airport. The rumor we heard was that the police had received a bomb threat, entered the plane with a couple of German Shepherd dogs, and removed from the plane not *a* bomb but *two* bombs. As we wondered about a possible third bomb, the flight to Nassau that morning was memorable.

And then there was the time that the huge L1011 plane reached the edge of the Bermuda Triangle and for seemingly no reason at all began an immediate fall, plummeting like a lead weight almost to the water. Unlike other white-knuckle flights where people get giddy with laughter, on this flight nobody was laughing. Instead, people were screaming and grabbing each other's arms and hands.

Yes, such times were memorable, and they still are. But these were isolated events. Most of the experiences became routine. The palm trees, the poinsettias, and the dark blue waters that turned a beautiful light green near the white, sandy shores all became routine and soon were ignored. But the Bahamas offered one thing that would never be ignored or taken for granted. This was the people who inhabited the islands. Some were natives; others were temporary residents, most having come from the former or current colonies of Great Britain. This was evident in their British accents. (It is also a safe generalization, because at one time over half of the world was under the British Empire.)

The Bahamians are warm and hospitable. At Christmas they showered me with gifts. Have you ever passed through customs with bottles of rum or frozen lobsters? A jigger of coconut rum put into a batch of pancake mix fills your house with a wonderful aroma. But the quality that made these people so special to me was partially due to my role, for I was their teacher. Although I had lived and taught in the Mother Country, where I discovered an appreciation for books that I had never before seen, I had never witnessed such an unquenchable thirst for knowledge. The year was 1975, and the Bahamas had declared its independence just two years earlier. As a developing nation, these people knew that the only way they could prosper was through education. Each Saturday, I lectured for eight hours. Throughout the day, and even at the end of each day, the entire class was literally hanging onto the edge of their chairs as they reached out mentally and firmly grasped every concept and every word.

As you read these words, they may be meaningless to you. But to me they are my life, and I shall continue to treasure them. Only at writing workshops do I experience the level of intensity that I found in the Bahamas. Only at writing workshops am I able to relate so personally with other kindred spirits who share my excitement. For I know what they want; I know what it can do for them; and I am determined to deliver it.

REASONS TO WRITE

People can be placed in two groups: the talkers and the doers. Some people enjoy just sitting around talking about writing, telling why they don't write for publication. One person said that he doesn't write for publication because "there are just too many mediocre books and articles out there, and I don't want to associate with mediocrity." Others talk a lot about the writing they plan to do, but they never seem to get around to it. Then there are the doers. Often the big difference between the two groups is that *serious writers have specific goals to reach through their writing.*

Initially you may not be able to articulate these goals for fear that you may never reach them or for fear that others might be critical; but few goals are ever reached before they become clear to their pursuers. And, for this reason, those who are serious about becoming writers must clarify at least to themselves their own reasons for writing.

Unlike being a student or working for a supervisor or boss, writers usually don't have people to spur them on. The world is full of people who dream about becoming something they aren't but who haven't the initiative to do the work that must be done to become whatever they wish to become. Most people who aspire to become writers are aware of some of the benefits of writing. They know that when you are a writer you are very much your own boss. You can decide *what* you want to write, *when* you want to write it, and even *where* you want to write. Authors can even choose their audiences. Writing offers opportunity to earn recognition. Few professionals enjoy more admiration than successful writers. Most people also know that *writing offers authors an opportunity to apply their creative talents.* When you write, you invent; and then you share your creation with as many others as possible. *Our society places much value on creativity.*

On university campuses professors write to share their research findings, to promote their disciplines. For the most fortunate, dissertations and theses become lifetime pursuits. These professors use their publications to disseminate their findings, thereby contributing to the advancement of their professions.

Some people find that writing helps them clarify their own thinking. As strange as it may sound, they write to find out what they think and to remove inconsistencies in their own thinking. Some professional people, like college professors, are told that they must publish before they can earn tenure, promotions, or merit pay. But writing is a proactive endeavor, and nobody can be forced to write. People write because they choose to.

Still others choose to write to earn money. Our society has moved through a period when the main thrust of individuals was to compete with the Joneses, earning more money and buying more goods. Then our society experienced a period when the major thrust was to join and support group movements. Today, the greatest trend among our population is for individuals to improve their own talents and capabilities. Many people write to improve themselves. In their book *Megatrends 2000,* Naisbitt and Aburdene (1990) offer ten megatrends to the twenty-first century. Among these is the triumph of the individual. The authors say:

> *The great unifying theme at the conclusion of the 20th century is the triumph of the individual. . . . [I]t is the individual who creates a work of art, embraces a political philosophy, bets a life's savings on a new business, inspires a colleague or a family member to succeed, immigrates to a new country, has a transcendental spiritual experience. It is an individual who changes himself or herself before attempting to change society. (p. 298)*

Writing is an empowering activity. Many individuals enjoy the power they derive from writing and the power derived from subsequent publication.

For example, professors enjoy the respect they get from colleagues and students when their articles and books are used in classes. Business people enjoy the power that writing gives them within their organizations. Perhaps the most meaningful empowerment is internal. Having a manuscript accepted for publication is evidence of your power; just knowing that your article has been approved by a national panel of experts in your field reassures you that you are on the cutting edge.

Often scholars view publication as a way to contribute to their professions. Some say that throughout their school years they took from the profession and that now, having completed their education, it is time to give knowledge back. Writing for publication provides a means for rendering this service. Professional people who hold this philosophy do not need the pressure of earning tenure, promotions, or merit pay to motivate them to write for publication. Perhaps this explains why many seasoned professionals, including retirees, continue writing and attending writing workshops. Incidentally, most participants in a recent week-long Phi Delta Kappa summer Writing for Publication workshop at Indiana University were retirees. Some entrepreneurs write to promote their businesses. For example, a realtor may write an article for a realtors' journal or the director of a medical clinic may write to publicize successful use of innovative approaches.

Some professionals see writing for publication as essential to their grant writing efforts. For example, one group of engineers whose entire profession is grant writing asked for a special workshop. They had two reasons. First, they wanted to improve their technical writing skills. Second, they wanted to increase their visibility through publication in professional journals because they knew that this would further enhance the acceptance of the group's future proposals.

Physicians, nurses, and nurse educators attend many of these workshops. They feel a need to share their expertise with their colleagues throughout the country. Clearly, many individuals write for publication because they anticipate benefits both to themselves and to others.

I asked some contemporary writers why they write. Here are their responses.

As a medical records administrator, I contributed articles to our local and state newsletters and to our national journal. Since becoming a dean, my writing efforts are devoted to technical pieces, employer-mandated documents, and correspondence. Although this type of writing is not for publication in the real sense of the word, the time and effort that goes into it and the tools I use are much the same as one would use for a magazine or journal article or even a book.

I have been a dean for five plus years now and have a few good articles in me from this new profession of mine. I find it much easier to write from experience, write from "What you know."

Yvonne Bergland, Dean
School of Mathematical/
Social and Natural Sciences
San Diego Mesa College
San Diego, California

The reason I write for publication is fairly simple: I occasionally have something to say—some idea or set of related ideas that organizes itself in my mind and stays there until I do something with it. When you have a good idea, it doesn't seem right to keep it to yourself.

Richard Burke, Professor
Educational Psychology
Bowling Green State University
Bowling Green, Ohio

My fourth-grade teacher, Mrs. Goldberg in P.S. 66, The Bronx (New York City) was the reason I began writing. I still remember that very first poem I ever wrote (at age nine):
    Eskimo-land with its icy cold snow
    And its high bold winds that always blow,
    The seal and the walrus, the polar bear too,
    The arctic fox and the caribou,
    They all live in Eskimo-land!
Higher education is the perfect "home" for someone of my ilk. We are rewarded for research and publications, and those may be what I do best. Thirteen books and 300 published articles later, I remember Mrs. Goldberg and how she released—or created the opportunity for development of—a talent I might never have realized.

Rita Dunn, Professor
Center for the Study of Learn-
ing and Teaching Styles
St. John's University
Jamaica, New York

Regardless of their discipline, many professors enjoy the craft of writing. As they continue writing they gradually but consistently hone this craft until it becomes an art. Elliot Eisner cherishes the opportunity that writing provides him to improve his thinking and his expression.

I write for publication because it is through the process of writing that my own ideas get clarified and revised. When one is speaking, words have a very short life. In the process of writing, they are fixed on paper and they can be modified, expanded, and made more potent. In a sense, writing is an artistic activity in which matters of voice, precision, transition, and organization are critical. In fact, as a former painter, I see in writing a process analogous to painting: I am interested in creating an aesthetically coherent, insightful, and cogent statement. Painters too are interested in such an outcome.

Thus, for me writing is a way of learning to think more rigorously about ideas that I possess or want to develop. In fact, the act of writing is an invitation to discovery, to the location of new intellectual seas on which to sail. It is an act of exploration that provides the satisfactions that come from trying to make something beautiful.

Elliot W. Eisner, Professor
Education and Art
Stanford University
Stanford, California

Jesus Garcia uses writing as a way to draw others into his area of professional interests.

I write for publication because I believe I have insights from my teaching experiences and work at the university that might be of interest to the educational community. While I attempt to write to a wide audience, I keep the classroom teacher in mind when I develop a manuscript.

I was encouraged to write for publication soon after finishing my dissertation. One of my doctoral committee members suggested that I should be able to "squeeze out at least one article from my dissertation." At that time little was written in the area of multicultural education. Because I believed I had something to contribute, I decided to carve a niche in this area. If I have any national exposure, I would say it is in the area of "evaluation of curriculum materials (i.e., textbooks and tradebooks) for the portrayal of societal groups."

Jesus Garcia
Department of Curriculum and
Instruction
College of Education
University of Illinois
Champaign, Illinois

Writing has a degree of permanency that many professors enjoy. Editor David Gilman appreciates this quality.

As a practitioner I had a lot of ideas, ideas that were important, and I wanted to share them. I thought you had to have a Ph.D. and teach at a university to get things published. Now that I am editor of a national magazine, I realize that articles written by practitioners can be extremely valuable.

Writing also helps me clarify my thinking. Often, after I've written a sentence or paragraph, I find myself reading it back and saying, "I didn't know that." I really did know it but the writing helped me realize it.

Articles that are written and published are then indexed and will influence students, practitioners, and administrators forever.

David Gilman, Professor
and Editor
Contemporary Education
Indiana State University
Terre Haute, Indiana

Researchers appreciate writing for the means it provides them to reflect on their own thoughts and mistakes. Thomas Good explains.

Writing for professional publication provides an opportunity to conceptualize, explore, and on occasion reformulate one's understanding of a topic. It presents an opportunity to consider what one understands and perhaps more importantly to confront one's misconceptions and one's limits. Writing is often frustrating, tedious, and forced. At other times it is spontaneous and rewarding. However, it is always the perfect medium for self-reflection and professional growth.

Thomas L. Good, Professor
Educational Psychology
University of Arizona
Tucson, Arizona

While research is a part of every professor's responsibility, some professors prefer working with people. Such professors, like Dave Hanson, may prefer applied research and writing over empirical research and esoteric writing.

At the outset I must say I'm much more a practitioner than an academician. I'm into applied psychology more than scientific psychology. Thus, research and publication is not my forte, but working with people is. When I do write, it's because, as a trainer of school psychologists, I want to comment on or share my thoughts about information, issues, or techniques that I think might be especially meaningful to other persons . . . like practicing school psychologists, or trainers, or students. In other words, my goal might be to disseminate information more broadly in order to advance the state of the art of offering help to pupils, parents, and teachers. For *instance, I read a book on intelligence by Robert Sternberg and subsequently wrote a review of it because I thought others would find his work informative and helpful. My values are more person-centered than science-entered.*

I might add that, as a managing editor of a professional journal, I help others get their works into print. (My background as an undergraduate English major comes into play here!)

Dave Hanson, Professor
Department of Psychology
James Madison University
Harrisonburg, Virginia

While many professors choose to write because of the opportunity it offers to clear out the cobwebs, some describe writing as an inquiry process.

Publishing allows one's ideas to be examined critically; to be tested and affirmed or refuted. No other form of communication of ideas allows for such critical examination. Herein lies the real essence of publication, that of inquiry. Writing as scholarship is directed toward understanding of the nature of the world; whether that be the physical world or the world of human thoughts, we strive to elucidate that which we cannot fully understand. To do so we extend and refine theories, we propose new directions for research, we argue regarding perspectives on the world all in an attempt to understand.

Finally, and personally, writing provides coherence and insight into one's own thoughts. While writing can be a painful process, it forces individuals to critically examine their ideas. Writing creates a forum within which thoughts must be organized, refined, deleted, rearranged, and finally presented for scrutiny. Writing forces critical review as well as creative production; it is the essence of scholarship; it provides for growth; it is thought.

Steven M. Hoover,
Associate Professor
Educational Psychology
St. Cloud State University
St. Cloud, Minnesota

Some professors use writing as a means of joining the rest of their professional group to explore their professional frontier beyond its current limits.

I write on topics about which I have strong feelings. Usually, I am frustrated that the world in general does not see things the way I see them, so

I attempt to communicate what I believe is an important message and hopefully to have some influence on research, policy, or practice. I also see writing as a way to interact with the top thinkers and writers in my field and to push our collective thinking a few steps further.

My personal goal is to write in a very straightforward way that helps people see in a new way things they deal with on a daily basis. It's always nice when someone says "I've read a lot of your stuff," but it is really rewarding when they say, "Your work is really helpful and clear. It really tells it just the way it is." When this happens, I feel like maybe I am contributing a unique piece of the puzzle and that makes it worth the time and energy it takes to develop a really comprehensive piece of writing.

Leslie Huling-Austin,
Director
LBJ Institute for the Improvement of Teaching and Learning
School of Education
Southwest Text State University
San Marcos, Texas

Some writers claim that they do not enjoy writing. Like Mary Renck Jalongo, they are willing to suffer the pain to enjoy the rewards at the other end.

Allow me to clear up two common misconceptions about what motivates authors. First, most people believe that "all authors just like to write." Not me. I do not enjoy the writing process any more than a passenger in a small aircraft looks forward to turbulence. The pleasure comes from a safe arrival, not in the travel. Second, I don't find writing easy. Most of the time, it is difficult—yet, its perpetual challenging holds my interest. Each time I attempt to communicate with a different audience, to write in another style, or to achieve some new purpose, I find new obstacles to overcome.

My personal reasons for writing fall into two categories; selfish and social. On the selfish side, I write because writing enables me to discover new things, express my feelings, clarify my thinking, improve my teaching, and participate in the ongoing dialogue published in professional journals and books.

On the social side, writing is sharing as I think aloud and along with other writers. Pieces of writing are often vehicles for mentorship as I draw upon my experience to offer guidance and encouragement to other authors. One great social reward of authorship is the esteem of colleagues and stu-

dents. I feel humble or yet proud when someone says, "I read your article and it just flows. I want to be able to write like that."

Mary Renck Jalongo,
Professor
College of Education
Indiana University of
Pennsylvania
Indiana, Pennsylvania

Over the years, a process that many pursue out of a sense of duty can become enjoyable. Elaine Jarchow has experienced this change.

When I began my career in higher education 18 years ago, I wrote because I truly believed that I could advance the curriculum theory knowledge base. My training at Kent State University, my exposure to curriculum reconceptualist thinking, and my experience as a liberal '60s secondary English teacher led me to believe that I would influence both theory and practice. My first publication in Curriculum Inquiry *was the result of several revisions—revisions, I would never have undertaken had the editor not signed his letter, "Be encouraged." Of course, in those early years, I also wrote to be promoted.*

Today I write because I like to, and I write about international education because that is now my focus. Most of my publications are neither research nor theory based; they fall into the wisdom or how-to category. I believe that I can influence the field by suggesting ways to internationalize the teacher education curriculum.

Elaine Jarchow, Dean
College of Education
Texas Tech University
Lubbock, Texas

Librarians like Leah McIlvain and others enjoy writing because it expands their knowledge to other disciplines.

Not only does writing for publication keep me current with what is taking place in my profession, it also enables me to branch off into other disciplines which hold special interest for me. Writing for publication also helps me serve as a role model for my colleagues, to encourage them that, if I can write, then they can as well.

Leah McIlvain, Librarian
Model Laboratory School
Richmond, Kentucky

All of these goals are worthwhile and admirable. As some have confessed, writing is hard work. At times it is lonely. So, if you are going to spend your time writing, do it right and make it pay off. *The main purpose of this book is to help you prepare to write articles and books that will get published.* These are immensely practical objectives and, as long as your writing is honest, they are perfectly honorable reasons for learning to write. This book is written for people who are committed to self-improvement and who want to enhance their professional and personal lives.

But even people who write for such practical reasons as earning merit pay and royalties must acknowledge that some people seek to learn to write because they hold a deep respect for the beauty that lives in eloquent writing. Pragmatists may question the wisdom of spending their time and energy with only the goal of making something pretty; yet, even they can appreciate knowing that others are willing to devote their writing to this end. To conclude that writers of prose seek only this end would be wrong. Many of the most eloquent writers have deep-seated purposes, and they use their writing skills to achieve these purposes. For example, we should appreciate the forceful nature of Eric Severied's writing. When he wrote the following lines, he had been serving as news correspondent from the beginning of the United States' involvement in World War II (Severied, 1976, pp. 497–498):

> The last battle would be fought just across the river. . . . The Germans did not know that this was the last day when the endless war would still be a war. Tomorrow the great German raid against the human race would be all over save for the meaningless odds and ends. . . . The whole situation was selfishly satisfying, and I savored it. I, an ordinary man with a name and origin of which Caesar (Hitler) was ignorant, was standing a couple hundred yards from his camp knowing the secret of his fate and the fate of his empire. And he didn't know. I, one of his intended slaves, was so much mightier than he. I, who had never kicked a Jew, or looted a village, or burned a bank, or stolen a country, or killed anything larger than a hare, was standing with empty hands looking into his final citadel, possessed of the biggest, brightest fact in this moment in eternity—the fact that the terror and tyranny of our times would come to an end this night. . . . Now that I am here, I'll represent the whole human race, all the millions of people who haven't done the things Caesar has done.

These few lines reveal the awesome power that rests in the hands of a skilled writer. Few activities offer us power to represent the entire human race. Writing does even more; the skilled writer can actually change the values and the behaviors of thousands or even millions of people.

If you value writing enough to pursue it, as you probably do if you are reading this, you will appreciate the words that John Steinbeck set to paper when he was asked to deliver a speech to the Kansas State Teachers Association (1959, p. 71).

My eleven-year-old son came to me recently and, in a tone of patient suffering, asked, "How much longer do I have to go to school?"

"About fifteen years," I said.

"Oh! Lord," he said despondently. "Do I have to?"

"I'm afraid so. It's terrible and I'm not going to try to tell you it isn't. But I can tell you this—if you are very lucky, you may find a teacher and that is a wonderful thing."

"Did you find one?"

"I found three," I said.

My three had these things in common—they all loved what they were doing. They did not tell—they catalayzed a burning desire to know. . . .

I shall speak only of my first teacher because, in addition to other things, she was very precious.

She aroused us to shouting, bookwaving discussion. She had the noisiest class in school and didn't even seem to know it. We could never stick to the subject, geometry or the chanted recitation of the memorized phyla.

Our speculation ranged the world. She breathed curiosity into us so that we brought in facts or truths shielded in our hands like captured fireflies.

She left her signature on us, the signature of the teacher who writes on minds. I suppose that, to a large extent, I am the unsigned manuscript of that high school teacher. What deathless power lies in the hands of such a person.

I can tell my son who looks forward with horror to fifteen years of drudgery that somewhere in the dusty dark a magic may happen that will light up the years, if he is very lucky. . . .

I have come to believe that a great teacher is a great artist, and there are as few as there are any other great artists. It might even be the greatest of the arts since the medium is the human mind and spirit.

Steinbeck knew how to hold on to the reader's attention. Equally important is the ability to grab the attention of today's busy readers. In his opening lines of *A Tale of Two Cities*, Dickens shows his ability to grab and hold readers' attention.

It was the best of times, it was the worst of times, it was the age of wisdom, it was the age of foolishness, it was the epoch of belief, it was the epoch of incredulity, it was the season of light, it was the season of darkness, it was the spring of hope, it was the winter of despair, we had everything before us, we had nothing before us, we were all going direct to Heaven, we were all going the other way.

A special chapter is included in this book to help you develop this skill.

At the beginning of *The Auctioneer,* Joan Samson (1975) used her words like an artist who carefully manipulates a brush to paint a picture. Her picture is full of motion and details.

> The fire rose in a perfect cone as if suspended by the wisp of smoke that ascended in a straight line to the high spring sky. Mim and John dragged whole dry saplings from the brush pile by the stone wall and heaved them into the flames, stepping back quickly as the dead leaves caught with a hiss.
>
> Four-year-old Hildie heard the truck coming even before the old sheep dog did. She scampered to the edge of the road and waited impatiently. It was Gore's truck, moving fast, rutting deeply in the mud and throwing up a spray on either side. John and Mim converged behind Hildie, each taking stock of what might be wrong to bring the police chief out to the last farm on the road.
>
> Bob Gore swung himself out and hooked his thumbs in the pocket of his jeans. He shifted from foot to foot for a moment as if his great belly were seeking a point of equilibrium. Gore had a taste for two things—trouble and gossip. By either route, he could talk away an afternoon without half trying. John glanced over his shoulder at the fire. (pp. 7–8)

Somewhere out there, someone may learn to write as eloquently as John Steinbeck, as forcefully as Charles Dickens, or as descriptively as Joan Samson. But most of us will never reach those superb levels of writing. Fortunately, though, you don't have to write eloquently or elegantly to become a successful writer and reach your goals. This book stresses simple, direct, and clear writing. The experts know that such skills give the author the ability to write assertively and forcefully. *This book provides the knowledge and opportunities needed to become a highly skilled author.* We should all take comfort in knowing that there are always good markets for important information that is clearly written.

Although the pay-offs for writing are clear, the investment one makes to become a writer is far less frequently understood. Writing is hard work even to those who enjoy it. It requires self-discipline and self-denial. Becoming a successful, published writer requires becoming a good writer. Publishing is a buyer's market, and the writer is the seller. In publishing, the supply always far exceeds the demand. Publishers are always flooded with manuscripts, many of which are mediocre or worse, but there are always enough good ones to make writing for publication a competitive activity. To succeed, you must compete with and outperform many others who are just as bright and just as knowledgeable as you. The one saving grace is that few would-be writers are willing to invest the time and energy required to transform their mediocre skills into the sharp, refined skills required to compete in this buyer's market. For this reason all serious writers should rejoice. By taking time to develop sharp skills and by taking time to revise, improve, and polish your manuscripts, *you can dramatically increase your odds of succeeding.*

With today's hectic schedules, most writers find the answer to their need for more time in their ability to improve their self-discipline. Elaine Jarchow writes:

> *When I have a writing task—a grant proposal or an article—I know that I must engage in rigorous self-discipline to find the time to write. My obligations as associate dean, consultant, wife, and mother don't leave much writing time. I find my writing time from 4 to 6 A.M. I try to retire by 10 P.M. and arise promptly at 4 A.M. I proceed immediately to the dining room table where the writing space is organized (my books, supplementary materials, pens, pencils, scissors, paper clips, and paper) are all arranged symmetrically in neat piles the night before! I begin writing immediately. These early morning hours are great for me—no interruptions take place, and I produce text quickly and effortlessly. Although there are two computers in our den and although I am certainly computer literate, I produce my important writing pieces in longhand. I genuinely love seeing my pen move across the page, switching from print to cursive, crossing out, and drawing arrows to insertions. I also love delivering the text to my efficient secretary who quickly produces the computer printout.*
>
> *At 6 A.M. I take a 30-minute walk; then, I shower, awaken my daughter and proceed into the day. I also use all-day Saturday and Sunday marathons to complete a writing task. Of course, this "dining room" approach means we can't have dinner guests until I finish the task!*

Others find writing so stimulating that for them it seems to demand the necessary time. Rita Dunn has said,

> *It's what I like to do most. I can come home exhausted at 10 P.M. after a long, stressful day, feel as if I can't wait to get into a hot bath and bed, but sit down at the computer and, three hours later, realize the time . . . , but keep going until 4 A.M. At that point, common sense dictates that I have to get up in the morning and* must *get some sleep!*

A TIME AND PLACE FOR EVERYTHING

A well-known verse in the Old Testament says that there is a time for everything. Writing is no exception. Knowing where and when to apply your energy to this pursuit strongly affects your degree of success. My work with hundreds of aspiring writers in dozens of workshops and courses has produced many excellent questions. Of these many questions, the most frequently asked (and one of the most difficult to answer) is, How do you find time to write? In fact, this question was so frequently asked that it prompted me to write an article, "How to Find the Time You Need," for *The National Businesswoman.*

When we speak of "finding time," we are implying that time is a tangible object. When we travel, we speak of *making up* time that was *lost* because of mechanical failures or inclement weather. Actually, time—perhaps the most valuable commodity of all—is never created by humans, nor is it found. Usually, when we say that we should find time to do something, what we mean is that we should give that activity more of our attention. To do this we must learn to schedule our activities more carefully and assign more time to those activities that are most important.

The remark, I don't have time to write, actually means I have committed all of my time to other things or I have not yet learned how to effectively budget my writing time. Surely, in our busy world, this is no strange feeling to any of us. Yet, at this juncture you must make a decision. You must either choose to continue doing all the things that you are currently doing, in which case you should dismiss the idea of writing, or you must carefully examine your weekly calendar and *replace some of the less important activities with writing for publication.* (This may mean giving up an hour a day in the coffee room.) For most of us it requires giving up a few hours of television each week.

Once individuals do replace a few of these passive activities with writing, they often realize that the activities that were chosen to relax them are far less relaxing than writing. Paradoxically, *writing for publication is both exhilarating and relaxing.* Have you ever noticed that, after a hard day's work, an evening spent in front of the television leaves you exhausted? Why? Because you weren't so much physically tired as emotionally drained; and passive recovery is slow. Writing is different. It puts your brain in gear, enabling your frayed nerves to heal. Writers say that writing stimulates them mentally while relaxing them emotionally. Writing is good therapy; it lets you express yourself. Trading an evening of reruns for an evening of writing may be the best decision you've made in a long time.

WHEN IS THE BEST TIME TO WRITE?

Some writers do most of their work late at night, while others prefer to get up very early and write for a few hours before the day's obligations begin. Some writers carefully schedule a combination of mornings, afternoons, and evenings. Your own schedule should be determined by first considering your personal preferences. If you begin nodding and dozing off by 8 or 9 P.M., you should try to schedule your writing at other times. But, if you are the type who likes to stay up late and sleep late, an evening writing schedule will probably suit you best.

Next, check your daily obligations. Your present job may dictate that some times are unavailable for you to write. (Don't worry. Some of the most prolific writers are shut off from writing between 8 and 5 P.M. daily). You may have to block out time for carpooling children to and from school, helping with homework, preparing meals, cleaning the house, washing the clothes, or cutting the grass. Consider whether you need large blocks of time and whether you need to be free from noise or disruptions. Such concerns may restrict the *quality* times available to you for writing to late evenings or early mornings.

One final but important suggestion. *Be realistic about the amount of time you set aside for writing, and then, honor your commitment.* Save time for tennis, or golf, or exercise, or reading, or watching a special television show. If you are married, ask for the support of other family members. Let everyone know your writing schedule, and, when the phone rings during your assigned writing time, let someone else answer it. Instruct your family members to say that you are not free to come to the phone if the call is for you. Other disruptions—such as uninvited guests, door-to-door salespeople, or charity workers—can destroy your writing time. Taking time to solicit your family's cooperation can help ward off such interruptions from the outside and will impress on your own family members the importance of their respect for your writing time.

In the following passages, Robert Maddox tells about his strategies for getting time to write.

> *Finding time to write is one of the toughest parts of writing. I have found that it helps to set aside blocks locks of time that are devoted exclusively to writing. When I make up my schedule for the upcoming semester, I will block my calendar out for class times, office hours, and also blocks of time (minimum of one-half day in a block) just for writing. It is much easier, if I have committed myself to these time periods, to "stay on schedule."*
>
> *If I am writing in my office, I close the door and put the phone on voice mail only. That way, it doesn't ring, but I know that I won't miss any important calls. I also use a beeper type pager which my family uses if they have an urgent reason to reach me.*
>
> *I do, however, maintain a faculty study in the library just for writing, and try to do nearly all of my writing there. It has no telephone and no name on the door. I have it equipped with a computer and printer. I have a similar computer in my office and another at home so that I can move to*

the office if the library is closed (weekend, evenings, holidays, etc.), and
also continue working at home, just by carrying a diskette with me. (I used
to lug around a portable computer, which was a real chore.)

Robert Maddox
Department of Management
College of Business
Administration
University of Tennessee-
Knoxville
Knoxville, Tennessee

Many writers do not have easy access to even one computer or to an
answering machine. But, when available, this equipment and a hideaway
office can make a major difference in an author's level of productivity. Perhaps you have found other ways to make your writing easier.

In addition to planning writing time into their weekly schedule, successful writers know how to capture additional valuable writing time. A
writing friend who lives in New York and frequently travels to the West
Coast has been accused of praying for delays. For her, the airport becomes a
writing office. Such discipline has led this professor, housewife, and mother
of six children to author some 20 books and 200 articles. Other writers take
similar advantage of the time spent commuting to work on trains and planes.

TOOLING UP THE JOB

Having a definite amount of time set aside each week is indispensable to
most successful writers. Yet, the success of these writing sessions hinges on
the writer's having the proper tools for the intended job. The importance of
having the proper tools available is easy to understand if you have ever
tried to repair a machine or cook a meal without the necessary equipment.

People often ask me what tools I consider essential for my office. I usually flinch a little and then remind them that the tools that one writer considers essential may offer no value to other writers. When pressed further, I
give the following list of tools which, in addition to office supplies, proper
lighting, and solitude, some writers consider staples for their offices:

1. Typewriter or word processor
2. Dictionary
3. Thesaurus
4. Book of Quotations
5. Books in the writer's special field of study
6. Journals in the writer's special field of study

7. Style manuals (e.g., *The Chicago Manual of Style, American Psycholog-ical Association Manual,* 3rd ed.)
8. Grammar books (e.g., *The Elements of Style* by W. R. Strunk, Jr., and E. B. White)
9. Publishers' Guides
10. Scissors
11. Tape and dispenser
12. Tack-it-tabs

A writer friend, Doug Brooks (a professor at Miami University of Ohio), explained the significance of having these tools on hand at the time he sits down to write. To him, "writing is like digging a well by hand." As you dig deeper and deeper, you must begin everyday by climbing down into the well and then climbing back out of the well when you are done for the day. Much energy and time are spent entering and exiting the well; therefore, the efficient well digger will be sure to have all the necessary tools waiting at the bottom of the well. Likewise, *the writer must have all the necessary tools waiting.* As trite as this may appear, having to leave the office to sharpen a pencil or fetch paper or a dictionary often leads to diversions that delay and prevent the writer from getting on with the real task at hand—writing.

THE BEST PLACE TO WRITE

The more I think about my library, the more I realize that it is unique and critical to me in my writing. First, it contains those resources with which I am very familiar. For example, I have those textbooks that I used during my doctoral program. Because I had not done my undergraduate or masters work at the institution where I was pursuing my doctorate, I knew absolutely no one on the faculty. Recognizing that many of my classmates had already earned two degrees at this university and being aware that many of them knew our professors as friends and knew which researchers and authors would be stressed in classes and on exams, I needed a strategy to even the odds for my success. By inquiring, I learned which textbooks were most widely used in each of the four areas covered by my forthcoming qualifying exams. I chose the two most widely used texts in each area and spent ten hours a day for one full semester virtually memorizing these books. When exam time came, I was prepared to quote those authors and studies that were so familiar to the professors who would be constructing and scoring my qualifying exams.

The preparation process was so successful that I began tutoring the next class of doctoral students, preparing them for the educational psychology part of the qualifying exam. The adage, "to teach is to learn twice," took on a new meaning. Needless to say, I became so well versed on this content area and so familiar with these textbooks that I will never forget much of this material. This is my best library of all; it is by far the most accessible because it's in my head. To make it even more valuable, I keep those source books in my library, and I still quote the classic studies found in them. What I am suggesting here is that you search out those books that are special to you and make them part of your library.

There is another unique aspect to my library. Each time I receive a professional journal or a research report, I scan it to identify areas of interest. Because I write on curriculum, educational psychology, teaching methods, and writing, I scan the table of contents for such topics. When I find one, I flag it with a tack-it tab and write the subject on the tab. Then, I shelve my journals with the open side outward. This means that I can sit at my desk and pull every resource that I own on any given topic—and this is exactly what I do when I begin writing an article or book chapter. In two minutes I am able to place all of my sources of information on any topic on my working table. I do this before writing a single word. So, when I do start writing, I can write for hours without even getting out of my chair.

Though you may not have shared my way of preparing for doctoral exams, chances are good that you became very familiar with a substantial body of knowledge in your field. This familiarity makes the content even more valuable, but only if you develop a system that permits you to use it. My system works for me. You may have already developed a system that works for you.

Whether you use a highlighter pen to accentuate the major points in everything you read, you keep files of quotes to use over and over again, or you develop a computerized database on your computer, your personal library will undoubtedly be your most powerful resource as a writer. Alter it in any way that will make it more "user friendly."

The exact location of your office may be dictated by several physical realities. For example, your house or apartment may be too small to accommodate writing at home, or a young child may render your home environment impossible for serious writing. Or you may not own the reference books and journals that you need when you write, making a local library the best writing space for you. Some writers use more than one location to write. These writers have a portable office housed in their briefcase. The number of portable offices has increased by severalfold in the last decade. The next time you are on a plane or commuter train notice the number of workers who carry their office in their briefcases.

My grandmother, whom we all affectionately called Mama, was a woman of great determination. When Mama made up her mind to have something, she had it—*her* way. There were at least two problems, however. The first was that her grandchildren were responsible for delivering on whatever she had decided. The other problem was that, once Mama set her determined mind on a target, she had an unsurpassed capacity for changing her mind.

Mama's greatest single source of indecisiveness was hats; so, whenever she mentioned that word "hat," her grandchildren disappeared for days. On one occasion my cousin and I were a little slow on the escape, and we ended up driving six miles to town for a hat Mama had seen in a display window. But by the time we drove to town and back, she had decided that the hat was just plain wrong for her. We dutifully returned it—only to have her regret sending it back. We made a third trip to town—and a fourth. Having traveled 48 miles, we arrived back on her front porch—with no hat!

Because most of us need more time than we currently have to write and we never know when we will be asked to make trips like the one I just described, many writers keep notepads and writing tablets in their vehicles. When asked to drive someone to the mall or elsewhere, the notepads are available to jot down ideas for topics or to make a quick and crude outline of a forthcoming article. Writing books and writing journals are also excellent topic sources and should be kept in the car or on the nightstand for idle reading.

For example, I had driven my son downtown to the music store to take a guitar lesson. While there, I was thumbing through a list of Reasons People Give for Not Writing. Noticing that the list contains some false beliefs or myths, I got the idea for an article. While waiting for my son to take his guitar lesson, I wrote an article titled "Six Myths That Haunt Writers." When I returned home, I wrote a query to *The Writer,* a favorite journal for professional writers. Sylvia Burack, editor of *The Writer,* liked the topic, so I sent her the manuscript "on inspection" (which means she was not obligated to accept it). Had she rejected it, I had identified two other journals for which this manuscript would have been appropriate.

Ms. Burack decided to use my article in a column called "The Rostrum" in the *The Writer.* That column usually includes short pieces that provide practical tips from authors. Although I would have preferred to have it appear as a feature article, I was happy to have it included in "The Rostrum"— especially when I learned later that it had been selected with articles by Dick Francis, Stephen King, Sidney Sheldon, and Mary Higgins Clark as one of the best 100 articles of the year. *The Writer's Handbook* also published this piece, placing it midway between articles by Stephen King and Sidney Sheldon. Not bad company for a writer who spent less than an hour drafting the piece, an hour that otherwise would have been spent waiting, daydreaming, and people-watching.

I confess that after my trip to the music store I spent additional time revising, rewriting, and polishing the manuscript, as I do for everything I write.

Even if the topic is one in which I have some expertise and my mind remains clear, I find that about a half-dozen rewrites are needed before the work begins to shine. Seldom do I submit anything before completing at least five or six rewrites. "Six Myths That Haunt Writers" appears in Figure 1–1.

TAKING INVENTORY

So far, this book has been quite blunt. It says that *successful writing is hard work.* It requires self-discipline and sacrifice—and the rejection rates for many journals and book publishers are astronomical. I maintain that serious writers must give up some leisure activities. Schedule time for writing, and discipline yourself to honor that schedule. To many people, such sacrifices appear foolish. Such individuals often criticize dedicated writers. For all this discipline and hard work the writer may get little more than criticism. Remember, it's a buyer's market, and the odds for success are indeed small.

I also maintain in this book that *successful writing is an activity that can be learned and mastered*—and that successful writing is not without rewards. Having mastered the craft of writing, you will have attained a variety of personal and professional goals, including earning money, advancing professionally, being creative, and being your own boss. Furthermore, such goals are within your reach if you are willing to demonstrate the self-discipline needed. The news even gets better; through practicing this advice *you can learn how to reverse the odds* of having your manuscript rejected.

In remaining chapters of this book, my aim is to help you master and use good writing skills. I hope you will use this book to gather the nuts-and-bolts knowledge of writing for publication. Decide what you really want to get out of writing, and use writing as a means to reach your personal and professional goals.

I have chosen to end this chapter with one writer's description of her personalized process. Perhaps you will find ideas that have potential for helping you.

> *First of all, I must be in the mood to write. Before putting the proverbial pen to paper, I have a ritual or process I follow. To be ready to write, I must contemplate the issue or topic. I jot down my initial thoughts in outline form adding marginal notes such as "requires research," "quote reference from . . . ," "see so-and-so for more information," or the like. Once this research/organization aspect is completed, I set it aside and just "think about it for awhile." I allow myself two to three days for this step. My trusty calendar keeps track of due dates, and I always try to allow enough time to produce the final product. My calendar-planner pad is designed in such a way that I can jot down new ideas about an assignment.*

FIGURE 1–1   **Sample article conceived and outlined while waiting for my son.**

Six Myths That Haunt Writers
By Kenneth T. Henson

Among the many things I have learned in conducting writers workshops on campuses across the country is that there are several false ideas, myths, that haunt most writers and often impede and/or block beginners. The following are six of these myths—and some suggestions for dealing with them.

1. *I'm not sure I have what it takes.*
I have found that on each campus, coast to coast, there is a superstar writer who, I am assured, has only to put his fingers to the keyboard or pen to paper and, presto, words, sentences, and paragraphs—publishable ones—flow. And, it is thought, these creations are effortless.

These tales are as ridiculous as ghost stories, but more damaging, since most people *believe* them. And like ghost stories, their purpose is to frighten.

If I were a beginning writer and believed that writing comes so effortlessly to some, I would be totally discouraged.

You admit that you, too, have heard of such a superwriter? You may even know such a person by name. Well, don't believe it. It's probably the creation of a person who doesn't intend to write and therefore would prefer that you don't either. The next time someone mentions this super-person, think of Ernest Hemingway, who wrote the last chapter of *Farewell to Arms* 119 times. Or think of the following definitions of writing: "Writing is 10 percent inspiration and 90 percent perspiration" and "Successful writing is the ability to apply the seat of the pants to the seat of the chair." Contrary to the myth, all writers perspire; some even sweat!

2. *I don't have time to write.*
You have heard this many times, and if you're like most of us, you have even said it yourself: "If only I had time to write." Ironically, most would-be writers have more time to write than most successful writers do. Some writers even have 24 hours a day to do as they please. But they represent only a small fraction of all writers. The vast majority of writers are freelancers who have either part-time or full-time jobs and pick up a few extra dollars, a little prestige, and a lot of personal satisfaction through writing articles.

The reason behind the bold statement that you have more time than most successful writers have to write is that, probably like you, most of them must earn a living some other way. Yet, these individuals have allotted themselves some time for writing: they took it away from their other activities. Good writers don't *make* time, and they don't *find* time. Rather, they reassign part of their time to writing. And that part of their lives is usually some of their leisure time.

I don't suggest that you stop golfing or fishing or jogging or watching TV, but if you are to be a successful writer, you must give up part of the time you spend (or waste) in the coffee room or bar and you must also give up the idea that you are too tired to write or that watching a mediocre TV show relaxes you. Writing is far more relaxing to most of us who return from our work emotionally drained; it provides an outlet for frustrations, a far more effective release than our more passive attempts to escape from them.

The next time you hear people say, "I don't have to write" or "I would write for publications if I had time," observe how those persons are spending their time at that moment. If writing is really important to you, replace the activities that are less important with writing. Let your friends and family know that this is your writing time and that you're not to be disturbed. Then tell yourself the same thing. Disciplined people have much more time than do undisciplined people.

3. *I don't have anything worth writing about.*

We've all heard this for years. A significant percentage of aspiring writers really believe that they don't know anything that is worthy of publication. If you are one of them, you're not learning from your experiences: either you don't make mistakes or you don't adjust your behavior to avoid repeating them.

The truth is that you possess a lot of knowledge that would be valuable to others. And you have the abilities that successful writers have to research the topics you wish to write about. I don't know any successful writers who don't feel that they need to research their topics. Start with the subjects that are most familiar, then enrich your knowledge of these subjects by periodic trips to the library, or by interviewing people, or by conducting surveys on these topics.

4. *The editors will reject my manuscript because my name isn't familiar to them.*

Of all the excuses that would-be writers give for not writing, none is weaker than, "If my name were James Michener or Stephen King, editors would listen to me."

But these people don't consider the fact that the Micheners and Kings didn't always have famous names; they started as unknowns and made their names known through talent and hard work. And they would probably be first to say that they have to keep earning their recognition through hard work. Of course, these writers have unusual talent, but you can be equally sure that they work hard and continue to do so to sharpen their skills, research their topics meticulously, and to create and invent new, fresh ways to express their ideas.

There's no guarantee that any of us can earn similar status and acclaim, but we can improve our expertise in our areas of interest and improve our communication skills.

5. *My vocabulary and writing skills are too limited.*

Many people equal jargon, unfamiliar words, complex sentence structure, and long paragraphs with good writing. Actually, though a good

Continued

FIGURE 1-1 *Continued*

vocabulary is a great asset to writers, so are dictionaries and thesauruses, for those who know how to use them and who are willing to take the time to do so. Jargon and long sentences and unnecessarily complex paragraphs harm writing more than they help it.

The sooner you replace words like *utilize* and *prioritize* with words like *use* and *rank*, the faster your writing will improve. Remember, your job is to communicate. Don't try to impress the editor. Editors know what their readers want, and readers seldom demand jargon and complexity.

6. *In my field there are few opportunities to publish.*

If your area of specialization has few professional journals (actually, some fields have only one or two), you may feel trapped, knowing that this uneven supply/demand ratio drives up the competition for these journals.

You might deal with this by searching for more general journals that cover your field, or journals whose editors often welcome articles written by experts in outside but related fields. For example, a biologist or botanist might turn to wildlife magazines, U.S. or state departments of conservation publications, forestry magazines, hunting and fishing publications, or magazines for campers and hikers.

Again, you could consider writing for other audiences, expanding your areas of expertise by taking courses in other disciplines, reading widely, and doing research in other fields to help you develop a broader range of subjects to write about.

Some fields have more journals than others, and some writers are luckier (and more talented) than others. But for those who are willing to work hard at their craft, writing offers a way to reach many professional and personal goals.

RECAPPING THE MAJOR POINTS

This chapter has introduced several important points. The following are well worth remembering:

- The competition among writers is keen. To succeed, writers must write excellently.
- Good writers are self-made, not born. By learning a few hard facts, you can master the skills needed to succeed in writing.
- Successful writing for nonfiction magazines, journals, and books requires—above everything else—the ability to write clearly.
- Plain, simple writing is preferred over sophisticated, esoteric, pompous, writing.
- Successful writers are organized. They have designated times and places for writing.

- In our busy society, nobody *makes* or *finds* the time to write. Successful writers assign a higher priority to writing than to other activities.
- Clear goals give writers direction and incentive.
- Self-discipline and self-motivation characterize successful writers. You are the only one who can give yourself the kick in the pants that is needed to get started.

REFERENCES

Dickens, C. *A Tale of Two Cities.* Intro. by D. G. Pitt. New York: Airmont Publishing Co., Inc., 1963.

Henson, K. T. Six myths that haunt writers. *The Writer* 104 (May 1991): 24–25.

Naisbitt, J., and Aburdene, P. *Megatrends 2000.* New York: William Morrow & Co., 1990.

Samson, J. *The Auctioneer.* New York: Avon Books, 1975.

Severied, E. *Not so wild a dream.* New York: Athenaeum, 1976.

Steinbeck, J. The education of teachers. *Curriculum Programs.* Washington, D.C.: National Education Association, 1959.

Strunk, W., Jr., and White, E. B. *The Elements of Style,* 3rd ed. New York: Macmillan, 1979.

2

Finding Topics

A former editor of a prominent journal tells the following story:

> I was in Chicago making a speech on the topic, "Writing for Publication." At the time, I was saying how easy it is for anyone to identify publishable topics, and I made the statement "All you need is one good topic. You don't need an unlimited number of ideas. All you need is one." It was precisely at this time when a small lady in the audience—very timid, yet serious and determined—raised her hand. What she said was the bravest thing I've ever heard. She struck straight to the heart of the fear that all writers, both new and experienced, feel at some time. In an almost inaudible whisper, she said, "But what if you don't have one good idea?" Then my hand went up and my mouth opened, because that's what speaking is all about. You always say something whether or not you have anything worth saying. Then I was stunned. For I realized that I didn't have an answer for that question. What if you don't have one good idea? So, I paused momentarily and with my hand raised high, I said, "Ahmmm. Let's take a break." And we did.

Later, the speaker confessed that he worried throughout the break because he didn't have an answer for the woman who posed the question. Many professors can remember occasions when, as young instructors or assistant professors, they went into their office for one purpose and one alone: to write. Knowing that their pending tenure and their future promotion to assistant, associate, or full professor depended on their writing manuscripts and having them accepted for publication in recognizable journals, all they could do it seemed was to sit with pen in hand searching the boundaries of their minds for topics. This is the same desperate and lonely feeling expressed in the woman's question. Most writers will acknowledge that often they did not have even one good idea for a topic!

When people ask about the source of ideas for topics, seasoned writers understand the courage it takes simply to admit that lost condition. Yet, to succeed as a writer, people must acknowledge their inadequacies. Paradoxically, the reason writers must admit their inadequacies is the need to build their self-confidence. We cannot gain confidence until we face ourselves. Our weaknesses make us stronger, if we take steps to remove these weaknesses.

The goal of this chapter is to provide knowledge and perspective so that you will no longer feel that awful, lonesome fear of not knowing what to write or the fear of being rejected. I hope you will learn to perceive your own questions and your recognition of limitations as what they *can* and *should* be—indicators of personal growth. The remainder of this chapter provides some suggestions that will help you build a storehouse of good publishable writing topics.

THE DISSERTATION: A SOURCE OF TOPICS

There are many sources of ideas for writing topics. For those who have pursued graduate courses, dissertations and theses are excellent sources for article topics. One individual whose dissertation was titled "An Identification of Earth Science Principles Pertinent to Junior High School Programs and An Examination of Currently Adopted Textbooks in Terms of the Principles Contained Therein" produced two or three good articles. An analysis of the title reveals that the study was divided into two major parts. Part One identified principles, and Part Two examined textbooks to determine whether or not they contained these principles.

Within a year following the completion of the study, an article by the author appeared in the journal, *Science Education*. The title of that article was "Contributions of Science Principles to Teaching: The History and Status of the Science Principle," and it was actually a summary of the *literature review* contained in the dissertation. The *review of literature*—usually the second chapter in a thesis or dissertation—can easily be rewritten to form an article.

Concurrently, in the journal, *School Science and Mathematics*, another article appeared by the same author titled "Representation of Pertinent Earth Science Principles in Current Science Textbooks." This article was an abstract of Part Two of the dissertation. *Many dissertations have multiple parts; often each part can provide the substance for an article.*

Both of these articles appeared within a year following the author's dissertation. This means that they were written and submitted either while the dissertation was being written or almost immediately upon its completion. As you might guess, this was no accident. William Van Til, a leading expert on writing for publication, says that dissertations are like fish and company; they spoil quickly. Unlike cheese and wine which improve with age, *as topics for articles, dissertations deteriorate rapidly.* If you have recently completed or are currently writing a paper, thesis, or dissertation, now is the time to draft articles.

If, however, you achieved this milestone earlier in life, and you fear that your thesis or dissertation has gone the way of old fish, don't worry. There is still hope. *To make your old dissertation a timely topic, you can always duplicate part of your original study.* The author of the science education dissertation did just that. Within a couple of years, an article titled "A Scientific Look at Science Textbooks in Indiana Junior High Schools" appeared in another journal, and still another article, "Applications of Science Principles to Teaching," appeared concurrently in the journal, *The Clearing House.*

By now you may be asking, How long can this milking process go on? The answer is, indefinitely. As long as you update your study or parts of it, you can generate excellent substance for more good articles. For example, two years following the appearance of the article in *The Clearing House, School Science and Mathematics* published "Contributions of Science Principles to Teaching: How Science Principles Can Be Used." Later, when the author had an opportunity to repeat approximately one-tenth of the study, *School Science and Mathematics* printed still another article, "Principles of Conservation of Clean Air and Water Pertinent to the General Education Programs in Junior High School."

I have taken the time to relate this entire sequence because several lessons are contained in this series of publication. Even if you have not written a dissertation or thesis, you can still benefit from a few truths found in these examples. First, all good theses and dissertations offer the substance for more than one good article. Second, the sooner the articles are written, the better—but, more important, it's never too late to use your dissertation or thesis to generate good articles. A close look at the titles of these science articles shows that one may be on the general theme of the study while others focus on parts of the study, such as the *Literature Review* section. The author may choose to use part of the findings, such as the article on principles of conservation of clean air and water, and ignore the remaining 90 percent of the study.

One final note about using dissertations as the source of article topics: the material can—indeed, *must*—be rewritten to become more interesting and easier to read. If you write for applied journals or for magazines, your articles don't even have to follow the rigid steps of the scientific method upon which most theses and dissertations are designed. In fact, for most journals, the scientific method is inappropriate.

YOUR JOB AS A SOURCE OF TOPICS

Whether or not you are aware of your strengths, *all workers perform some parts of their jobs exceptionally well.* This means that you have information that is valuable to others who hold similar positions. But, month after month and year after year, aspiring writers attend writing workshops and openly acknowledge that they do not believe they have anything worthy of publication. This conclusion is unwise and it is wrong. You *do* have knowledge that is worth sharing, and until you acknowledge this truth you will remain unduly handicapped.

One beginning writer, a former teacher, had a job that required him to supervise student teachers in a public school setting. This new vantage point enabled him to see some of the barriers that prevent students from learning the content that teachers try to impart. This new job led to the publication of a series of articles including "Student Teachers Unlock Learning Barriers," "What the New Teacher Should Know About Learning Barriers," and "The Teacher as a Learning Barrier." All of these articles appeared in different issues of the same journal, *School and Community.* By shifting from teacher to observer, this person discovered a series of barriers that inhibit learning. What an excellent observation to share with other teachers! What an excellent topic! This observer even made a list of teacher behaviors that interfere with learning. To non-teachers this may be inane information, but to the right audience it is valuable knowledge.

PROFILE

Nathan L. Essex received a B.S. degree at Alabama A&M University in 1964, an M.S. degree in Educational Administration at Jacksonville State University in 1971, and a Ph.D. in Educational Administration at the University of Alabama in 1975. He has served as a public school teacher and administrator; as consultant, bureau director, and program chair in Educational Administration for a state department of education; and Area Head of Educational Leadership. Dr. Essex, currently Dean of the College of Education at Memphis State University, has a long and distinguished record of involvement—with school boards, professional organizations, principals, and K–12 teachers—serving as a policy consultant and a staff development consultant. He has written and continues to write in both educational and business journals on legal issues and policy issues that have impacts on these organizations. He serves on a number of governing boards representing both public and private sectors. Additionally, he serves on a number of editorial boards in the areas of administration and leadership.

I write for publication as a means of enhancing my own professional development. Writing for publication enables me to remain on the cutting edge of developments in my field. It also provides me with a unique opportunity to share my research with practitioners who may find it useful in improving their practice. Writing for publication is one way that I can contribute to the knowledge base in my field and feel that I am offering solutions to the myriad of problems faced by practitioners today. I find it to be one of the most gratifying professional activities in which to engage. Lastly, an obvious pleasure comes from recognition by my peers who judge my works as ones that have the potential to make a contribution to our field.

Identification of relevant topics is an important decision in writing for publication. I consistently attempt to identify topics that have significance for those professionals with whom I work. Some of my topics are linked to problems encountered by administrators, teachers, and manag-ers. These topics surface during my interactions with them. Other topics come from problems that I identify during my consulting experiences. Since issues involving personnel and law are constantly changing as federal and state statues change, communicating these changes to administrators, teachers, and managers in clear and concise operational language is critical. I try to keep abreast of emerging issues in the fields of law and personnel and carefully select those topics that I believe are critical to the maintenance of effective organizations. I attempt to be as pragmatic as possible in my writing so that practitioners can apply manuscript content to improve their organizations. My primary objective in writing is to present relevant and current information in a useful format for the audience to whom the article is intended. I attempt to provide guidelines to be used by the reader whose organization is faced with a problem relating to issues discussed in the manuscript.

OTHER OCCUPATIONS AS SOURCES OF WRITING TOPICS

Too often, we limit our writing to an unnecessarily narrow field; *professionals in many different fields could benefit from your expertise.* To avoid this myopic trap, try to think of as many audiences as possible who could benefit from your articles. For example, a nurse might wish to write an article titled "Strengths and Weaknesses of Today's Nurses." Who cares? Well, even if you and I don't care, there are others who care immensely about the strengths and weaknesses of today's nurses. Nurse educators must actively seek out feedback on the performance of graduates of their programs—feedback on what students learned that helps them in their work, feedback from employers on additional skills graduates need. This knowledge is essential for program evaluation, program improvement, and accreditation.

Practicing nurses need to know what they do well, and what areas can be improved. Directors of hospitals and clinics need to know the strengths and weaknesses of today's nurses. Personnel directors must be aware of common weaknesses in the profession if they are to avoid hiring nurses who possess these weaknesses.

The author can now ask, *What do I know that is valuable to each of these audiences?* Practicing nurses? Nurse administrators? and Nurse educators? Each question may lead to a similar, yet different, article. Whatever your ideas for topics might be, you can multiply these topics by asking these questions: "Who would be interested in this topic? Who else?" For a list of expectations of nursing journals and journals in other disciplines see Appendix A.

REFERENCE BOOKS AS A SOURCE OF TOPICS

One of the richest sources of ideas for writing topics is the reference section found in every library. For example, the *Readers Guide*, the *Education Index*, the *Business Periodical Index, Psychological Abstracts, Index Medicus, Social Science Citation Index, Social Science Index, Humanities Index*, the *MLA Bibliography*—these are but a few of the available reference books that can be used to identify topics.

Suppose you decide to write an article on a given topic. By checking the most current bound volumes of the appropriate index, you can see what topics are being published. Furthermore, you can readily identify those journals that are giving this topic attention. This is very important because most journal editors have topics they prefer to include and topics they prefer to exclude from their journals.

Book publishers are even more topic-limited. Each book publishing company has topics with which it excels because it has cultivated teams of experienced reviewers and marketers for those subjects. Although companies occasionally do break new ground, to do so is the exception. The acquisitions editor is far more likely to pursue tried and proven topics. Inexperienced writers are likely to purposefully avoid contacting publishers who already have a successful book on their chosen topic. This is a mistake. When the markets are large enough to support several books in a given area, publishers often actively pursue additional manuscripts in a subject area so as to increase their own share of the total market and to leverage their existing presence in that market.

Some topics will require the use of several key words. For example, say you have chosen to write on bicycle repair. There may be no entries under *bicycle repair,* but there are entries under *repair,* and *small machines,* and still other categories. A similar search on another topic may turn up no articles; now it is time to consider a computer search. For a nominal fee, most libraries offer this service. In addition to telling you what is being published and by whom, the computer search produces a review of the literature which you can use to expand your own knowledge of the topic and which can be used in your references and bibliography. Additional uses of the library to locate good topics are discussed in Chapter 6.

But suppose that neither you nor the computer can locate any articles on the topic you selected. Don't be discouraged. There's always a first time for everything. If you really want to write on this topic, do it anyway.

In the following passages, Jesus Garcia, the University of Illinois professor mentioned earlier, talks about his topic-screening system:

> When I write, I take an idea through what I call a "critical analysis process." I begin by placing an idea on pager/screen and "weigh its worth" to the educational community. Is what I want to tell the public novel, thought provoking, and practical? I discuss my idea with colleagues, particularly classroom teachers. I outline what I wish to do with the idea and again share the idea with colleagues. Third, where appropriate, I attempt to include suggestions that teachers would find useful for classroom use. Fourth, I do the research, begin writing, and continually sharpen the focus of the manuscript by returning to the original idea. The process is further heightened if I coauthor a manuscript, which I do regularly.
>
> I find this process beneficial because I can look at an idea from multiple perspectives. More often than not, I am able to generate more than one manuscript from an idea. This process also allows me to generate other ideas. As ideas are scrutinized, others surface. Moreover, I find that the process helps me to grow as I reinforce my commitment to an idea, modify my position, or reject an original idea.

FORECASTING THE FUTURE

By this time it should be obvious to you that with a little practice you will have no trouble identifying innumerable ideas for article topics or book topics. But this alone is not enough; *you must be able to identify topics that will be popular next year.* You see, the topics that you read about today are at least one or two years old. If you write about them and are lucky enough to get your work accepted, when your work is published it will be at least two years old! This figure is derived from taking a year-old topic; spending three months preparing, polishing, and submitting the manuscript; and waiting another nine months for it to be published. Does this place you in the seemingly impossible position of having to forecast the future? In a way, it does. But there are several strategies you can use—flawless strategies—to predict what topics will be popular in your field *one* or even *two* years from now. Here are three strategies that I use.

Using Speakers to Predict Future Topics

One effective way to identify topics of the future is to identify today's leaders in your chosen writing field(s). Take advantage of every opportunity you have to hear these leaders speak. The next time you visit a convention or hear a noted speaker, if at all possible, don't leave until you've spoken to this person. There is a sure-fire way to get most speakers' attention. Buy a copy of the speaker's latest book and, at the end of the speech, ask for an autograph.

As you stand in line waiting your turn, listen to the speaker's conversation with other members of the audience. Invariably, someone will ask about a recent article or book. Although the speaker did, indeed, write the article or book, the individual will be puzzled to learn how vaguely the author recalls the specifics of the work. Why is the author so vague?

Though far from obvious, the answer is simple. Before you suspect the author of plagiarism, consider the age of this work. Although the book or article carries a recent publication date, it has been at the publishing house for at least a year. Meanwhile, the author has moved forward to other topics. In fact, at this moment the admirer who has recently read the work has a better knowledge of the work than does its own creator.

Before taking time to talk to our speaker, we were looking for some ways to identify topics that will be popular one or two years from now. Actually, we haven't left our main path of pursuit because our side-track discussion introduced the best single way to identify next year's "hot" topics—*attend a conference or any assembly that affords you an opportunity to hear a speech by a recognized leader in your field of interest.*

The topic doesn't matter. You will know that it is on its way to becoming a popular item because the leaders in any field shape their field of study. While others are writing about the author's recently published, yet year-old works, the author is writing about something very different. Since the leading authorities in any field have a way of getting their manuscripts accepted (this technique is known as good writing skills) and since effective authors have a knack for getting mileage from their work, (the subject of a forthcoming chapter) you can rest assured that this speaker's speech will be found alive and well dwelling in a book or an article (or both) in the next year or two. You can do far better than your competition if you take notes and prepare your own article, not on the author's book or article but on the much more current topic of the evening's speech.

Using Journal Editors to Predict Future Topics

A perhaps less exciting but equally effective way to discover the topics of the future is to contact the editors of the journals in your field of work. Ask these editors for a list of coming themes. Most nonfiction journals run a high percentage of theme issues. Editors always know the forthcoming themes for their journals at least a year or two in advance.

Using Professional Association Yearbook Editors to Predict Future Topics

Another excellent way to identify topics that will be popular one or two years from now is to contact your professional societies and ask for the topics of their forthcoming yearbooks and for the chapter titles in these books. Why is this method better? Because only the *best* of the *best* experts in the profession are invited to write a chapter in the yearbook. A trip to the reference desk of your local library can quickly identify the current members of the yearbook committee and the members of the journal publications committee.

Should you decide to write for popular magazines, examine your hobbies. A survey to determine sources of writers' first articles found the most common topic source to be personal hobbies.

Chapter 6 explains how writers can use their libraries to identify topics. With a little effort in the shape of purposeful planning, you can identify several excellent topics on which to focus your writing. With experience, you will be amazed to learn that locating topics is no problem. On the contrary, you will instinctively and unintentionally discover more topics—*good* topics—than you will ever have time to pursue.

RECAPPING THE MAJOR POINTS

This chapter has pointed out that, although having good timely topics is essential for all writers, beginning writers often search desperately for suitable topics. You can always have a supply of topics if you remember these points:

- Dissertations, theses, and papers are excellent sources for journal articles.

- When possible, articles based on dissertations, theses, and papers should be written while those projects are still underway.
- Authors of dissertations can return to that document and duplicate part of the research to produce substance for a timely article.
- Your job (or any activity you do well) is an excellent source for article topics.
- You *do* have something to say that would make a good article topic.
- You can increase the mileage of each topic by considering the various audiences who would find it pertinent. This produces one or more articles for each audience.
- Topics that are popular today will lose their popularity in the year or two required for their publication; therefore, you must seek topics that will be popular a year from now.

3

Getting Started

THE RIGHT TITLE

The skeptic asks What's in a title? The answer is, only the most important key for the writer. *A good title captures the reader's attention.* Without this, the book stays on the shelf, and the article is instantly and painlessly flipped out of the reader's life.

When I was a small child, taking vacations was something special, something to really get excited over. My brother and I were barely tall enough to look out ahead above the tall seats in Dad's big Buick. But occasionally we saw something that was well worth the strain. The company that made Burma Shave, a popular shaving cream, had created a new way of advertising its product—a clever saying would be broken into phrases, and each phrase was painted on a simple sign which was then positioned strategically beside the highway. For example, on one stretch of road, the first sign read "Why is it." Then, around the next curve we saw another sign, "when you try to pass." And over the next hill, a third sign appeared, "the guy in front." Quickly, we would try to guess the ending. Around another curve we saw it, "steps on the gas?" And always the last sign read simply "Burma Shave."

Maybe today's high-tech, "flash and trash" world of advertising finds that earlier lifestyle boring; more likely, today's advertisers recognize that adults read only a small percentage of road signs and only a slightly higher percentage of books and magazines. Instead, today's readers are very selective. They know they haven't time to read even a small percent of the books and articles with which they come into contact. Today's readers have two reasons for reading. They read for *information* (nonfiction) or they read for *fun* (fiction), hoping to get lucky and find material that delivers both information and fun.

An astute author can capitalize on this knowledge. As you search for the right title, select one that hooks the reader's interest and/or promises to deliver information the reader deems important. Consider, for example, Tipper Gore's book, *Raising PG Kids in an X-Rated Society.* To catch the reader's attention, Gore uses a little levity, playing on motion picture ratings. Her title also makes a definite promise to the reader. Experienced writers know that to protect their integrity their writings must deliver whatever the title promises. Whether a book title or an article title, the reader will feel disappointed if the work fails to deliver.

The writer must also remember to *keep the audience in mind at all times.* With a title like *Raising PG Kids in an X-Rated Society,* it is clear that Gore's intended readers are parents and guardians, so each paragraph and each sentence must be written to provide information that parents and guardians need. This title contains an implied promise to help these people meet the challenge of raising good kids in a less-than-wholesome society.

Once such a promise is made, it must be kept. It might help to remember that as a writer you are creating a product that you want to sell. Therefore, your product must provide something of value in return for the reader's time, attention, and money. In a society as busy as ours, a person's time and energy are precious. As a writer, you are competing with many other vendors for people's time. In every sentence, you must be sure that the reader won't feel shortchanged. Give something valuable to the reader, and you will have gained a loyal customer; but break your promise, and you will lose the reader's support.

Consider the following titles. Do they hook *your* attention? Does each make a promise?

- *How to Turn $15 into a Money-Making Business*
- *Megamergers*
- *Breaking Up Is Hard to Do*
- *The One-Minute Manager*
- *Finding the Freedom of Self-Control*
- *Existentially Speaking*
- *39 Forever*
- *Help for the Battered Woman*
- *Thoroughbred Handicapping as an Investment*
- *The Facts on FAX*
- *How to Save Your Child From Drugs*
- *Eating on the Run*

A quick glance at this list tells the reader that these are nonfiction books. They promise to provide useful information and help the reader.

Titles of fiction books and articles may be far less descriptive because the purpose of fiction is to entertain. Consider the following list of current fiction titles:

- *Many Waters*
- *Leave a Light on for Me*
- *The Down Side of Up*
- *Foxcatcher*
- *Speaker of the Dead*
- *Windmills of the Gods*
- *After the Rain*
- *Out on the Rim*
- *Something Shady*
- *The Treasure of Pawley's Island*

Although fiction book titles may or may not be descriptive, they usually stir the imagination. For example, the reader doesn't have to know that *Foxcatcher* is about espionage to find the title captivating. Good fiction writers know that their readers are imaginative, and good writers use this knowledge when choosing titles.

Choosing Titles for Nonfiction Journal Articles

Writers of nonfiction journal articles have a special opportunity to use titles to engage their readers. Knowing that their readers have even less time to dedicate to their reading than fiction readers who read for fun, successful authors of nonfiction articles make even more definite promises to their readers. For example, consider the following article titles and their respective audiences.

Article Title	Audience
• Ten Ways to Avoid Litigation	Physicians
• Six Ways to Resolve Discipline Problems	Junior high school principals
• Knowing Your Clients' Needs	Realtors
• Interviewing: Accentuating Your Assets	Job applicants
• How to Make Your Car Last 150,000 Miles	Car owners

All of these titles promise to help the reader, but what is more important is that finding solutions to the problems addressed is perceived by the intended audience as being very important. With litigation on the rise, in number of cases and in the number of dollars and number of awards to patients, what physician could ignore an article titled "Ten Ways to Avoid Litigation"? What junior high school principal, who must deal daily with children of the most awkward and rebellious age, could fail to be intrigued by an article that promises to make his or her own life easier?

The two titles just mentioned also contain another element to attract the reader. The first title specifies that *ten* concrete suggestions will be provided to the reader, and the second offers *six* substantive solutions. When asked what he looked for most in an article, the editor of a research journal responded: "I suppose that what I want more than anything else is that each article makes some contributions." Readers of research journals and readers of applied journals want—even demand—substance from the articles they read.

The last title on the preceding list, "How to Make Your Car Last 150,000 Miles," is an article that appeared in *Consumers' Digest.* Interestingly, the first page of this article carries a chart that lists the 10 least expensive cars to maintain to 50,000 miles and a corresponding list of the 10 most expensive cars to maintain to 50,000 miles. With just a glance at this first page, this chart immediately tells the reader that this article offers substance. The author did his homework and researched his topic, which means that he reviewed the literature to discover new and helpful information to enrich his article. Incidentally, he reprinted the charts with the permission of *The Car Book* and gave that source credit. Good writers use lists, charts, and graphs so that readers won't have to "sniff out" or look for the main ideas in their articles.

Another important aspect of selecting a title is that a good title gives direction to the author. The importance of having each sentence throughout your document advance your theme cannot be overstressed. A specific descriptive title can put you on track and keep you there. The right title can help you select words and construct sentences to make this direct, straight-line advancement happen. *Use your title to guide the writing of each page and each paragraph.*

Often during the writing process an author will discover ways to improve the work by shifting the direction of the manuscript. Such a short interruption to explain or offer an example is fine as long as the end result does not alter the theme to the extent that the document no longer delivers on the title. This need not be a problem—the title can always be revised to correct the mismatch. Even the best writers make such adjustments. To neglect to do so would either result in a title that doesn't live up to its promise or an article written in one limited direction, with limited creativity.

WRITING THE FIRST SENTENCE

The author of nonfiction must immediately tell the reader exactly what this article or chapter will do. This is the function of the lead (or leading) sentence. For example, the first sentence may introduce a problem; the rest of the lead paragraph will explain how and to what degree the author will solve this problem. Or the article might begin with a question, and the rest of the lead paragraph tells exactly what this article is going to do about answering the question. The remainder of the manuscript must then step-by-step, sentence-by-sentence, paragraph-by-paragraph begin resolving the issue, solving the problem, or answering the question.

Fiction writers may have no question to answer or problem to solve, but they must use the first sentence and paragraph to begin establishing the climate, introduce and develop characters, and introduce conflict. Early attention to these tasks enables the writer to capture and hold the readers' attention.

A wide variety of types of lead sentences is available to writers. Factual statements are among the most common, although they are not necessarily the most captivating. You be the judge of what constitutes an interesting lead sentence. Examine the following three examples to see which type you prefer.

- Early Sunday evening Tom Simms walked into the dimly lighted parking lot, unaware of the plot against his life.
- Americans are killing themselves, and they don't even know it.
- What is your consumer I.Q.?

These three examples are all good lead sentences, but they differ greatly. One is fictitious, one is factual, and one asks a question. Like all good lead sentences, they *hook the reader to want to know more.* What is it about these sentences that compels the reader to read the next sentence? Each one focuses on a topic that contemporary Americans find important. Crime continues to rise. Concern and commitment to better health are evidenced in the sale of exercise videos and books. Consumer awareness is a deep concern because of the increase in all types of fraud—credit card, mail-order, and investment, not to mention the customer-service fraud such as medical malpractice or interstate auto mechanics fraud.

A nonfiction article should begin with a lead sentence that addresses the topic revealed in the title, and it must extend this topic in a logical way. For example, an article titled "Our Foods Are Poisoning Us" may begin with the following sentence: Americans are killing themselves, and they don't even know it. The next sentence is very important, for it must reveal the purpose of this article. If the author plans to write about cholesterol, this sentence might read, "Each day Americans consume more cholesterol than . . ." Or, if the writer wishes the article to focus on salt consumption, the next sentence might read, "Each day we eat 10 times as much salt as our bodies need."

While still in the first paragraph, the author must articulate the purpose of this article. Here the author must tell readers what the article offers that will enable them to cope with this problem or situation. For example, the next sentence may read, "Fortunately, through planning, we can control our consumption of . . .". This sentence implies that the rest of the article will tell the reader how to do this planning, and the rest of the article—each paragraph, each sentence and each word—should be used to deliver this promise.

Examine again the first sample lead sentence. "Early Sunday evening, Tom Simms walked into the dimly lighted parking lot unaware of the plot against his life." Although this sentence could be used to start a nonfiction article, it seems more likely to be the beginning of a fiction piece. Assume that Tom Simms is a leading character and that he will survive the parking-lot scene. The author must now let the reader know who Tom is by describing his appearance and his personality. The reader can appreciate this story only by knowing and perhaps identifying with Tom Simms. To assure that the reader will read on, the author must continue to build Tom's character, explaining why he behaves as he does.

As you have seen, authors often use more than a single lead sentence just to grab the reader. Consider the following article opening: "It's happening on college campuses everywhere. It's exciting, and it isn't even illegal. But it should be." These three short sentences are written to stir your curiosity and make you wonder, what's happening everywhere? What's exciting? What isn't illegal but should be?

This was the lead I used for an article in the *The Chronicle of Higher Education* warning writers about publisher rip-offs. The title of the article is "When Signing Book Contracts, Scholars Should Be Sure to Read the Fine Print." Once past this hook, I immediately begin describing the traps, using lists and subheadings to highlight each one. This shows that the article has substance and makes the content easily visible to even the most casual reader. (See Appendix B for a reprint of this article.)

PARAGRAPHING

Two mistakes account for a large percent of the poorly written materials. Both of these mistakes concern paragraphing. Inexperienced writers seldom know when to end a paragraph. Some writers use the surveyor's approach. They step back and look to see how much of the page has been used, then hit the return key. Other writers just keep on writing and writing until their pens and ribbons run dry. You can do better.

The paragraph is an important tool available for all writers who know how to use it. As readers read, they make associations between the sentences. The author can help shape these associations so that the reader thinks as the writer thinks. This is important if the reader is to draw the author's intended conclusions. By lumping the related sentences together, the author tells the reader which sentences to associate. By correctly assembling the sentences, the author helps the reader comprehend the overall meaning of the paragraph. However, many authors fail by packing too much information into one paragraph. There is a simple rule: *one major theme per paragraph.*

A second useful way to determine the best length of a paragraph is to purposefully keep each paragraph short enough so that you (and the reader) can remember all of the ideas contained in the paragraph. Usually half of a double-spaced typewritten page is as much as a reader can retain. Remember the reader, and *keep your paragraphs short.*

Paragraphs can be simplified by using a process which psychologists call "chunking". Consider the following numbers: 386914. Try to remember them. If you succeeded, you may have put the numbers in groups such as 38–69–14 or 386–914. This is chunking. Now try to remember the following paragraph.

> *A good way to add power to your writing is by keeping your subject and verb in close proximity. Good, strong, paragraphs have only one major idea and good, strong sentences start with concrete nouns and use action verbs. Writing can be weakened by hiding the subject in the middle or at the end of the paragraph.*

Now consider how much easier it is to remember this same information when it is organized into chunks:

> *There are three ways to make paragraphs powerful: (1) use concrete nouns, (2) put the subject up front, and (3) follow it quickly with an action verb.*

Once you complete your manuscript, read through it to see if each paragraph advances the ideas in previous paragraphs. If not, the paragraphs must be reordered. There is a good way to do this. Those who use the pencil or pen can write each paragraph on an index card and then sequence and rearrange the order until you are satisfied. Those who write on computers also have unlimited flexibility to experiment until they find the best sequence.

GO AHEAD AND WRITE

The first and foremost job of a writer is to write. Recognize that you do have something that is worth saying. Identify your target audience and ask yourself: If I were in their shoes, what would I want to know? What would I find interesting? Helpful?

Some people find it helpful to make an outline. They say that making an outline forces them to rethink and sequence their ideas. It helps them identify the most important issues. But other people find that making an outline stifles their creativity, and they prefer not to be restricted by an outline. But what about *you*? Should you use an outline? The decision is simple. If you like to work with outlines, use one. If not, don't.

The main thing to remember about getting started is to forge forward without worrying about errors in spelling or punctuation and without trying to avoid superfluous words and sentences. All of these errors can be corrected later. Don't make the mistake of perfectionists who ponder over word choice even during the first draft. Don't worry that you may be stray-

---

PROFILE

Arnold B. Cheyney received bachelor's and master's degrees from Kent State University and a Ph.D. from Ohio State University. He began his career as an elementary school teacher, principal, and supervisor in Canton, Ohio. Now University of Miami Professor Emeritus he lives in Wooster, Ohio. Jeanne Cheyney, his wife, attended the Cleveland School of Art, graduated from Kent State, and taught in Ohio and Florida at elementary schools. She is a professional writer, illustrator, and novelist.

They have done 12 GoodYearBooks, a series of curriculum books for primary teachers. In addition, the Cheyney's curriculum materials for primary grade Sunday Schools are used throughout Canada and the United States.

Arnold Cheyney's book, *The Ripe Harvest: Educating Migrant Children,* (U M Press, 1972) was selected by the American Library Association as an outstanding academic book for 1972–1973. He has published over 500 articles in newspapers such as *The Miami Herald, Detroit Free Press,* and the late *Chicago Daily News.*

Jeanne Cheyney's novels include *Captive's Promise* (1988) and *The Conviction of Charlotte Gray* (Zonderrean, 1988) which are now being republished in condensed versions by a book club; *A Patch of Black Satin* (Silhouette, 1985); and *The Secret of Giltham Hall* (Cook, 1980). She has several other novels completed and ready to make the rounds of publishers.

The Thirteen Cheyney Maxims for Would-Be-Published Writers

1. Know for whom you want to write, send for writer's guidelines, and follow them explicity.
2. Read widely and much, especially in the area in which you intend to write.
3. For practice, copy exceptional paragraphs when you find them in your reading, and analyze them. Do the words flow? Why are the words the writer used good choices? Do the sentences describe a scene in as few words as possible?
4. Be sure the first paragraph in your book or article captures your reader's interest.
5. Become familiar with the latest issue of *Writer's Market*. It gives you editor's needs and how to prepare manuscripts and queries. Your public library has a copy.
6. Send only your very best work.
7. Keep to deadlines.
8. Proofread and proofread again.
9. Do not take rejection of your manuscripts as a personal affront.
10. Do not talk about what you are writing—if it's publishable, others will find out in due time.
11. Let your manuscript rest in a drawer for seasoning, and read it again before sending it to an editor.
12. Be kind but honest when evaluating your collaborator's writing.
13. Read all lists, tips, and maxims on writing with suspicion.

---

ing from the title. Writing is a creative process, even nonfiction writing. So just write. Whenever you think that you might have something to say, just write it down. The first draft doesn't have to be good. *Getting something on paper is half of the challenge. You can do it. Just write.*

RECAPPING THE MAJOR POINTS

Getting started is the most difficult challenge that writers face. The goal of this chapter has been to help you begin getting words on paper. Getting started will be easier if you remember these points:

- Choose topics that are interesting to the reader.
- Begin by writing a title that describes your forthcoming article.
- Feel free to stray from your title; you can always change the title at a later time.

- For nonfiction articles, choose a title that makes a promise to the reader, then use the article to deliver that promise.
- For fiction articles, write a title that hooks the reader's attention.
- Use the first sentence to tell the readers exactly what the article will do for them.
- Make every sentence extend the message found in the preceding sentence.
- For nonfiction articles, use the first paragraph to tell what the article is going to do to help the reader.
- For fiction articles, begin developing the characters in the first paragraph.
- Keep your paragraphs reasonably short, limiting each to one major idea and a reasonable number of supporting ideas.
- If you like outlines, use them; if not, don't.
- During the first draft, ignore any need that you might feel to make your article grammatically correct.

REFERENCE

Henson, K. T. "When signing book contracts, scholars should be sure to read the fine print." *The Chronicle of Higher Education*, October 24, 1990, p. B2.

4

About Style

In your quest for facts and tips on becoming a better writer, nothing is more important than style. What is the meaning of style? It might help if you think of someone familiar like, let's say Fred Astaire, whom most people recognize as having style. Ginger Rogers had it, also—she did everything Fred did except she did it backwards and in high heels. People with style are poised and confident. They are eager to display their talents, yet they never "toot their own horns"—their performance and behavior speak for them.

Style is not just the particular combination of dance steps; it's *how* the dancer takes those steps. Style is not just the words a writer chooses; it's also *how* the writer uses them. Here's where many beginning writers trip on their own thoughts. Their failure to see their own potential and purpose for writing limits their ability to master an effective writing style. Style requires a few basic understandings. These understandings shape how writers think; and, in turn, how they think shapes how they write.

To appreciate the role that style plays in writing, refer to the passage from *The Auctioneer* by Joan Samson (see page 13). Suppose, instead, she had written:

The man and women were burning brush. Their daughter was with them. She saw a truck coming toward them and went over to get a better look. It was Bob Gore, the police chief.

Instead, Joan Samson chose to have the dead leaves hiss, the truck tires rut, the mud spray, and Gore's belly seek a point of equilibrium. This writing style is entertaining, and it puts the reader on the scene. Obviously, Joan wanted the readers to share this experience and enjoy it. But, most of your writing may be for professional, academic journals. There, you will not choose to entertain but to inform. Consider your other reasons for writing, and develop a style that will serve your purposes. For example, if you write to earn promotions, tenure, or merit pay, consider the qualities that your evaluators will be looking for, and work those qualities into your manuscript. A good way to develop this sensitivity and flexibility is to write a manuscript for a specific audience, and then rewrite it for a different audience.

Now, it's time to dispel some common myths that impede the development of writers. Among these is the common belief that *It's who you know* that determines your success as a writer. It's visible and audible. Skepticism is in the eyes of aspiring writers, and some beginners are bold enough to announce it openly. Some just bear their souls and say, "I don't know if I have what it takes to become a successful writer." At this point let me share a little good news. Although it may sound deceptively simple, to become a successful writer, you must set aside your modesty and believe in yourself. My promise to you is that *anyone of average or above intelligence can become a successful writer.*

Occasionally skeptics will openly challenge this assertion. They say, "Sure, it's easy for people like you. You have published so much that the editors recognize your name. But what about me? Nobody knows me!" Although mine isn't a household name to most editors, I will admit that having editors recognize your name probably causes them to consider your manuscript a little more carefully, resulting in a slight edge. But, I emphatically insist that having an editor recognize your name is far overrated. Any advantage is good to have, but you don't need this edge to get published. All you need to do is to turn out a good product, and you can do this by learning a few simple, but essential nuts and bolts about writing. Then you carefully apply this knowledge to developing your own writing style.

Let's examine a little logic. Suppose you were the editor working for an important magazine, journal, or book publisher. It's fair to assume that most people would consider important any journal that happened to be their source of income. As an editor, your own success hinges on your ability to give your journal subscribers or book buyers what they want and need. If you succeed and your readership increases, your board of directors will be happy, making the company president happy, your boss happy, and you happy. Why would any editor who values success let friendships and familiar names seriously influence the decision to accept or reject a manuscript? Only a very shortsighted (and probably short-tenured) editor would run such a risk.

For several summers I have enjoyed traveling to college campuses to give writing workshops. Part of the enjoyment comes from visiting journal offices. For example, I have been shocked at the smallness of the staffs of some premier journals and with the physical smallness of other offices. Most readers would be surprised to learn that the amount of released time from teaching given to some editors is only one course per term; some get none.

Sometimes the editors of these journals share some interesting stories. For example, on one visit I learned that one of the most respected leaders in his field, both nationally and internationally, received a rejection letter for an article he submitted to a journal for which he had previously served as senior editor. In fact, it was generally acknowledged that this journal had been elevated to a rank unsurpassed by similar journals during this author's editorship. His manuscript was rejected because he had failed to give his own manuscript the attention and hard work that it needed to meet the standards of that journal.

If not a recognizable name, then what does one need to become a successful writer? Some say luck. It's hard to deny that luck does play a part in the success of writers. But many insist that real winners make their own luck. Rather than waiting for luck to come to us, each of us can *develop* an effective writing style that will increase our odds of success. What is the best style? One that works for you.

Now let's get specific about writing style. Basic to success for both nonfiction and fiction writers is the ability to write clearly, succinctly, and positively—to communicate. And whether writing fiction or nonfiction, all successful writers are able to communicate ideas, thoughts, and feelings with clarity and accuracy.

WRITING CLEARLY

In writing, clarity is best achieved through the use of a simple, concise, straightforward approach. Writing simply and clearly sounds easy, but for most people it is not. Why? There are two reasons. First, most beginning writers believe that the task before them is to impress the editor. Second, they think the best way to impress the editor is to use big words, complex sentences (well-seasoned with jargon), and long paragraphs. Both of these ideas are dead wrong. The way to impress an editor is to communicate clearly. This is not easy for most academicians who are steeped in jargon. Experienced writers and editors know that *anyone can take an easy topic and make it appear difficult, but only a skilled writer can take a complicated topic and make it appear simple.* Furthermore, the author's job is not to please the editor: it's to please the readers—the people who subscribe to the journal or buy the books or magazines. Editors have a common expression that sounds strange to the novice but has precise meaning to other editors. Editors are often heard saying: "It's *right* for our journal" or "It's *not right* for our journal." Good editors develop a keen and accurate sense for what their readers want and expect in terms of both content and style.

By now, perhaps you are asking, "How do I know what content and style are right for a publisher?" There are two easy, sure-fire ways to learn what editors expect from their writers. First, get a recent copy of the journal and study its style and content. Second, you can contact the editor to request a list of needs, future themes of the journal, and guidelines for contributors.

Write Concisely

In their classic reference book *The Elements of Style*, William Strunk, Jr. and E. B. White (1979) say:

> Vigorous writing is concise. A sentence should contain no unnecessary words, a paragraph no unnecessary sentences, for the same reason that a drawing should have no unnecessary lines and a machine no unnecessary parts. (p. 23)

Good writing is achieved by deleting unnecessary words and arranging the remaining words in active order. By this standard, parts of some translations of the Bible exemplify some of the best writing we know. For example, John 11:35 reads, "Jesus wept." Although our educational background may tell us that such simple writing should be avoided, this is powerful writing. Ironically, it is difficult to shed the pedagogical jargon that we have learned to use so effectively to cloud our meanings. For most of us, developing a good, simple writing style requires *unlearning* years of poor word selection and complicated sentence structure. But, with determination and practice, you can master the art of straightforward, simple writing.

It is now time to learn how to write clearly and simply. Figure 4–1 contains an editing exercise designed to help you recognize stylistic problems. Try to simplify each of the following statements by deleting unnecessary parts of each sentence. Be careful not to change the meaning of the sentence. Then refer to Figure 4–2 for an edited version of the exercise.

Although your results may vary from the revisions in Figure 4–2, you probably will agree that most of these statements are improved over those in Figure 4–1. If you look carefully, you will discover even more ways to shorten some of these sentences without changing their meanings. For example, sentence 7 still contains the superfluous words, "There is no doubt that." These words are excess baggage. Delete them. Sentence 8 has the useless words, "The reason is that." Sentence 9 could be shortened further by deleting "no doubt" and by changing "was right in finding" to "correctly found." It is important to note that this editing takes place in steps, and each step improves the quality of the product. This is precisely how good writers work. The popular belief that good writing is the product of geniuses

---

FIGURE 4–1   Editing exercise.

Delete the Unnecessary Words.

1. The truth of the matter is that the company was not successful.
2. The judge, who was a distant cousin, set him free.
3. She is a woman who does not usually stumble forward without giving considerable thought to the possible consequences.
4. His cousin, who is somewhat older than he, himself is, will stand a good chance to inherit the entire estate.
5. The fact is, he's finished.
6. His job is a highly demanding one.
7. There is no doubt but that he responded in a highly hasty manner.
8. The reason why is that the Hawthorne control group was shocked out of its complacency by the supervisor's presence.
9. There is no doubt that the jury was right in finding him guilty.
10. Were you aware of the fact that excessive salt produces hypertension?

---

is quite mistaken. Polished manuscripts result from a series of editing sessions, each bringing gradual improvement to the work.

Write Positively

Classes in public speaking teach us to speak assertively. When writing, we should write forcefully. Forceful writing results from writing concisely, actively, and positively. The present tense is usually more active and therefore more forceful than the past tense. Refer to the "close editing" examples in Figure 4–3. Sentence 1 can be made more positive and forceful by changing "not successful" to "unsuccessful." The words "does not" in sentence 3 can be replaced by the word "seldom" and, of course, the word "proceed" must be changed to "proceeds." Eliminating negative words such as "not" is often a key to making writing more positive and forceful.

Figure 4–3 shows the results of step-by-step editing of the statements from the earlier exercise. First, read a sentence in the left column and then follow that statement to the right to see how each editing step contributed to the improvement of the existing statement. Next, compare the statement in the left column with the final edited statement in the right column. Most of these examples show dramatic improvement. Finally, notice that the objective of the first two steps was to shorten the statements. In the last step, the objective is to make the statement more active. From these examples, can you make a statement about how writers can make their writings more

---

FIGURE 4–2   Effect of close editing.

1. The company was not successful.
2. The judge, a distant cousin, set him free.
3. She does not usually proceed without considering the consequences.
4. His older cousin will stand a good chance to inherit the entire estate.
5. He's finished.
6. His job is highly demanding.
7. There is no doubt that he responded hastily.
8. The reason is that the Hawthorne control group was shocked out of its complacency by the supervisor's presence.
9. No doubt the jury was right in finding him guilty.
10. Were you aware that excessive salt produces hypertension?

---

active? *To add power to their writing, good writers put the subject at the beginning of the sentence.*

Throughout most of the century, Americans have used the term "jump-start" to refer to the process of starting a stalled car engine. When former President George Bush applied the term to the country's lagging economy, suddenly it seemed as if we were jump-starting everything. Inexperienced writers often try to jump-start sentences with words such as "it" and "there" at the beginning—but these lifeless words are no more effective than using a dead battery to jump-start a car.

For example, consider the sentence, "It is a good practice to always lock your car." The first part of this sentence drags. You can read four words and still know nothing. Why not put a concrete subject up front? "Locking your car is a good practice." You might even make it a command: "Always lock your car."

The most common of these jump-start words is "there." This word should be used to give directions, yet it is often used to get sentences going. For example "There is a good chance that the person who buys the most tickets will win." Instead of this slow start, how about, "The person with the most tickets will probably win." Or "Buying more tickets increases your chance of winning."

Because the sentences we have been examining are exaggerated, they may seem contrived and ridiculously obvious. But many serious writings are full of superfluous words assembled awkwardly, and with passive verbs. Figure 4–4, however, contains sample sentences from the first draft of a book manuscript. This exercise will be more challenging.

After you have edited all of the sentences, examine Figure 4–5. The same editing process used in the previous exercise has been applied to these

FIGURE 4–3   Writing positively.

Original Sentence	First Revision	Second Revision	Third Revision
The truth of the matter is that the company was not successful.	The company was not successful.	The company was unsuccessful.	The company failed.
The judge who was a distant cousin, set him free.	The judge, a distant cousin, set him free.	The judge set him free. (Wrong valuable meaning is lost.)	
She is a woman who does not usually stumble forward without giving considerable thought to the consequences.	She seldom proceeds without giving considerable thought to the possible consequences.	She seldom proceeds without considering the consequences.	She thinks before she acts.
His cousin, who is somewhat older than he himself is, will stand a good chance to inherit the entire estate.	His older cousin will stand a good chance to inherit the entire estate.	His older cousin will probably inherit the entire estate.	
The fact is he's finished.	He's finished.		
His job is a highly demanding one. There is no doubt but that he responded in a hasty manner.	His job is demanding. He responded in a hasty manner.	 He responded hastily.	
There is no doubt that the jury was right in finding him guilty.	No doubt the jury was right in finding him guilty.	The jury was right in finding him guilty.	

more advanced statements. Because the original statements are more complex, the improvements are more pronounced.

Sentence 1 in Figure 4–4 has two major problems. First, it has a very weak beginning; and second, it is too wordy. *To give the sentence more force,*

FIGURE 4–4 Advanced editing exercise.

1. It will help if teachers will identify routines that need to be established.
2. Teacher preparation programs typically spend a great deal of time acquainting prospective teachers with how to teach information.
3. Such fear may well be a result of a lack of understanding of some ways of preventing problems and of responding to them once they do occur.
4. However, repetition should not be overdone, if it is, boredom can set in.
5. In general, people who are acknowledged to have a great deal of expertise in a given area exercise considerable influence over others.
6. Efforts are being taken in schools of nearly every industrialized nation to improve the quality of high schools.

---

put the subject up front. "Teachers should" or "teachers must" identify routines . . . give the sentence thrust. Shortening the sentence clarifies the meaning while making the sentence more powerful. The words "that need to be established" can be replaced with one word, "necessary." A reversal in the sequence of the last two words is needed.

Sentence 2 suffers from too many words and colloquialisms. By removing the colloquial expressions, you can reduce the number of words while removing the distractions. For example, use "much" instead of "a great deal of." Replace "how to teach" with "teaching methods" or "teaching strategies." Simply delete the word "information."

In sentence 3 replace "will be a result of" with "result from," giving the sentence more force. Change the remainder of the sentence to "a lack of awareness of ways to prevent and resolve problems." The expression "once they do occur" is superfluous since this is the only time one could respond to problems.

Sentence 4 begins with a conjunction, which is not as strict a taboo today as it once was; yet, don't do it casually. For example, sometimes starting a sentence with "however" or "but" can make a stark contrast to the previous sentence. Sentence 4 should read, "Excessive repetition causes boredom." Did you think of another way to eliminate the colloquialism "set in?"

Sentence 5 is far too wordy. You might begin by replacing "people who are acknowledged to have a great deal of expertise" with "experts," thereby reducing the number of letters and spaces from 61 to 7. This is economical writing through good editing. Good writers are good editors. The ending of the sentence, "exercise considerable influence over others" can be reduced to "influence others."

FIGURE 4–5   Good editing is a step-by-step process.

Original Sentence	First Revision (to shorten)	Second Revision (to shorten more)	Third Revision (to make active)
It will help if teachers will identify routines that need to be established.	It will help if teachers will identify necessary routines.		Teachers should identify necessary routines.
Teacher preparation programs typically spend a great deal of time acquainting prospective teachers with how to teach information.	Teacher preparation programs typically spend considerable time acquainting prospective teachers with how to teach.	Teacher preparation programs typically spend considerable time on teaching about methodology.	Most teacher preparation programs emphasize methodology.
Such fear may well be a result of a lack of understanding of some ways of preventing problems and responding to them once they do occur.	Such fear may result from a lack of understanding of ways to prevent problems and respond to them.	Such fear may result from a lack of understanding of ways to prevent and respond to problems.	Not knowing how to prevent and respond to problems can frighten teachers.
However, repetition should not be overdone. If it is boredom can set in.	Repetition should not be overdone. If it is boredom can set in.	Excessive repetition can result in boredom.	Excessive repetition can cause boredom.
In general, people who are acknowledged to have a great deal of expertise in a given area exercise considerable influence over others.	In general, experts in a given area exercise considerable influence over others.	Experts in a given area exercise considerable influence over others.	Experts often influence their peers.
Efforts are being taken in nearly every industrialized nation to improve the quality of their schools.	Efforts are being made by most industrialized nations to improve their schools.		Most industrialized nations are working to improve their schools.

The sentences in this second exercise are representative of those found in actual manuscripts. Writing an article or book requires several editings. Indeed, *good writing is the result of good editing, and good editing occurs in gradual steps.*

Treat Genders Fairly

The 1970s was the decade that brought concern for equal treatment of the sexes into the public consciousness, and that change was accomplished largely through our literature. As great efforts are made to portray the sexes equally and fairly, too often the results are awkward writing. Our society has moved from using the single pronoun *he* and *him* to the double pronouns *he or she* and *him or her*—we even take care to reverse the order much of the time. Then we learned to combine *she* and *he* by using a slash (s/he). All of these attempts to treat the genders fairly result in awkward reading. Some textbook authors have attempted to handle the problem by using masculine pronouns throughout and by prefacing the book with a disclaimer directing the reader to think masculine half of the time and feminine the other half of the time. None of these strategies is acceptable.

Two easy strategies will skillfully handle the gender issue in almost all circumstances. Either you can simply choose to pluralize the subject or the antecedent, or you can reconstruct the sentence so that the need for identifying the gender of the subject or antecedent is eliminated. Figure 4–6 provides an opportunity for you to develop skill in treating the genders fairly without disrupting the flow of each sentence. First, see if you can resolve the problem by using the pluralizing strategy. Then see if you can resolve the problem by reconstructing the sentences. For this exercise, ignore the superfluity of these statements, and do not edit for any purposes other than dealing with the gender problem.

Now that you have had an opportunity to apply these two strategies, examine Figure 4–7 and compare the changes with those you made. Should you find discrepancies, don't worry. Usually you will find several ways to

---

FIGURE 4–6 Treating genders equally.

1. There is no relationship between a learner's self-concept and the likelihood that he or she will develop acceptable patterns of self-control.
2. The teacher can continue to monitor the entire class at the same time that he or she is working with the small group.
3. If someone is liked and respected as an individual, people are more willing to accept his or her advice than if he or she is not liked.

FIGURE 4–7   Eliminating sexism through pluralizing and restructuring.

Original Statement	Pluralizing	Restructuring
There is no relationship between a learner's self-concept and the likelihood that he or she will develop acceptable patterns of self-control.	There is no relationship between learner's self-concepts and the likelihood that they will develop patterns of self-control.	Self-concept has no effect on self-control.
The teacher can continue to monitor the entire class at the same time that he or she is working with the small group.	Teachers can continue to monitor the entire class at the same time that they are working with the small group.	The teacher can continue monitoring the entire class while working with the small group.
If someone is liked and respected as an individual, people are more willing to accept his or her advice than if he or she is not liked.	If people are liked and respected as individuals, others are more likely to accept their advice than if they are not liked.	Friends have more influence than enemies.

improve statements. Some improvements may be better than others, but *all* improvements are good!

Study Figure 4–7. Notice that for each statement, both pluralizing and restructuring methods are applied. Do you prefer the results of the revisions by pluralizing over those by reconstructing? Is your preference consistent for all three statements? This may give you some insight into how you want to handle this concern in your writing.

The net result of developing and using an effective writing style is capturing and holding the reader's attention—a goal that all successful writers keep in front of them at all times. The article that appears in Appendix C summarizes these stylistic goals.

Developing conciseness requires concerted effort. Figure 4–8 lists some of the most common examples of expressions that can clutter writing.

The expressions in Figure 4–9 are some of many that make writing unnecessarily wordy. Long words have already been identified as contributing to needlessly complex writing. A list of such words and their simpler substitutes appears in Figure 4–9.

FIGURE 4–8   Replacing long expressions with fewer words.

Bulky	Concise	Bulky	Concise
until such time as	until	on a daily basis	daily
a high rate of speed	fast	in a hasty manner	hastily
on account of	because	in close proximity	near
in the event that	if	there is no doubt that	undoubtedly
provides information	tells	administrate	administer/run
in the majority of cases	usually	a large percentage of	most
each and every one	each	once upon a time	once
has to do with	concerns	during the past year	last year
has the capability of	can	can't help but think	think
in spite of the fact that	although	almost everyone	most
cancel out	cancel	need to be established	needed
mandatory requirement	requirement	filled to capacity	full
at that point in time	then	give consideration to	consider
at this point in time	now	as to the question	why
in attendance	there	as to why	
improve the quality of	improve	rank order	rank
a new innovation	an innovation	as to whether or not	whether
in short supply	scarce	put in an appearance	attend
in the final analysis	finally	revert back to	revert to
continues to occur	reoccurs	a great deal of	much
in the forseeable future	soon	with the exception of	except
she is a woman who	she	in the amount of	of
in the majority of	usually	to have to tell you	to say
instances		have no other choice	must
in view of the fact that	since		

This list is intended to stimulate you to think of more two-dollar words that can easily be replaced with 25-cent words. Understandably, politicians hear a lot of fancy words that lack meaning. Texas congressman Maury Maverick coined the word "gobbledygook" to represent those words that sound fancy but have little meaning. For him, such words conjured up the image of a turkey gobbler which spreads its wings, struts around, and gobbles. Like the gobble-gobble sounds made by Old Tom, such words make their users look like turkeys.

You might be surprised to know just how often you use unnecessarily long words and expressions. John Locke said "We are what we do. Therefore, excellence is a habit." Obtuse writing is also a habit, and like all habits, it is difficult to break. Figure 4–10 provides further opportunity to practice using shorter sentences and shorter words.

---

use
FIGURE 4–9   Writers should ~~utilize~~ small words.

utilize	use
prioritize	rank
medication	medicine
origination	origin
established	set
irregardless	regardless
administer	run/give

When you have completed the exercise in Figure 4–10, examine the following edited version:

If you attended the meeting last year, you know why the room was full and why that meeting usually improves our sales. She can give each innovation a boost.

Consider the difference this type of editing can make when applied to an entire manuscript.

For several years, I have taught a course on writing for publication. Most students in this class have published. To earn an A, students must produce two completed, edited, polished, and mailed manuscripts. Half as much is required for a B. No student has failed to earn a B, and half have

---

FIGURE 4–10   Additional editing practice.

In the event that you were in attendance at the most recent meeting this past

year, you have a pretty good understanding of why that presentation improves

the quality of our sales, at least in the majority of instances. You also have a

good understanding as to why the room was filled to capacity.

I have to tell you that she has the ability to give each new innovation a boost.

earned As. But, notice that the course does not require manuscript *acceptances*; only that the manuscript is mailed to a national journal. Acceptance is not required because the turnaround time for some of the journals is longer than the entire semester.

One student shocked herself, her classmates, and me by breaking the world's speed record for acceptances *and* by a premiere journal whose acceptance rate is about 5 percent. As a class we edited her manuscript on Friday. The following Friday this student announced to us the acceptance of her manuscript. Her article appears in Figure 4–11. It seems an appropriate ending for this chapter.

FIGURE 4–11 Sample student article.

One-Pulse Words: Short, Sweet, and to the Point
by Ann Davis Toppins

Once a day I try to state in short words what I think. The words I use are words of one pulse. The rest of the day I use words that are two-, three-, or six-pulse words—just the way school folks ought to talk. But each day for a short time I work at plain speech. My aim is to clear my head.

I learned this mode of speech a few years back. Dave Blum wrote of the Club for One-Pulse Words, a group of friends who write and speak this way as much as three hours a day. The group lives by these rules:

1. Use no words of more than one pulse.
2. Words that make use of a small mark (such as "don't") are fine but should be used with care.
3. Folks' names that have more than one pulse should be changed to code words.
4. Don't be a pest.

Their point is that "words don't have to be long to be good."

To help you get a grip on this kind of speech, look at how I have changed what most school kids say each day:

I pledge my troth to the flag of the states that are joined in this land and to the form of rule for which it stands; one large state with trust in God, not to be split, in which all can be free and for whom the law is just.

See what I mean? Some of this may seem forced, and it is. I'm new at the task, and it's hard to speak in one-pulse words. The art is to use them so well that they sound smooth. Those skilled in the craft have done this for years. The Bard, whose first name is William and whose last name is a blend of shake and spear, left us a store of one-pulse quotes. "To thine own self be true." "Out, damned spot! out, I say!" "What's in a name?" "To be or not to be." And what school child was not stirred by:

Continued

FIGURE 4–11   *Continued*

Give a man a horse he can ride,
  Give a man a boat he can sail;
And his rank and wealth, his strength and
health,
  On sea nor shore shall fail.

That 12-line verse, by a scribe named James whose last name tells us he was Tom's son, has just two words of more than one pulse in the whole work.

The fair sex, too, have used this form to say what they feel. The maid whose first name is the same as the queen of the Brits and whose last name is Brown with an -ing on the end wrote:

How do I love thee? Let me count the ways.
I love thee to the depth and breadth and
height my soul can reach. . . .

Much of our lore—the truth passed on from one group to the next—is found in words of one pulse: "Where there's a will, there's a way." "Where there's smoke, there's fire." "A bird in the hand is worth two in the bush." "All things come to him who waits." "Three's a crowd." And the well-known Book of God has a large stock of one-pulse lines. "And God said, 'Let there be light.' " "You shall know the truth and the truth shall make you free." No doubt you can think of more.

Since I have learned this game, I find strings of one-pulse words in use each day by all sorts of folks. When I read a book, talk with a friend, or watch the tube, I hear such things as, "Let me give it to you straight." "What shall I do with my life?" "You can't mean that!" "Keep your chin up." "This is a piece of cake." "Are you out of your mind?" "Where's the beef?"

I once asked a class to write a thought in one-pulse words. Some could not. Some would not. Some slipped in a few two-pulse words and were shocked when I found them. Most thought the task was weird. Three or four vowed not to choose my course the next term.

At times I try to get my peers to talk with me this way. A few laugh and join in the fun, but some look at me as if I were on the wrong train. Most who teach in my field want to stretch their words, not cut them short. They have heard that they must write or die. And they think that what they write needs to sound big if it is to be seen in print. So they add -ize, -tion, or -ing to plain words and hope that they sound wise.

You may think I write these lines with tongue in cheek, so to speak. In a way I do, but my point is that great truths can be said in one-pulse words. Who knows? My own thoughts may last if I can do the same. And, as the words carved on the tomb of the wit John Gay make clear:

Life is a jest, and all things show it,
I thought so once, and now I know it.

Reprinted with permission of Anne Davis Toppins, Associate Professor Emerita, College of Education, the University of Alabama.

RECAPPING THE MAJOR POINTS

While learning how to write concisely, actively, and positively, you are well into the process of developing an effective writing style. Take every opportunity to edit your own writing and the writings of others. Only with practice will your skills continue to improve. As you continue your writing, remember these points:

- Most editors base their decisions to accept or reject manuscripts on the quality of the manuscript and its relevance to the readers.
- Nobody has time to write. Successful writers must reassign time for their writing, time which they need for other activities.
- Everyone with average intelligence has much information that would make an excellent article, if correctly written and aimed at the right market.
- All good writers must write, edit, and rewrite each manuscript several times.
- Writers should place clarity above all else.
- Rejections don't always imply low quality.
- Good writing is more plain than fancy, more simple than complex.
- Editors and writers are partners who share the same goal: to produce the best possible product for their readers.
- Authors don't need pomposity and arrogance, but they do need self-confidence.
- The best way to impress editors is to write clearly and accurately.

REFERENCES

Blum, D. "Some guys I know march to the beat of one weird drum." *Wall Street Journal* (July 15, 1982) p. 1.

Strunk, W., Jr., and White, E. B. *The Elements of Style.* New York: Macmillan, 1979.

Toppins, A. D. "One-pulse words: Short, sweet, and to the point." *Phi Delta Kappan,* 66(4), 286–287.

5

Organizing Articles

Conducting workshops for writers is a gratifying experience because of the many different people who attend them. Over one hundred such workshops, some with hundreds of participants, have had no known disinterested participants or, indeed, no participant who was only mildly interested. Unlike the members of many audiences who arrive early to get a seat in the back of the room, these people arrive early to get a front seat! Nor does the speaker have to strive to get their attention. They arrive motivated and, for the duration of the workshop, they remain motivated.

Educators tell us that learning requires only two factors: motivation and ability. The students must want to learn, and they must be capable of learning at the same level that the teacher is teaching. Aspiring writers are seldom short on either motivation or ability. When writing workshops fail, it's usually the presenter's fault. Too many participants blame themselves. *Never doubt your ability to succeed as a writer. Just set your goals and go for them. You can astound yourself.* This chapter will help you develop your organizing skills, and the ability to organize will help you produce a more successful manuscript.

The facts and tips on writing are easy to teach. Given highly capable and motivated audiences, most of the *how-tos*, the *what-tos*, and *what-not-tos* of writing are easily taught. This is not always true for helping people become better organizers. One aspiring writer was completely baffled over writers' abilities to assemble hundreds of pages of ideas. This confused but brave beginner asked a very simple, yet poignant question: How do you know how to organize a manuscript? The fact is, most people who are good organizers would be hard pressed to explain how they do it. They just do it. But they do it well. An answer such as this is of little help to individuals who have not yet mastered the skill of organizing writing. Fortunately for some of us who struggled with outlining assignments in our high school

English classes, organizing writing content for the purpose of publishing is easier than other types of organizing.

Have you ever watched while someone prepared a meal? If so, and if your acquaintance with the kitchen is limited to the refrigerator and microwave oven, you may have been amazed at the complexity of the task. (Some items are baking while others are skewering; and the cook is mixing others.) To a novice, just the timing alone is a miracle. But the experienced cook usually manages to have all the dishes and the bread and drink completed at the same time. This is organizing!

If you are an accomplished cook (which by my definition means that in two tries out of three you can prepare a simple meal without burning down the kitchen), then you are an organizer, even though you may find it difficult to explain how you do it. The same is true for writers. *Successful writers are good organizers* although they may not be able to help others learn how to organize. But there is good news. Organizing manuscripts for publication can be learned if you are willing to heed some advice that may sound elementary and trite. Maybe the following is just that, elementary and trite, but it is also a sure-fire way to improve your organizing skills.

ORGANIZING NONFICTION ARTICLES

Organization can be thought of as a separate tool that you can use to hold your readers' attention, make your writing clearer, and give your writing more force. There are skills that you can easily master and use to achieve better organization. These skills include establishing credibility, achieving substance, paragraphing, and using flowcharts.

Organizing Skill No. 1: Establishing Credibility

Nonfiction readers are critical of the authors whose works they read. When receiving a professional journal, the typical professional scans the index to examine the article titles *and* to see who wrote each article. They have a common thought in mind. "Who is the author? Who is he or she to be telling me about this topic? Does this person have expertise that I don't have?" In other words, "Why should I read this person's writings?"

Some authors may find such critical questions annoying, but many experienced authors recognize this as an opportunity to score a point with the reader while also scoring a point with the editor. But to accomplish this, you must be familiar with some of the sources of evidence that the reader finds credible. In almost every workshop, I ask participants to tell me what they consider good evidence that an author has necessary expertise to write on a given topic. Almost without exception the first response is the author's title. Running a close second is the author's degree(s). You can do better.

Far more convincing than degrees and titles is evidence that the author has researched the topic. Nonfiction authors can and should immediately show the readers that they have researched the subject. The article in Figure 5–1 shows how this can be done quickly and easily.

In the very first paragraph of their article, the authors leave no doubt that they have researched this topic. In this short, two-sentence lead paragraph, they cite eight references—an excellent model for establishing credibility early in the article.

Organizing Skill No. 2: Achieving Substance

Nonfiction readers go to the libraries and bookstores in search of substance just as grocery shoppers go to the supermarket. Just like the grocery shoppers, readers look over the products. They don't want just anything to fill their baskets. They want substances that have specific uses. The producers of every product in the stores know that their economic survival depends on their ability to help the customers find what they need. Through cleverly designed, eye-catching advertising, they make the advantages of their products known to everyone who comes down the aisle. Book and magazine buyers shop just as selectively. They browse through the bookshelves and the card files until they find something promising. Then they track it down and, opening to the table of contents, they resume their shopping. They check the article or chapter titles. Everyone knows that people today are selective, but few realize just how selective people really are. Newspaper publishers know. They know that only one reader in 10 completes reading a front page article that continues on another page. This is why papers such as *USA Today* don't extend many articles beyond one page.

Knowing that the readers are looking for specific content and knowing that the average reader will give only a few seconds to survey the table of contents of a journal or book gives you an advantage over your less-aware competitors. You have already learned how to select captivating titles. Now consider the reader's next move. After finding a title that promises content, the reader will either begin reading or will thumb through the article to see how long it is and what it looks like. Either way the author wins, so far.

This is where the experienced writer takes care to see that the reader doesn't take a quick glance and reject the article. This can be done by openly displaying the major parts of the manuscript. By clearly identifying the distinct parts and by structuring the article appropriately to display these parts, you can achieve the same effect that the washing powder producers hope to achieve by labeling their products with "Effective in hot or cold water" and

FIGURE 5-1   Establishing credibility.

Source Monitoring
Marcia K. Johnson, Shahin Hashtroudi, and D. Stephen Lindsay

A framework for understanding source monitoring and relevant empirical evidence is described, and several related phenomena are discussed: old-new recognition, indirect tests, eyewitness testimony, misattributed familiarity, cryptomnesia, and incorporation of fiction into fact. Disruptions in source monitoring (e.g., from confabulation, amnesia, and aging) and the brain regions that are involved are also considered, and source monitoring within a general memory architecture is discussed. It is argued that source monitoring is based on qualities of experience resulting from combinations of perceptual and reflective processes, usually requires relatively differentiated phenomenal experience, and involves attributions varying in deliberateness. These judgments evaluate information according to flexible criteria and are subject to error and disruption. Furthermore, diencephalic and temporal regions may play different roles in source monitoring than do frontal regions of the brain.

Past experience affects us in many ways. It influences the ease of identifying stimuli under degraded conditions (e.g., Jacoby & Dallas, 1981), changes the probability that we will think certain thoughts (e.g., Dominowski & Ekstrand, 1967; Kihlstrom, 1980), affects emotional responses such as preferences (e.g., Johnson, Kim, & Risse, 1985; Zajonc, 1980), manifests itself as expert or semantic knowledge (e.g., Chase & Simon, 1973; Tulving, 1983), and creates the potential for what we take to be memories of autobiographical events from our personal past (e.g., Rubin, 1986).

This review focuses on expressions of memory that involve judgments about the origin, or source, of information. The term *source* refers to a variety of characteristics that, collectively, specify the conditions under which a memory is acquired (e.g., the spatial, temporal, and social context of the event; the media and modalities through which it was perceived). This concept is closely related to, but somewhat more inclusive than, that of memory for context. A central claim of the source-monitoring approach is that people do not typically directly retrieve an abstract tag or label that specifies a memory's source, rather, activated memory records are evaluated and attributed to particular sources through decision processes performed during remembering.

The ability to identify the source of remembered information is critical for many cognitive tasks. In laboratory studies of memory, for example, it helps subjects differentiate between test items they recognize or recall from a study list and test items that seem familiar or come to mind from other sources. In everyday life, memory for source contributes to our ability to exert control over our own opinions and beliefs; if you remember that the source of a "fact" was a supermarket tabloid such as the *National Enquirer* and not *Consumer Reports,* you have information that is important for evaluating the veridicality of the purported fact. Perhaps most important, the subjective experience of autobiographical recollection—the feeling of

Continued

FIGURE 5–1 *Continued*

remembering a specific experience in one's own life—depends on source attributions made on the basis of certain phenomenal qualities of remembered experience. (When memory information enters consciousness without these qualitative characteristics, it is experienced as knowledge or belief.)

Inability to specify source information can be mildly disconcerting, as in not being able to remember whether the person to whom you are about to tell a joke is the one who told you the joke in the first place. Failures to remember source can also be profoundly disruptive, as in delusions (e.g., Oltmanns & Maher, 1988) and confabulation (e.g., Stuss, Alexander, Lieberman, & Levine, 1978). In fact, a severe disruption in remembering source is a salient feature of some, and perhaps all, forms of amnesia (Hirst, 1982; Mayes, Meudell, & Pickering, 1985).

Source monitoring refers to the set of processes involved in making attributions about the origins of memories, knowledge, and beliefs (Hashtroudi, Johnson, & Chrosniak, 1989; Johnson, 1988a, 1988b; Lindsay & Johnson, 1987; Lindsay, Johnson, & Kwon, 1991). There has been a recent upsurge of interest in such questions (e.g., R. E. Anderson, 1984; Eich & Metcalfe, 1989; Foley, Durso, Wilder, & Friedman, 1991; Hanley & Collins, 1989; Intraub & Hoffman, 1992; Jacoby, Kelley, & Dywan, 1989; Johnson & Raye, 1981; Kahan & Johnson, 1992; Masson, . . .

From *Psychological Bulletin* (1993) Vol. 114 No. 1, p. 3. Reprinted by permission.

"Gets out ugly stains." *Arrange your manuscript so that its major messages are visible to even the casual reader.*

The article in Figure 5–2 uses similar structuring techniques to communicate clearly that it, too, has something definite to say. This article, titled "Middle Schools: Paradoxes and Promises," identifies several major nuggets of material. Some of these nuggets are labeled "paradoxes" and some are called "promises." The paradoxes are listed sequentially and all of them are presented before the promises are addressed. Numerals are used to give emphasis to the fact that this article has a definite number of separate and distinct pieces of substance.

Organizing Skill No. 3: Paragraphing

English texts frequently discuss several types of paragraphs, such as introductory, emphatic, transitional, and concluding. As mentioned earlier, writers need to know how to write each of these types, but the major problem

FIGURE 5–2   Communicating visually through structure.

Middle Schools: Paradoxes and Promises
Kenneth T. Henson

Anyone who has read Charles Dickens' *A Tale of Two Cities* will recall the opening lines:

> *It was the best of times, it was the worst of times, it was the age of wisdom, it was the age of foolishness, it was the epoch of belief, it was the epoch of incredulity, it was the season of light, it was the season of darkness, it was the spring of hope, it was the winter of despair, we had everything before us, we had nothing before us, we were all going direct to Heaven, we were all going the other way.*

To the uneducated person, these lines may appear foolish, but the alert mind finds them stimulating. With these few lines, Dickens was able to tell his readers that they were about to set out on a journey full of suspense and action. Such is often the case with paradoxes; they challenge us to investigate, and yet they are difficult to understand.

The American middle school is one of the most misunderstood institutions in our society. It is also one of the most interesting and challenging concepts, with unlimited possibilities. Like Dickens' novel, the American middle school is full of paradoxes that not only make it a worthy challenge to study, but that also fill it with promises for becoming a better educational institution than any of its predecessors. The following presents some of these paradoxes and discusses some of the promises for hope and success of the American middle school.

Paradox Number 1
Teaching in the middle school is both frustrating and rewarding.

Interestingly, few students plan to teach the middle grades; yet, attrition alone assures that the number of middle school and junior high school teachers is greater than the number of high school teachers. Therefore, most middle school teachers begin their experiences somewhat reluctantly and without confidence. They find their students at a very awkward age. This brings an inordinate number of problems to the middle school teacher.

But after teaching this level of students for a year, many teachers find themselves hooked on this age group for life. The reason for this paradox is found in the rewarding feeling teachers experience when they help youths who have either no direction or too many directions in their lives. The middle school teacher is often identified as the one individual in a youth's life who is most influential and whom the students would most like to emulate.

> *I continued with two additional paradoxes and then introduced three promises as follows:*

Continued

FIGURE 5–2   *Continued*

Promises of the Middle School
Although the middle school offers contradictions and challenges, these should not be interpreted as indicators of a dismal future for the middle school. In recent years, research on classroom teaching offers much to counterbalance the limitations imposed by these paradoxes. Following is a generalized representation of the research that can make the future of the middle school increasingly bright and successful.

Promise Number 1
Many popular myths that limited progress in academic achievement have been disproved.
According to Hunter,

> *Current findings are in direct contrast to the former fatalistic stance that regarded I.Q. and socioeconomic status as unalterable determinants of academic achaievement. Gone also should be the notions that different ages, ethnic deviations, or content to be learned require a completely different set of professional skills, or that effective teachers must be born and can't be made.* (1983, p. 169)

Although no one denies that genetic inheritance sets limits on learning, recent research shows that many students' learning has been curtailed by their acceptance of limits imposed by intelligence-test scores, limits that have often been far below their real levels of ability. In fact, studies have shown that contrary to popular belief, a full 90 to 95 percent of all second-ary-level students are capable of mastering all of the content and objectives found in modern schools (Bloom, Hastings, & Madaus, 1981, p. 51).

> *I continued with Promises Numbers 2 and 3, and then wrote the following conclusions:*

Conclusions
The middle school has not failed in the many ways that the junior high school failed, and it will not likely achieve the poor image of its predecessor because, unlike the junior high school, the middle school has a clear set of purposes. Among these purposes is that of nurturing the emotional, social, and cognitive growth of students. Despite the many paradoxes that make these goals difficult to reach, recent progress in educational research gives reason to hope that all teachers at all levels will become more effective in their power to enhance cognitive growth in their classrooms.
   Since its origin, the middle school has been dedicated to nurturing the growth of its students, and middle school teachers have always viewed change positively. As research on classroom teaching continues to enhance cognitive attainment at all levels (K–12), these characteristics of the middle school and of middle school teachers should accelerate this progress among students in the middle schools.

I always count the number of references in articles in my intended journal and I purposely include a few more than average. Can you guess why? You'll find the answer in a later chapter.

References

Alexander, W. M., et al. 1968. *The emergent middle school* (2nd ed.). New York: Holt, Rinehart, and Winston.

Bloom, B. S., Hastings, G, & Madaus, J. T. 1981. *Evaluating to improve learning.* New York: McGraw-Hill Book Company.

Dickens, C. 1963. *A tale of two cities.* New York: Airmont Publishing Company.

Epstein, H. T. 1976, April. A biologically based framework of intervention projects. *Mental Retardation, 14:* 26–27.

Good, T. zL., & Brophy, J. (in press). *Third handbook of research on teaching.* New York: Macmillan Publishers.

Henson, K. T. 1981. *Secondary teaching methods.* Lexington, MA: D.C. Heath and Company.

Henson, K. T., & Saterfiel, T. 1985, January. Are recent state-wide accountability programs educationally sound? *NASSP Bulletin* 23–27.

Hudson, L. 1968. *Contrary imaginations: A psychological study of the English school boy.* Middlesex, England: Pegasus Books, Inc.

Hunter, M. 1983. Knowing, teaching, and supervising. In P. L. Hosford (Ed.), Using what we know about teaching. Alexandria, VA: Association for Supervision and Curriculum Development.

Konopka, G. 1973, Fall. Requirements for healthy development of adolescent youth. *Adolescence, 8,* 10–11.

Offer, D. 1969. *The psychological world of the teenager.* New York: Basic Books.

Saylor, J. G. 1982. *Who planned the curriculum? A Curriculum reservoir model with historical examples.* West Lafayette, IN: Kappa Delta Pi.

The Clearing House, Vol. 59, issue 8, pp. 345–347, April 1986. Reprinted with permission of The Helen Dwight Reid Educational Foundation. Published by Heldref Publications, 1319 18th Street, N.W., Washington, D.C. 20036–1802. Copyright 1986.

that writers experience with paragraphs is their inability to identify one. That's right. Many struggling writers don't know a paragraph when they see one! Furthermore, they often fail to recognize one when they, themselves have written it. A review of a few journal articles will show that some published writers fall into this category. As simple as it sounds, without the spacing and indenting, could you tell where another writer's paragraphs should begin and end? Would you see paragraphs exactly the same as another writer sees them? Probably not.

Your elementary or junior high science class probably first introduced you to concepts. There, you learned that concepts are categories made up by people. What a friend considers a long pencil with a soft lead, you may consider a short pencil with hard lead. So it is with paragraphs; yet, some general guidelines are available. As was discussed in Chapter 3, each paragraph should focus around one major idea. When the author progresses to a new idea, a new paragraph should be used. Sounds simple, but is it? For example, examine this paragraph that you are now reading. Does it focus on one idea? Two? More? Should it be divided to form more than one paragraph? If so, where? Figure 5–3 consists of the first two pages of an article—but all of the author's paragraphs have been removed. Take some time to decide where *you* would begin each new paragraph.

Ideally, new paragraphs begin every time the author moves from one clear idea to another. If you would like to see how the author of this article used paragraphing, refer to Appendix D.

Learning to paragraph takes practice. Don't be too harsh on yourself if your paragraphs and the author's are not identical. Paragraphing remains an art; some variation is to be tolerated. In fact, variation is expected, since the author's personal preferences affect the length of each paragraph.

Paragraph Sequencing

Writers are often confused over the search for the "correct" sequence for their paragraphs. Sometimes the sequence of paragraphs is of little significance. It usually doesn't matter which set of pros and cons follows another set or which axiom follows another—but it is always good to *check to see if a logical paragraph sequence exists.* For example, in an article titled "Ten Ways to Increase Your Safety at the Ice Rink," an author might put *follow the direction of the crowd* before giving advice about exiting the rink. Perhaps you noticed in the article about the myths of corporal punishment that Myth Number One is introduced first because the other myths explain the basis for Myth Number One.

The advent of the word processor has eased the paragraph sequencing task for many contemporary writers. If you do not use a word processor (although perhaps you already know you should), an alternative is to write each paragraph on an index card. When all paragraphs are written, you can simply organize and reorganize the cards until they are in the sequence that makes the most sense to you. Remember that each paragraph, from the first sentence to the last sentence in the article, should advance the discussion.

FIGURE 5–3   Paragraphing exercise.

Two hundred years after the French Revolution, when the division between Left and Right began to be used to map political alignments, it seems obvious to many that such clear-cut political differentiation has lost its meaning. Certainly, it is argued, that Left no longer can be said to have reality—with the collapse of international communism, the decomposition of the Soviet bloc, the abandonment of socialism by those living under its "actually existing" form, and the recent conservative drift of politics in many Western countries. I want to argue, however, that we still need "left" and "right" to signify certain essential political and cultural differences. I want to propose that what is dying is a particular type of political mobilization. It is, I want to suggest, the Left as Party which has come to an end. The Left is, first of all, let us say, a tradition—a relatively distinct body of belief and action that began to have a coherent character at the time of the American and French revolutions. An enormous variety of ideological perspectives and a host of labels constitute that tradition: socialism, anarchism, communism, pacifism, radical democracy, feminism, certain variants of libertarianism; in the United States, instead of these relatively specific labels, leftists typically refer to themselves by using such ideologically euphemistic terms as progressive, liberal, populist, and radical. Left ideological perspectives have often been propelled by organizations created to advance those perspectives. The proliferation of ideological perspectives, of variants within them, and of organizations representing these perspectives who are competing for support has meant that the tradition of the Left has been deeply structured by internecine struggle. Given the ideological divisions and warfare on the left, what warrants the assertion that there is nevertheless a shared tradition? What, if anything, do the Left fragments have in common? One answer is that there is an essential idea that underlies these ideological differences. That idea, it seems to me can be best captured by a statement like this: Society and economic life should be arranged so that every member of society has the chance to have some voice in shaping the conditions within which their lives are lived; socioeconomic arrangements in which a few can decide the lives of the many should be replaced by arrangements based on collective self-government; social life should be structured as much as possible on the basis of reasoned discourse among society's members, rather than by the exercise of power or by chance (or the working of impersonal markets). In short, the Left tradition is the cumulative struggle to envision and practice a fully realized democracy. Most of the ideological differences within the tradition of the Left have revolved around issues of power and strategy. Disputes over what kinds of power—economic, political, military, sexual—have primacy, and over the agencies, levers and processes of . . .

From "The Party's Over—So What Is To Be Done?" by Richard Flacks, *Social Research*, Vol. 60, No. 3, Fall 1993. Reprinted with permission.

Organizing Skill No. 4: Using Flowcharts to Organize

Another way to organize your article or book chapter is to develop a visual diagram of flowchart. The illustration in Figure 5–4 is an example of how authors can use a picture to explain a concept described in their article.

If you share my frustration with authors such as William Faulkner who with all ease slip into and out of trains of thought, you can appreciate the power of flowcharts such as the one shown in Figure 5–4 to simplify the writing job as well as the job of the reader. The horizontal lines are used to enable the author to branch off from the article or chapter's major message or theme and later return at will.

For example, suppose you are writing an article to explain a new program. Your purpose is to enable other institutions to use this program. You could identify several vertical steps and write a question for each. Step One: What is this program? Step Two: What does it achieve? Step Three: What are its parts? Step Four: How effective has it been? Step Five: How could it be improved? At each of these vertical steps, a horizontal line could be used to list those ideas to be covered. For example, at Step One you might wish to list several factors such as defining the program, giving its purpose, and telling why it is important to your institution. At Step Two you could list several advantages or benefits of such a program. At Step Three you could list all of its parts and perhaps briefly discuss each.

RECAPPING THE MAJOR POINTS

Learning the how-tos, the what-tos, and the what-not-tos of writing is easy, but learning how to organize an article is not so simple. In this chapter you learned the following:

- Trust yourself. You have the ability to develop essential writing skills.
- Successful writing requires good organizing skills.
- Immediately establish your credibility.
- You must show your readers that your article contains substance that they consider valuable.

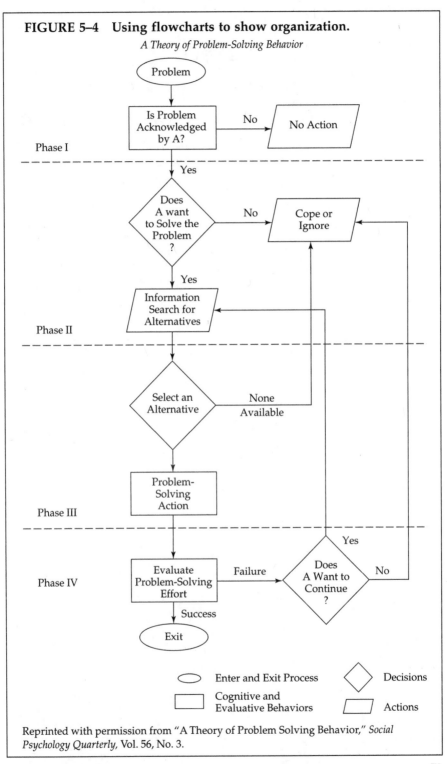

FIGURE 5–4   Using flowcharts to show organization.

A Theory of Problem-Solving Behavior

Problem

Phase I

Is Problem
Acknowledged
by A?

No → No Action

Yes

Does
A want
to Solve the
Problem
?

No → Cope or Ignore

Phase II

Yes

Information
Search for
Alternatives

Select an
Alternative

None
Available

Problem-
Solving
Action

Phase III

Phase IV

Evaluate
Problem-Solving
Effort

Failure →

Does
A Want to
Continue
?

Yes

No

Success

Exit

Enter and Exit Process   Decisions

Cognitive and
Evaluative Behaviors   Actions

Reprinted with permission from "A Theory of Problem Solving Behavior," *Social Psychology Quarterly,* Vol. 56, No. 3.

REFERENCES

Johnson, M. K., Hashtroud, S., and Lindsay, D. S. "Source Monitoring." *Psychological Bulletin,* 114(1), 3–28.

Henson, K. T. "Middle Schools: Paradoxes and promises." *The Clearing House,* 59(8), 345–347.

Flacks, R. "The party's over: So what is to be done?" *Social Research,* 60(3), 445.

Tallman, I., Leik, R. K., Gray, L. N., and Staford, M. C. "A theory of problem-solving behavior." *Social Psychology Quarterly,* 56(3), 157–177.

6

Using Journals, Libraries, and Surveys

USING JOURNALS

For years higher education institutions have encouraged their members to write and submit their works to journals for publishing. Major research universities have held the strongest expectations for their academic employees, often requiring them to publish in research journals. Recently, however, many regional, private, and parochial colleges and universities also have begun requiring their ranks to write and submit their manuscripts to professional journals.

Whether writing for a research-type journal or other professional journals, writers can begin improving their skills in this craft by using the journals as models. Few novice writers and perhaps only a few experienced writers make maximum use of the journals to perfect their writing and publishing skills. Editors will tell you that you should begin writing each article by reading a few recent issues of the journal to which you plan to submit your manuscript. This chapter will present other ways that you can use the journals to increase the likelihood of acceptance of your manuscripts.

Physical Characteristics

Interestingly, readers can read every issue of a journal for years and still know very little about the physical makeup of the journal. Think about a journal that you often read. If asked, could you accurately describe this journal's average article length, average reading level, the average number of references per article, frequency of themed issues, whether manuscripts are sent out for review and if so to what degree? Each of these questions is very important to the aspiring writer; each one can increase the chances of manuscript acceptance—and the answers are in the journals. The secret to understanding what the editor thinks is right for a journal can be unlocked by studying that journal's physical characteristics.

Article Length

One of the most obvious physical properties of any journal is the length of its articles. You want to know the minimum, maximum, and average lengths. Determining these lengths requires examining only one or two recent issues. Simply count the pages of each article and note the longest article and the shortest article. Use the lengths of all articles in the issue(s) to compute the average. Then your answers must be translated from journal pages to manuscript pages. The conversion is simple. Each typed manuscript page has about 250 words. So, to change from journal pages to manuscript pages simply count the number of words on an average journal page, multiply by the number of journal pages, and divide by 250.

$$\frac{\text{words/journal page} \times \text{no. of journal pages}}{250} = \text{no. of manuscript pages}$$

Now you have the average number of manuscript pages per article. Try to keep your article length between the length of the shortest article and the average article length for that journal. The reason for aiming at the shortest length is that editors often need a short manuscript to finish out an issue. Because your manuscript is short, it may be chosen over others that are equally well written.

Reading Level

A somewhat less obvious quality of manuscripts that makes them "right" in the editor's eyes is the manuscript's reading level. Some journals have high reading levels; others have low reading levels. You can easily determine the reading level for your journal by following these steps:

1. Randomly select a page from each of three articles, and count out 100 words for each, starting with the beginning of a sentence in each article. Count each proper noun, acronym, and numeral group as a word.
2. For each 100 words, count the number of sentences, estimating the length of the last sentence in tenths.
3. Count the number of syllables in the passage.
4. Compute the average sentence length and average number of syllables. Then use the graph in Figure 6–1 to plot the point where the two

FIGURE 6–1   Graph for estimating readability—extended.

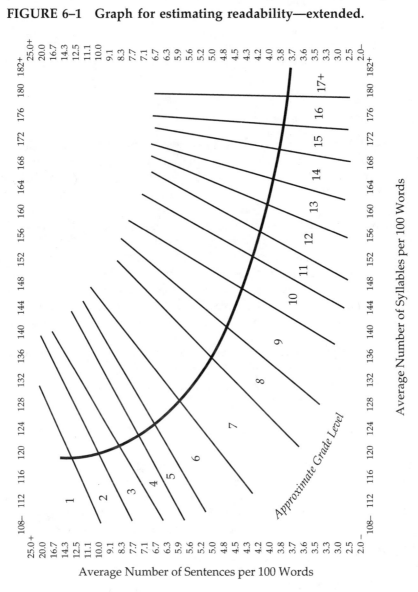

Average Number of Syllables per 100 Words

Average Number of Sentences per 100 Words

Reprinted from "Fry's Readability Graph: Clarifications, Validity, and Extension to Level 17," *Journal of Reading*, Vol. 21, No. 3, 1977, p. 249.

lines intersect. Most reading charts use grade levels to calibrate reading levels. This answer is the approximate grade level of the journal.

The readability level of your manuscript should approximate the level of readability of the target journal. If your manuscript's reading level varies substantially from that of the journal, examine the sentence lengths and the lengths of the words in the two, and edit your manuscript accordingly.

Guidelines for Authors

Most professional journals have a page or two of instructions or guidelines for authors to follow when writing and preparing a manuscript for the particular journal. Check your target journal. Most guidelines resemble the ones in Appendix E. They may be labeled "Suggestions for Contributors," "Information for Authors," or "Manuscript Guidelines." Study these guidelines carefully. They are the quickest route to understanding those qualities that can make your manuscript fit the particular journal. Notice the style and be sure to put your manuscript in this style. If the guidelines call for a 50-word summary, prepare a 50-word summary. If the guidelines forbid tables, charts, or figures, don't include these in your manuscript. Most guidelines ask for a self-addressed stamped envelope (SASE). Whether or not your journal asks for this item, *it is always appropriate to include a self-addressed, stamped envelope with your manuscript.* If the journal you have targeted has no guidelines for authors printed in it, simply request a copy. But a precaution is necessary. Editors are proud of their journals. They like to think that most members of the profession are familiar with their journal, and asking for a copy of guidelines may be interpreted as a lack of familiarity with the journal, which surely is not in your best interest when you are about to submit a manuscript. There is a way out of this dilemma.

Instead of writing or calling the editor, phone or write your request to the managing editor, the editorial assistant, or the secretary. These individuals can fill your request, freeing the editor to edit and without calling the editor's attention to your lack of familiarity with the journal.

Another way to learn the expectations of journals is through directories and journal articles. For example, the expectations of several types of journals are given in Appendix A.

Call for Manuscripts

Occasionally professional journals issue a "Call for Manuscripts," "Call for Papers," or "Request for Manuscripts." See Appendix F for a sample. These items usually appear when a journal is new, has new management, or is altering its goals or operating procedures. Whatever the specific reason, when you see a Call for Manuscripts you know that the journal is searching for material to publish. The common supply/demand ratio that makes writing a buyers' market puts you at a major disadvantage as you try to get editors to accept your manuscript. The Call for Manuscripts tells you that if you act quickly, you can submit your manuscript at a time when the editors need more manuscripts. *Don't miss the opportunity to act when the odds are in your favor!*

Coming Themes

A recent survey showed that editors receive about three or four times as many manuscripts for general issues as for themed issues. Thus, solicitation of manuscripts on upcoming themes is not unusual. (Appendix G shows an announcement of coming themes.) Notice that each theme is accompanied by a corresponding deadline for submission. Clearly, your chances of having your article accepted are enhanced by preparing your manuscript well and ensuring its arrival at the editor's office prior to the deadline.

Reviewers' Guidelines and Rating Scales

Many journals rely on a cadre of content specialists to judge the appropriateness of manuscripts for publication. These reviewers are given a set of guidelines and a rating instrument, which helps to maintain objectivity.

Rating scales help editors attain consistent information from all reviewers of the same manuscripts. The reviewer's job is also simplified in that the rating scale tells the reviewer what qualities to look for in the manuscript. (By sending a self-addressed, stamped envelope and a note to the secretary at the journal address, you can obtain a copy of the rating scale used by reviewers.) *But more important to you, rating scales can tell you, the writer, what qualities to put into manuscripts.* Figure 6–2 shows a rating scale with seven criteria against which manuscripts submitted to this journal are measured. Notice that the first item on this scale is "significance to teacher education." How important is it that authors choose topics that are considered pertinent by the audience who subscribes to the journal? Actually, for this particular journal and many others, this is the most important quality of its articles. According to the journal's editor, failure to write on topics pertinent to the journal's audience is the most frequent reason that manuscripts sent to this journal are rejected. These seven criteria are typical of those included in many journal rating scales.

Writers often ask, "Which, if any, of these criteria are indispensable?" Although the answer may vary slightly from journal to journal, it is safe to say that most editors consider criteria 2 and 6 indispensable. As for the quality of writing, writers often ask, "If the content in an article is accurate

FIGURE 6–2   **Rating scales raise the quality of manuscript evaluations and simplify the evaluators' work.**

JOURNAL OF TEACHER EDUCATION
Reviewer Response Form: Manuscripts

Assessment of Manuscript Quality

CRITERIA	ASSESSMENT				
	Weak	Marginal	Accept-able	Strong	Excellent
1. Significance to teacher education	1	2	3	4	5
2. Suitability for JTE audience	1	2	3	4	5
3. Stimulating quality of material	1	2	3	4	5
4. Originality	1	2	3	4	5
5. Accuracy of content	1	2	3	4	5
6. Quality of writing	1	2	3	4	5
7. Overall manuscript evaluation	1	2	3	4	5

CRITIQUE (Please type):

From the American Association of Colleges for Teacher Education.

and important, won't editors just rewrite manuscripts that meet the other six criteria?" The answer is almost always a resounding no because editors usually have an abundance of good, accurate, well-written articles from which to build each issue. Why should they be willing to use their time to do work that the writer should do?

Only on the rare occasion when editors receive an *unusually* important and timely manuscript will they be willing to rewrite the manuscript. One editor said that in a *decade* of editing a journal, only once had he bothered to rewrite a poorly written manuscript. The message, here, is that authors should study these criteria and consider each one essential to getting their manuscripts accepted.

Most rating scales contain a place for the reviewer to recommend action on the manuscript, or the editor asks for the recommendation in his initial letter to the reviewer. Usually, reviewers must recommend one of three actions:

1. Acceptance as is.
2. Conditional acceptance (provided that the author makes specific, requested changes).
3. Rejection.

Authors often ask what they should do if an editor asks them to alter their manuscripts. Unless you think the changes misrepresent your manuscript or distort your intended meaning, you should be eager to make those changes. The additional time and energy put into fulfilling an editor's request are usually much less than you would spend sending the manuscript to another journal. The greatest benefit of making the requested changes is the time you will save on the life of the manuscript. In most cases editors' requests for changes significantly improve the quality of the article. We will discuss this topic further in Chapter 9.

USING LIBRARIES

Most experienced authors spend endless hours in libraries. They spend most of this time researching their topics. Even those writers who are leading experts in their field of study realize that their writings should reflect the current literature, and the only way to do this is by reading the most current books, journals, magazines, and monographs on the topics they have selected.

Unfortunately, many novice writers only use the library for research. Some experienced writers get far more writing help out of libraries. You, too, can get many valuable writing benefits if you learn how to make maximum writing use of the library. The following profile suggests a method for using the library to perform several writing functions.

PROFILE

Sharon O'Bryan (also O'Bryan-Garland) received her BS, MAT, and Ed.D degrees from Indiana University. Her teaching experience includes 10 years in Indiana public schools and 16 years at the university level in Illinois, Texas, and Missouri. She also taught at Texas State University at San Marcos where she attained full professor rank and received a Fulbright-Hayes grant to study in Bogata, Columbia. For the University of Alabama, O'Bryan spent summers teaching Caracas, Venezuela and Mexico City, Mexico. Before assuming her current position, she was Department Chair of Education and Physical Education at William Woods College in Fulton, Missouri, and Director of Student Teaching at Indiana University. In 1990 she was recognized as one of the nation's 70 Leaders in Teacher Education. It should come as no surprise that her main writing area is teacher education, although she writes as a generalist across the curriculum.

Writing for publication, to me, is as if I were leaving footsteps on a path for others to follow. It tells not only where I have been, but by my contributing to the reader's knowledge, that person can come along with me. By taking abstract theory and presenting it in such a way that it becomes concrete and practical, then I have contributed to a common pool of knowedge. I am making myself understood by colleagues.

Moreover, publishing my writing is important to me because it is a source of immortality. If I am in a meeting and I verbalize an idea, it becomes a part of the group of ideas generated that day. However, I can receive full credit for my original ideas in print.

Sometimes I use the library for research purposes, but more often than not I go to the library to absorb the atmosphere of thoughts in progress. If I feel that I am under the gun to do some serious writing and the natural flow is not forthcoming, then I use the library as a catalyst. I seek a floor or space which has people concentrating. I place myself in their proximity. Not to be distracted by them, rather (as spooky as this sounds) to meld with the higher thought processes going on around me. Being around others when they are thinking brings out some of my best creativity. I guess I use the library as a muse in this way.

I have a deep reverence for the place that houses the ideas that human beings put down on paper. I have often been teased about my fascination for libraries. It is a love of knowledge.

After formulating the initial concept for a piece, I search my mind for the ultimate question that I will strive to answer during the course of the article. This creates my focus. Sometimes I will actually type this thesis sentence (or question) on a small piece of paper and tape it to my computer.

I begin by convincing my intended audience that the problem under discussion truly exists, in order for the reader to be drawn in and concerned, it is important to get that reader to agree with me that the problem is worthy of discussion and ultimately a solution or some type of action. After stating the issue, I then unravel it. It gives me great joy to take a complicated issue and make it understandable to others. Linking one thought to another in such a way that is unique to my set of experiences and cache of knowledge is truly a thrill for me. The reader and I then work our way through the problem in a logical, straightforward manner. While remembering my focus, I try to incorporate distinctive elements that will appeal to the reader. Finally, I end the article with the implications for the issue. My purpose is to give others a formula that can be applied and modified to suit them.

In my mind, I equate writing with problem solving. Although I realize that natural ability does come into play, generally, a good writer has the ability to follow directions. I thrive on being an idealist with practical ideas. Setting them down on paper with a little bit of charm and flourish keeps the reader receptive to my ideas.

Identifying Topics

Experienced authors learn to identify good topics much as news editors learn to "smell" a good story. As they go about their daily work, experienced writers carry a big question in their subconscious memory: What would be a good topic for my next article or book? Then they filter all of their observations through this perceptual screen. Consequently, at any one time, experienced writers can tell you several topics they plan to write about.

Unfortunately, beginning writers often do not have on hand this supply of good topics. Consequently, they spend a lot of valuable time trying to "think up" good topics. This process is too slow, and it seldom results in quality topics. You can do better.

Chapter 2 provided detailed information that you can use to perfect your topic selection skills. But, you may feel that you do not have time to become a master at this task. You may want a quick way to identify a topic so that you can get on with the author's business at hand—writing. Here's where the library can help.

The library is the best, richest source for identifying good topics, topics that editors and readers will find captivating. Here's how the process works. First, locate your library's reference periodicals. They may be in the reference room, but in some libraries they are kept in the periodicals room or in yet another room. Find the *Business Index, Medical Index, Education Index* or whatever annual reference index your discipline offers. Begin by examining the annual topics list if your index has such; if not, examine the most recent issue. Scan through the categories of topics until you find a topic that relates to one of your own professional roles. Now, see how many articles are being published on this topic. You want a topic that has some degree of popularity in the literature. Repeat this process until you have found a topic that you find interesting. *Don't worry if you don't currently possess enough knowledge to write on this topic. One benefit of writing is to enlighten the writer on new topics.*

Identifying Target Journals

Suppose you have an idea for a topic. Let's say that you decide to write about the case study as a teaching method. As you think about this topic, you realize that there are several audiences who would benefit from learning more about the case study method. Elementary, middle, and high school teachers could surely profit from learning more about this method. In fact, many junior college and university professors make extensive use of case studies; so another audience would be higher education faculty. Since teacher education colleges prepare teachers, teacher educators should know about the case study method. Today, K–12 school administrators are perceived as instructional leaders and are held accountable for the achievement level of all learners in their schools; thus, many administrators would be interested in learning about the case study method.

You could continue identifying target audiences but to do so wouldn't be a good use of your time. It is now time to tentatively identify a target audience and direction for this topic. Suppose you decide to write for teacher educators. What journals are written for this audience? Which of these journals would be interested in your topic? Some of them include *Educational Forum, The Journal of Teacher Education, Action in Teacher Education, The Professional Educator, Theory Into Practice,* and *Phi Delta Kappan.* This is an opportunity to really use the library to improve your writing for publication. Most contemporary libraries have computer facilities. Most have programs that you can use to do quick searches on topics.

If your library does not offer this facility, don't worry; a simple reference index such as *Business Guide* or *Education Index* will do well. Looking under "Case Study Method," you will see several articles on this topic. Now, see what journals published these articles. This tells you that the editors of these journals consider this topic relevant for their readers. If the list is short, a few alternative topics such as methods of teaching, lecture, simulation games, questioning, discovery, and inquiry can extend the list. Any editor who has published articles on any of these topics would probably welcome a manuscript on the case study method.

So far, you have used the library to collect data on publishers. Now you can use these data in two ways. First, you know which journals are interested in your topic. You will remember and use this information when you begin selecting a journal to consider this manuscript. You also have more immediate use for this information. You can use it to shorten your search for data to use in writing this article.

Take a full-size writing tablet and follow these steps. First, draw three horizontal lines one-third and two-thirds down the page, dividing the sheet into three equal parts. (See Figure 6–3.)

FIGURE 6–3   Systematic research method.

Donham W.B. "Business teaching by the case system," in *The Case Method of Instruction*, ed., C.E. Prager (New York: McGraw-Hill, 1931).

"The distinguishing characteristics which make the case system of teaching law, in the hands of a competent instructor, an instrument of great power is the fact that it arouses the interest of the student through its realistic flavor and then makes him, under the guidance of the instructor, an active rather than passive participant in the instruction."

- -

Dewing, A.S., "An Introduction to the Use of Cases," in *The Case Method at the Harvard Business School*, ed. M. P. McNair (New York: McGraw-Hill, 1954), p. 3.

"Of the many theories of education, there are actually only two. Education is the gathering of important information accumulated by human kind through the ages, followed by its refining, categorizing, and systematizing before presentation to students."

"Human thinking and the new human experience are indissolubly bound together. If we teach people to deal with the new experience, we teach them to think. In fact, power to deal with the new and power to think are pragmatically the same." p. 4.

- -

Biddle, B. J., and Anderson, D. S. "Theory, Methods, Knowledge, and Research on Teaching." *Handbook of Research on Teaching*, 3rd ed. M. C. Wittrock, ed. (New York: Macmillan, 1986), pp. 230–252.

"Case studies provide an open invitation to generalize."

"Correctly used, the case study method will allow students to draw many conclusions, some of which the instructor may not even be aware."

Second, at the top of each one-third section on your note tablet, write complete bibliographical information for an article that sounds promising. *Caution: Do not abbreviate or omit any of the bibliographical information.* Should you have to return to look up this information you may spend several times as long searching for the information as is required to copy it down at this time. A similar search should be made of books, using the card catalog or computer. This task is easy and fun. You just look over the lists as though you were shopping and you have the money to buy anything you want. You will need several pages completed with three articles and/or books listed on each page.

Third, scan each article or book. Copy verbatim one or two quotes. Look for quotable quotes—those that say something meaningful and say it clearly.

Suppose the search revealed that the journal *Educational Forum* has recently published several articles aimed at improving teaching methods through improving practices in colleges of teacher education. Then, perhaps you should tentatively choose this journal and audience as targets for your article. Figure 6–3 also shows some quotable quotes from books, one of which date back to 1931. Were this the only reference used in our article, it would be too old; yet, this is a valuable source of data. Because the journal article quotes are recent, the age of the references will be balanced. The most sensible approach is to begin your journal searches with the current issues and work backward.

Read the second quote by Dewing in Figure 6–3. This is a powerful testimony supporting the topic on which you may wish to write. Having quoted verbatim from the books, you can now choose between paraphrasing and quoting.

Using Your Own Expertise

As you plan and research your article topics, remember that prolific writers don't start at square one or point zero with each article. On the contrary, you must draw upon your own previously accumulated material. Suppose you have previously written a research paper or conducted research for a professional convention presentation where the paper or speech topic was "The Role Concepts Play in Learning." Suppose you also read in John Goodlad's school reform report, *A Place Called School,* that teachers must help students identify major concepts in their discipline. Go back to that study and find a quote that says concept identification is important to teaching, and one that explains *why* concepts are important to teaching. Your goal is to use your existing repertoire of quotations to enrich and embellish this article. You might also look up "concept teaching" on the library computer or in the *Education Index* to gather another current reference. Continue your search until you have as many good references as you need to write your article. Appendix H contains an article that was written by following precisely the steps just discussed.

USING SURVEYS

A recent survey of the requirements of over 50 journals found that 90 percent report some research, and two-thirds of all the articles published in them cite some research—either the author's or that of others. This means that all serious writers should report research, and whenever feasible some portion of that research should be original.

Correctly designed and implemented, a survey can easily produce a large amount of important information. Furthermore, the survey can facilitate the writing of articles. The questionnaire in Figure 6–5 has produced a series of articles for several premiere journals. By comparing this questionnaire with the list of articles it produced, you can readily see a correlation. (See Figure 6–6 for the list of articles.)

Carefully examine the survey questionnaire in Figure 6–5. This questionnaire was designed by simply asking those questions the author would ask should he meet with the editors. The questions were sequenced with a number of article ideas in mind. For almost a decade now, this questionnaire has been revised and readministered biannually. The results have been four articles in the *Phi Delta Kappan,* one article in the *Training and Development Journal,* one article in the *NASSP Bulletin,* and a chapter in the *Writer's Handbook.*

When first used, this questionnaire had a 75 percent return rate. By its fourth use, the return rate had increased to 98 percent. This unusually high return rate can be attributed in part to the covering letter (see Figure 6–6). The letter explains that there will be an advantage to the editors for completing the questionnaire. Two follow-up letters were sent, and one follow-up phone call was made to each editor who failed to respond to the second mailing. Notice that the cover letter for the 1990 survey (Figure 6–7) was revised to save the editor time, which also helped to increase the return rate.

When designing questionnaires remember to:

1. Select a topic of importance to the respondents.
2. Keep the questionnaire short—no longer than one page whenever possible.
3. Word each question so that it can be answered easily and quickly.
4. Answer the questions, yourself. When you find a question ambiguous, rewrite it.
5. Keep your article in mind, and sequence the questions accordingly.
6. Ask a couple of colleagues to complete the questionnaire and, if clarification is needed on any question, rewrite it.

FIGURE 6–4 Sample survey questionnaire.

EDITOR'S INFORMATION FORM

Name of Editor _____

Name of Journal _____

Address _____

1. a. _____ Approximate number of subscribers.
   b. Your primary audience is _____

2. _____ % of the contributors are university personnel.
   _____ % are graduate students, and _____ % are K–12 classroom teachers;
   _____ % are K–12 administrators; _____ % specialists; _____ % other:

3. Refereed 10 yrs ago? _____ Refereed now? _____ If yes, nationally?
   _____ , or in the office? (by the editor and/or the editorial staff)
   _____ If refereed, is it anonymous? _____ Other? _____
   Please explain _____ .
   Do you provide the referees with a rating instrument? _____ .

4. _____ % of the articles in your journal report research data, i.e., what percent of the articles report the results of a study conducted by the author(s)? _____ .

5. _____ % of the total number of articles published in one year relate to a particular theme issue.

6. _____ % of all manuscripts received are accepted for publication.

7. _____ days lapse before we answer query letters. (please estimate)

8. _____ days lapse before we acknowledge receipt of a manuscript.

9. _____ weeks lapse before we make the publishing decision.

10. _____ months lapse between acceptance and actual publication.

11. _____ manuscript pages is our preferred article length. Our max. length is _____ pp. Our min. length is _____ pp.

12. In addition to the original, how many photocopies do you require? _____ .

13. Required style: APA _____ , MLA _____ , Chicago _____ , Other _____ .

14. Accept dot matrix? _____ Letter quality? _____ Photocopies? _____ .

15. Good black & white photos would enhance acceptance in this journal? none _____ , possibly _____ , likely _____ .

16. To inquires about possibly submitting a manuscript, do you welcome query letters? _____ , phone calls? _____ Which do you prefer? _____ .

17. Some common mistakes made by contributors.

18. Recommendations to contributors:

Copyright © 1989 by Kenneth T. Henson.

FIGURE 6–5   Articles produced by periodically readministering the survey to editors.

Henson, K. T. "Writing for professional publication." *Phi Delta Kappan.* December, 1984, 65, 635–637.

Henson, K. T. "Writing for publication: Playing to win." *Phi Delta Kappan.* April, 1986, 67, 602–604.

Henson, K. T. "Writing for education journals." *Phi Delta Kappan.* June, 1988, 69, 752–754.

Henson, K. T. "Writing for education journals: Some facts to consider." *Phi Delta Kappan.* June, 1990, 71,   .

Henson, K. T. "How to shake the six myths that haunt all writers." *The Writer.* May, 1991, 24–25.

Reprinted in the 1991 *Writer's Handbook.* Chap. 13, pp. 53–56.

Henson, K. T. "How to write for education journals—and get published." *NASSP Bulletin.* September, 1991, 75(536): 101–105.

Henson, K. T. "Six ways to capture and hold the attention of nonfiction readers." *Writers' Journal.* Jan.–Feb., 1993, 19–20.

Henson, K. T. "Writing for successful publication: Advice from editors." *Phi Delta Kappan.* June, 1993, 74(10): 799–802.

Henson, K. T. "Writing for education journals: Some mistakes and suggestions" in *NASSP Bulletin.*

Toppins, A. D., Henson, K. T., and Solezio, E. "What editors want: How to get published in HRD Journals." *Training and Development Journal.* March 1988, 26–29.

When sending questionnaires, you can assure a high return rate by:

1. Alerting each recipient of the forthcoming questionnaire.
2. Promising to send the results to those subjects who wish to see them.
3. Thanking respondents for their cooperation.
4. Enclosing a self-addressed stamped envelope.
5. Sending a follow-up letter to recipients who fail to respond within a certain time period.
6. Following up the letter with phone calls to those who still have not responded.

FIGURE 6–6 **Sample questionnaire cover letter.**

_____ , Editor

Journal of _____

Street Address

City, State 00000

Dear _____ :

During the autumn of each odd year, I collect information to help prospective contributors improve the quality of manuscripts that they submit to education editors. I then attempt to report the results in a journal article.

If you would like to have your journal included in this report, please complete the enclosed questionnaire. For your convenience, I am enclosing a self-addressed, stamped envelope. I realize that your schedule is very demanding and thus will be most grateful of your time. Hopefully, the information you provide will save you time by reminding your future contributors of your requirements. Thank you for your consideration.

FIGURE 6–7   Revised questionnaire cover letter.

_____ , Editor
Journal of _____
Street Address
City, State 00000

Dear _____ :

    Enclosed please find a questionnaire that you completed for a survey several months ago.

    The last time this questionnaire was mailed one editor suggested that, to save all the editors some time, I might return the last questionnaire and ask everyone just to note any changes, an excellent suggestion. So, will you please examine your questionnaire carefully and note any changes at your journal. I have erased the last two items to provide room for your suggestions. Thanks very much for your participation.

                    Gratefully,

The questionnaire shown in Appendix I, violates the guideline on length—it is six pages long. Its construction, mailing, and interpretation took two years; so the decision to use such a complex questionnaire should be made only if you are confident that it will generate more than one article. Each major part of this particular questionnaire was designed to generate data for one article. The articles are listed in Appendix J.

Another consideration in undertaking large research studies is the possibility of collaboration. Novice authors often ask if they should work with other colleagues. The answer depends on whether you have colleagues who are congenial, whose areas of expertise complement your own, and whose work habits are efficient. For example, the middle school survey just discussed proved to be highly productive because each collaborator had a unique area of expertise. The team included a researcher, an editor, and an author—all of whom were task oriented. In addition, each member had harmonious working relationships with the other two.

RECAPPING THE MAJOR POINTS

- By modeling your article after the characteristics of the articles in a journal, you can significantly improve your chances of acceptance in that journal.
- You can determine the average manuscript length of a journal's articles by counting the words in an average line, multiplying by the number of lines in the article, and dividing by 250.
- You can increase your manuscript's chances of acceptance in a journal by keeping it near the length of the shortest article in the journal.
- The reading level of your article should approximate that of articles already published in the journal.
- The surest and easiest way to make your manuscript fit a particular journal is to read a couple of recent issues of that journal and design your article accordingly.
- Most journals have a set of author guidelines. If these are not printed in the journal, you can get a copy by writing to or phoning a secretary, assistant editor, or managing editor.
- Journals are inflexible; therefore authors must follow the guidelines closely.
- Most manuscripts are rejected because they are not appropriate for that publication's audience.
- Only *rarely* will editors rewrite a poorly written manuscript.
- The *Education Index* and similar reference guides can be used to identify appropriate article topics and to identify appropriate journals for given topics.

- Prolific writers relate their writing topics to their previously acquired knowledge enabling them to use references with which they are already familiar.
- References should always include a few current entries.
- Whenever possible, surveys should be kept to one page. Long surveys have lower return rates.
- The return rate for surveys can be increased by choosing a topic of concern to the respondents and by designing the questions so they can be answered quickly and easily.

REFERENCES

Biddle, B. J., and Anderson, D. S. "Theory, methods, knowledge, and research on teaching." *Handbook of Research on Teaching*, 3rd ed. Edited by M. C. Whittrock (New York: Macmillan, 1986), pp. 230–256.

Copeland, M. T. "The development of principles by the use of cases." *The Case Method of Instruction.* Edited by C. E. Fraser (New York: McGraw-Hill, 1931).

Tallman, I.; Leik, R. K.; Gray, L. N.; and Stafford, M. C. "A theory of problem-solving behavior." *Social Psychology Quarterly,* 56(3), 1993, 157–177.

7

Common Errors in Writing for Journals

THE NATURE OF WRITING

Almost every college campus has its own story of a resident genius superwriter who has only to pick up a pen or put the fingers on the keyboard, and—presto—words, paragraphs, and pages begin to flow. Even more astounding, this superwriter doesn't have to edit or rewrite: the first draft comes out perfect. The story must be true because it is told often by the superwriter's own colleagues, and it is told with conviction.

Why would anyone purposefully distort the truth to such a degree, knowing the harm that it does to aspiring authors? Could the purpose of such a fib be to demolish the would-be authors who are merely human? Indeed, many novices who are already insecure about their ability to write publishable articles must be devastated by the thought that for some of their peers perfect writing is an effortless process, a gift granted at birth.

James Raymond (1986) used the title of his book to remind would-be writers that *good writing doesn't come naturally or easily.* Raymond's book is titled *Writing (Is an Unnatural Act).* William Zinsser, author of *On Writing Well* (1988) cautions would-be writers that successful writing requires clear thinking, which must be learned. Says Zinsser,

> *Thinking clearly is a conscious act that the writer must force upon himself. Just as if he were embarking on any other project that requires logic.* (p. 12)

James Kilpatrick, author of *The Writer's Art,* (1984) says, "The construction of a good, solid sentence is no more a matter of instinct than the putting together of a dovetailed drawer, (p. 11). Although to many aspiring writers these comments may appear trite and unnecessary, they obviously are quite necessary because contributors to journals and magazines continue to make the same mistakes over and over. But you can do better. By knowing these mistakes before you write, you can avoid them.

The rest of this chapter reports, in order of their importance, the mistakes that editors say their contributors make most frequently. This information is based on 172 editor responses to two open-ended questions: What are the most common mistakes made by contributors? and What recommendations would you give to contributors? The answers are reported verbatim as they appeared on the questionnaires returned.

MISTAKES AND RECOMMENDATIONS

Mistake: Lack of Familiarity with the Journal and Its Readers

Ignorance about the target journals causes the most common error that contributors to these journals make—failure to design their articles so they fit the intended journals. Of all the comments that these editors made, the advice they offer most frequently is for authors to read some recent issues of the journal. A former editor of the *Journal of Teacher Education* says that one of the most frequent mistakes made by contributors to that journal is "not addressing a topic of concern to their readers." For example, such journals as *The Journal of Teacher Education, Action in Teacher Education, The Teacher Educator,* and *The Professional Educator* are published for a specific audience: teacher educators. Yet, many, if not most of the manuscripts sent to these journals are written for classroom teachers—clearly the wrong audience. The following comments are taken from the questionnaires returned by editors of many well-known journals.

"(The authors) do not understand the journal's purpose."

"Read articles in the journal to which you are submitting."

"Most mistakes . . . could be avoided if authors studied our journal . . beforehand."

"Read the journal before submitting!!"

[A common error of contributors is] "not reading past issues to become familiar with the types of articles we publish."

"[Authors] need to read the editorial [in the journal to which they plan to submit] to find out what's appropriate."

Another editor advised, "Read a few copies." This will help acquaint you with both the audience and the journal. In Chapter 6 it was noted that editors often use the expression, "It is not right for our journal." This can mean that the manuscript is directed to another audience or it may mean that the way the article is written is unsuited to the audience. For example, the article may be either too research oriented or too pragmatic, too long or too short, too pedantic or too elementary; or it may mean that the article uses the wrong style for footnoting and referencing.

The two article excerpts in Figure 7–1 show the wide range in style among journals in the same field. Part One shows a complete article; Part Two is but a short paragraph taken from a very long article. Suppose you have prepared a manuscript for submission to one of these journals. In what ways would it be inappropriate to submit this article to the other journal? In addition to submitting their manuscripts to journals within their fields, most prolific writers also have a group of journals outside their subject specialty to which they occasionally submit manuscripts, which further increases the diversity of journal styles. It is essential to make certain that your manuscripts are adapted to fit each journal to which you submit.

"It's not right for our journal" might also mean that the topic is not a topic of interest to the journal's readers. It could also mean that the language is inappropriate. Once again, examine the two articles in Figure 7–1. One journal is read by professors and doctoral students; the other is read by practicing teachers. As you compare these, listen to the tone of the language. Is one more pedantic? Scholarly? Chatty? One of the articles has no references; the other has 26. Can you tell which audience is professors and doctoral students? How?

Now consider how much better the editors of these journals know their readers. The next time you hear an editor say "It's not right for our journal," realize that the editor has discovered a polite way to say that you haven't done your homework. It's your responsibility to study the journals and make your articles fit the audiences' expectations. You must write about topics that have special appeal to those who read the targeted journals, and you must learn to be flexible, adapting your writing style to conform to the style of each journal. By examining the table of contents of a few copies of each journal, you can easily develop a sense of what these readers consider important. By studying the style of each journal—i.e., the topics, the reading level, tense, amount of research reported, and the amount of statistical description—you can prepare manuscripts that will appear familiar to the readers. You *can* do it, and you must.

Mistake: Wrong Style

Rita Dunn (1986), who has authored and collaborated to produce more than 300 articles and monographs, says that she has learned that the journals won't change, nor will they make exceptions to accommodate the style of

FIGURE 7–1　PART ONE　Sample article style A.

SCHOOL & COMMUNITY
Student Teachers Unlock Learning Barriers
Kenneth T. Henson

The degree of learning which develops in any classroom is affected by the atmosphere in that classroom. The experienced teacher knows this varies so much that each class has its own personality. This atmosphere of "personality" is somewhat determined by a number of factors present in the class which present or disrupt the learning process. These factors may be labeled "learning barriers." The method which the teacher uses successfully today to remove learning barriers may not work so well tomorrow. A method successful with one class may be a failure with another. A method successful for one teacher may never be successful for another. Such variations have prevented the discovery of methods which can be prescribed to overcome learning barriers in all situations; however, this is no indication that research cannot contribute to the removal of learning barriers.

Each teacher should be aware of the existence of learning barriers and of several methods for overcoming them. A number of methods affords selection of alternatives when the first attempt is unsuccessful. Analysis can identify these barriers and provide the teacher with a selection of methods and the knowledge of the degrees of success achieved through their use in situations similar to his own.

Following is a record of responses of ten student teachers of high school mathematics to some learning barriers which developed during a semester of student teaching. A conference was held with each student teacher immediately following each teaching period. During this meeting, the student teacher was reminded of his attempts to overcome barriers which threatened to disrupt the learning process during the preceding period. He then explained why he selected the particular method to deal with each situation.

Introducing a Concept:

Mister Wells observed that in his classes certain behavioral problems which disrupt the learning process are most abundant immediately following an introduction of new subject material and decrease after the students began to grasp an understanding of the new material.

This suggested to him that failure to understand is often the cause of inattentiveness and a special effort should be taken to make sure that the boisterous students understand new lessons. Since more misunderstanding is present during this period, the teacher should avoid traveling at a pace which students cannot follow. He should be careful to explain newly introduced material thoroughly, not assuming that students have information which is basic to the new concepts, but assuring that each student has this necessary background, before proceeding into the new area.

Henson, K. T. , Student teachers unlock learning barriers. *School and Community,* 56 (February 1970): 43–44. Reprinted by permission.

FIGURE 7–1   PART TWO   Sample article style B.

THE ELEMENTARY SCHOOL JOURNAL

Long-Term Academic Effects of the Direct Instruction Project
Follow Through
Linda A. Meyer

There are generally high correlations between MAT and WRAT end-of-third-grade reading scores and ninth-grade reading. Third-grade MAT total reading scores and ninth-grade total reading scores correlate .78 for cohort 2 and .81 for cohort 3. The end-of-third-grade WRAT reading scores and ninth-grade reading scores correlate .47 for cohort 1, .71 for cohort 2, and .73 for cohort 3. End-of-third-grade WRAT math scores correlate with ninth-grade math scores .49 for cohort 1, and .39 for cohort 1 and .49 for cohort 2. Ninth-grade math scores and Slosson IQ scores correlated .20 for cohort 1, and .49 for cohort 2.

Meyer, L. A., Long-term academic effects of the direct instruction project follow through. *The Elementary School Journal* 84(4) (1984): 380–394.

---

manuscripts. Journals that use *The Chicago Manual of Style* by The University of Chicago Press will not accept manuscripts that use the style of the American Psychological Association and vice versa. Journals that accept 10- to 12-page manuscripts are unlikely to accept 20- to 30-page manuscripts and vice versa.

Just inside the front cover, most journals tell prospective contributors which style to use. If the style is not mentioned, authors can write or phone for a copy of the guidelines.

Many manuscripts are rejected because authors fail to follow the journal's designated style. Following are some style-related reasons for rejection particular editors give.

- "Not (failure to use) APA style."
- "Need to use the APA format."
- "Not (failure to follow) Chicago style."
- "Failure to follow style guidelines."
- "Wrong style, level, and focus."

Many other editors in this same survey cautioned their contributors to follow the author guidelines, which always address style.

When your manuscript is completed, always make a final check to see that the citations (or footnotes) in the manuscript match those at the end of the article.

Mistake: Failure to Check for Grammatical Errors

How serious is this error? One editor says that he counts grammatical errors the way an umpire counts strikes. Incidentally, he allows some errors, but just one mistake over the number allowed earns the manuscript a place in the rejection file.

Nobody can avoid mistakes; yet, you can and should refuse to share your errors with editors. Never let the editor be your first reader. Several of these editors recommend that you let at least two or three colleagues read your manuscript before sending it to anyone. Preferably those readers should read critically and react honestly. You need someone who offers specific feedback and suggestions, not a doting spouse, not an envious colleague, but an objective critic who will offer specific suggestions and who will tell you if the manuscript is confusing or shallow.

Another suggestion is to give your manuscript a cold reading. This means put it aside for a few days before your final reading. This allows errors to crystallize and become visible to the author. A good practice is to begin writing another manuscript immediately upon completing the current one. Some authors work on several manuscripts simultaneously, putting each aside for a day or two and returning later with a fresh perspective.

Mistake: Failure to Include Substance

When researching the art of writing for research journals, Halpin and Halpin (1986) asked the editors, "What is the most important quality that you look for in a manuscript?" An editor responded, "I suppose that the most important quality is that the article makes some unique contribution, however small." Yet, the comments of the editors in my more recent survey reveal that many manuscripts fail to offer anything new. Responding to the question about the most common mistakes that contributors make, the editor of *Contemporary Education* said, "Old Hat; Old Stuff." The editor of *Vocational Education* said, "Rehash of well-known information." The editor of another journal said, "Much ado about nothing."

An examination of some of the other responses gives a definite clue as to how writers can avoid this criticism. The editor of *The High School Journal* lists as a common mistake, "No data base." The editor of *Journal of Research in Science Teaching* says, "Not making a new contribution."

These comments imply that not all writers should write for research type journals. Unless your employer requires such, your time and energy can be much more economically invested in writing for journals that do not follow the research format. Nonresearch formatted journals, such as journals written for practitioners, usually have higher acceptance rates; they are far less demanding on authors; and they have a much shorter turnaround (response) period, which permits authors to move their publishing program at a much faster pace.

If, however, you do intend to write for research-type journals, remember that you are not limited to reporting your own research; relevant data and the opinions of other experts in the field can be used to buttress your article (see Figure 7-2).

But beware of including lines and lines of quotes. Like William Faulkner's and James Joyce's stream of consciousness style, very long quotes take the readers off course. If and when the reader realizes what has happened, the point you were attempting to make has been lost.

To avoid this confusion, break up long quotes and just talk to the reader. Offer examples. These will serve two purposes; they will clarify the meanings hidden in the long quotes, and they will remind the reader that they are still in the quote.

FIGURE 7–2   Referencing the work of others.

[T]eachers must first learn proper methods of using inquiry learning. When using inquiry, the main role of the instructor is that of a catalyst to encourage students to make and test their own hypotheses,[22] since "case studies provide an open invitation to generalize." [23]

Finally, the instructor can use the case study method to cross-examine the students. Although we typically recognize the word "cross-examine" as a legal term, this approach is also widely used in business education programs and has been cited by some as the most desirable way to use the case method in business.[24]

These four approaches are the most common for using case studies.[25] Instructors should mix and sequence these approaches so that their students will be exposed to the benefits of all of them, while simultaneously learning to enjoy a variety of activities in their daily classes.

A recent variation for using the case method is the development of case study computer simulations. According to Zappia, "Many computer simulation games are designed so that they provide all the positive elements of the case method, but games have an added dimension . . . they permit the students to see the actual consequences of their decisions." [26]

When using the case study, all decisions should be based on involving the students in positive ways. As Ahmadian explains, "The key to capturing potential (that has got to be tapped) is to cause students to become deeply involved, both emotionally and intellectually, in the analysis and resolution of cases. It has been found that case analysis and resolution must be supported by textual material and instruction guidance." [27] Used in such a way, the case study method becomes a tool that can help instructors bring meaning to the increased field experience components of their programs.

From Henson, K. T., Case study in teacher education. *The Educational Forum*, Vol. 52, No. 3 (September 1988) p. 240.

A similar common error among research articles is quoting the same source too often. Pretty soon the readers begin to wonder why they are reading your article when they could be reading the original source.

Some other errors that you will recognize include:

- Referring to data in the singular (data are always plural).
- Personifying the document (e.g., this paper will . . .).
- Using abbreviations.
- Using an acronym without first spelling it out.
- Referring to yourself in the third person (e.g., the author, the investigator, or the researcher).
- Pairing a singular subject with plural antecedent or vice versa. Perhaps the most common cause of this problem is the word each, as in "*Each* of the researchers shared *their* findings."
- Claiming "research shows" but failing to immediately cite a study. If you say that research studies have found, you should immediately cite *two* or more studies.
- Using colloquialisms including:

—Used to (did).
—Come up with (discovered or introduced).
—Has to do with (concerns).
—On the other hand (in contrast or conversely).
—Brings to mind (recalls or reminds).

Mistake: Failure to Write Simply and Clearly

Having something to say is one thing; saying it simply and clearly is another. Time after time these editors made emphatic statements addressing this need. Tying the two needs together, the editor of *American Middle School Education* said, "Articles [in our journal] are evaluated for substantive content and quality readability or thought flow." The editor of *Contemporary Education* said that his journal often rejects manuscripts because they "lack coherence."

First, the article must have a distinct message, and this message must be clearly stated in the title. Then, the message must be clarified in the first paragraph. The comments of the editor of *Middle School Journal* captured both of these ideas: "Entice your reader with a title and (with your) opening paragraph." Communicating the purpose of the article immediately is absolutely essential. The *NASSP Bulletin* editor said, "Contributors do not write interesting opening paragraphs. If editors aren't excited with openings, how will readers react?" The editor of *Journal of Reading Behavior* said, "Including identifying information in the body of the manuscript which the editor must sniff out."

The editor of the *Journal of Allied Health* advised contributors to, "Avoid too much professional jargon. Be concise, be consistent, be thorough, be direct, and avoid administrative language." The editor of *Theory and Research in Social Education* advised, "Be thorough, clear, factual, and scholarly." *The Social Studies* editor added a valuable suggestion, "Avoid passive voice." The common thread in all of these comments is the message to authors that their number one objective should be to attain clarity.

Just how important is getting your idea across clearly in the beginning of your article? Think of yourself as a salesperson. If your income came from the sales you made, you would find a way to clearly and quickly communicate the strengths of your product. *Writers, too, are salespeople who must compete with all other writers who submit to the same journal.* Like potential customers who purchase goods, readers of professional journals will turn to other sources rather than labor to understand your meaning.

One editor emphasized his desire for simple language when he cited "overuse of jargon" and "pedantic style" as common problems with manuscript. The editor of *The Reading Teacher* and *Journal of Reading* echoed this concern by deploring "writing in pompous, academic style." She advised, "Write in a straightforward manner as if speaking to practitioners." *Educational Record's* editor says, "We look for nonacademic [writing style]." The editor of *Theory Into Practice* makes an excellent suggestion to improve clarity: "Examples should be used to explain difficult concepts."

Following are some additional suggestions to improve clarity:

- If the journal permits, use headings. A brief survey of a current or recent issue can provide this information.
- Use short, familiar words. For example, the word "use" is preferable to utilize, "change" instead of "effectuate."
- Use short sentences and short paragraphs.
- Avoid cliches.
- Edit your work. As you reread your drafts, remove unnecessary paragraphs, sentences, and words.
- Read and follow the advice in such works as *The Elements of Style*, by William Strunk, Jr., and E. B. White.

Never settle for the level of quality of your writing so long as anyone reading a single sentence has to reread the sentence for understanding.

In summary, the most common mistakes that contributors to professional journals make are:

Common Mistakes	Recommendation
• Lack of familiarity with the journal.	• Read a few recent issues.
• Wrong style.	• Check inside the front cover for directions. If there are none, write for a copy of the journal's guidelines for contributors.
• Grammatical errors.	• Proof and correct. Wait a few days and give it a cold reading. Ask associates to read and critique your articles.
• Failure to include substance.	• Consider using a survey to gather data. Review current articles and important books and reference these works in the body of your manuscript.
• Pedantic writing.	• Avoid using unnecessary jargon. State your message in the title. Use familiar words, short sentences, and short paragraphs.

Although the preceding errors are the most common mistakes contributors make, they are by no means the only mistakes. The editors responding to the questionnaire offered the following recommendations to help eliminate mistakes.

Recommendation: Select Your Target Journals in Advance

Even before you begin writing, you should take time to select some target journals. Only then can you design your manuscript to make it fit these journals. The assistant editor of the *Peabody Journal of Education* says, "Scholars should do their homework when selecting a journal." This task is just as much a part of becoming a successful writer as writing the manuscript itself. This is why the editor of *Educational Record*, wrote "Read our magazine before your submit (or ideally, [before you] write) an article." Failure to select your target journals and tailor your articles to them could lead to the problem referred to by a former editor of the *Journal of Teacher Education*— "Not addressing a topic of concern [to our readers]."

Recommendation: Identify Coming Themes

Most professional journals publish some themed issues each year. Alexander L. Pickins, editor of *Educational Perspectives*, was referring to these themes when he suggested, "Inquire regarding forthcoming themes—write toward a theme for which your expertise exists." Some journals have no themed issues; others have *only* themed issues. But most journals have both themed and general issues, and considerably fewer manuscripts are received for the themed issues than for the general issues. Often three or four times as many manuscripts are received for general issues as are received for themed issues. This means that *you have an opportunity to increase your chances for acceptance by 300 to 400 percent.* To achieve this goal, you must write your article and submit it before the deadline date. You can learn about forthcoming themes and deadline dates for submitting to the themed issues by examining several recent issues of each journal. At least one issue will carry this information for the coming year.

Recommendation: Find a Good Title

Responding to the question about common mistakes contributors make, the editor of *Middle School Journal* wrote, "Terrible titles." Entice your readers with a title that is inviting and that describes the content of your manuscript. Whenever possible, use your title to make a commitment to your readers. (See Chapter 6).

Recommendation: Focus on the Opening Paragraph

Like the title, the opening paragraph should hook and hold the reader's attention. Like those boring speakers who use the first few minutes to get to the subject of their presentation, many would-be writers use the first paragraph or two to begin focusing their writing. By the second or third page, they attain clarity in their own thinking about the article, and the reading picks up. Unfortunately, many readers will become bored and give up before reaching the "good stuff."

The editor of the *NASSP Bulletin* listed as a common mistake, "Contributors do not write interesting opening paragraphs. If editors aren't excited with [the] opening, how will the readers be?" To make your opening paragraphs more stimulating, immediately tell the reader what the article is about and what you intend to do about it. Too often, writers fail to achieve this goal.

Recommendation: Avoid Provincialism

The preceding recommendations were taken directly from responses to a recent survey. Now permit me to make a couple of additional recommendations which my workshop participants have led me to consider essential.

Beginning writers have a tendency to write about their own experiences. Perhaps the best advice that can be given to fiction writers is to write about the people and places they know best. This usually translates to mean that you should write about your own community. Maxwell Perkins, editor for such writers as F. Scott Fitzgerald and Ernest Hemingway, advised Marjorie Rawlings to stop trying to write Gothic novels of which she knew very little and instead to write about her own community and the people she knew. Rawlings had moved to Florida to become a writer. With each hopeless manuscript that she sent to Perkins, she described her new friends and neighbors. Her letters were so interesting—and her manuscripts were so bad—that Perkins advised her to stop writing the novels and write about her friends and neighbors.

At first, Rawlings was angered at being told that she didn't know enough about her favorite type of novel. After all, for years she had spent most of her leisure time reading Gothic stories. Fortunately, like most good writers, she was determined to try anything, even her editor's advice. In her Florida swamp, she wrote about her neighbors. Her book, *The Yearling,* won a Pulitzer Prize in 1939. Just three years later she completed her autobiography as a backwoods dweller. This book, *Cross Creek,* was a best seller.

Without much effort you can think of great writers in your own locale—Zane Grey, Eudora Welty, Samuel Clemens, or James Street—who were successful because they captured the lifestyles of the people they knew best. Yet, for the nonfiction writer, provincialism can become a deadly trap. So, you are an entrepreneur who wants to write about the business that you personally nurtured to health against overwhelming odds. Fine. This is a story that should be told. The dilemma is that few people will want to read a nonfiction business book unless they can identify closely with the circumstances—so closely that they can transfer your story to their own situation. Here's where you must help. *By offering examples, you can make your story pertinent to other types of businesses and to other geographic areas.* A novice writer in Eastern Kentucky is currently writing about a partnership program between a local school system and a coal mining industry. Initially the author wrote specifically about her home town, providing names of the town, industry, local school superintendent, and company officials. Unlike the characters in well-written fiction, her characters were not developed so that the reader could identify very strongly with them. Therefore, to talk extensively about them is inappropriate. Her intent was not to have the reader feel compassion, anger, or other emotions about the characters. Introducing the name of the town, the industry, and the people was not inappropriate, but talking extensively about them would run the risk of shutting out entrepreneurs in other areas and in other types of business.

A second approach to overcome provincialism is to offer examples to explain how people in other businesses in other locations can benefit from your article. The writer could tell how other partnerships could be developed. Figure 7–3 is an example of such an article.

FIGURE 7–3   Expand application beyond one geographical region.

The Teacher in Residence Partnership Program

Introduction

The central theme of the commission reports and task force studies has been that we must improve the quality of education. These reports have not prescribed standardized answers, but they have encouraged entrepreneurship at the state and local levels. Collaborative efforts and programs have been initiated to lubricate the wheels of progress. These include programs between state and federal levels, schools and communities, businesses and schools, and colleges and schools. The focus of this "Promising Practice" is on a partnership program among the Tuscaloosa City School System, the Tuscaloosa County School System, and The University of Alabama's College of Education.

The program, titled "Teacher in Residence (TIR) Partnership Program," involves two outstanding classroom teachers selected to serve as regular full-time faculty members in the College of Education's Early Childhood and Elementary Education undergraduate teacher preparation programs.

Planning sessions were held between the two superintendents of the local city and county school districts, the dean, the Head of Curriculum and Instruction, and the Chairperson of Early Childhood and Elementary Education. After approval from the appropriate boards, the following guidelines were instituted.

Fellows

An outstanding primary (1–3) grade teacher would be cooperatively selected from the County school system and an outstanding intermediate (4–6) level teacher would be selected from the City school system. The TIR Fellows would serve as faculty members with the University in a fashion similar to an adjunct or visiting professor.

Qualifications

The following objective requirements were set: current classroom teaching experience at the designated grade levels; tenure in the respective school systems; and a Master's Degree. Additionally, affective qualifications included the ability to work with university students and faculty, and a positive and enthusiastic manner.

Selection

In June of 1985, teachers in the two participating school systems were sent letters of notification regarding the program. Interested candidates were asked to submit to their Superintendent's Office an application, a one-page statement of educational philosophy, and any additional facts which might favorably influence their selection. The Assistant Superintendents for Personnel (Dr. Nora Price for the City system and Dr. Sydney Poellnitz for the County system) and the Chairperson of Elementary Education reviewed the applications and selected finalists. The Area Head of Curriculum and Instruction and the Chairperson conducted the final inteviews during July. In future cycles of the program the selection process will be conducted during the spring to allow greater transition time.

Duration

The TIR positions are for one academic year and are renewable for a second year upon mutual agreement. Teachers serving two years as a Fellow are guaranteed a return to the same school and grade level from which they left. The two-year time frame was selected as the optimal time length because of the breadth of learning that would be required of the Fellows. A period of time less than two years would reflect more of a novelty approach rather than a sustaining program. The school systems agreed to reverse the primary and intermediate levels of the teachers for the next cycle of the program in 1987.

Salary

The University contracts with the respective school systems for the services of the teachers. The Fellows' salary and benefits will continue in accordance with their permanent positions. Salary checks are issued by the participating school systems. This program was not designed to save money by hiring non-doctoral personnel for the University. The teachers' regular salary exceeds the salaries that would be paid to starting assistant professors on nine-month contracts. If the Fellows choose to teach during summer school, their salaries will be paid directly by the University on a visiting professor basis.

Schedule and Assignments

During the Teacher in Residence Program, the Fellows follow the annual and daily University schedule as do regular University faculty members.

Their assignments revolve around a 12 semester-hour core of teaching undergraduate courses. Regular faculty teach 9 semester hours, generally including at least one graduate course, and are assigned 3 semester hours of research and publication time. The Fellows also serve on program committees, advise students, have voting power on departmental issues (excluding promotion and tenure), and generally function in the same manner as regular faculty members. They enjoy having equal status with other full-time faculty members as is reflected in one of the TIRs, Mrs. Jo-Ann Schweer's, comments: "The opportunity to be chosen as a participant in this program has been a highlight of my teaching career."

Evaluation

Fellows serve as members of the Early Childhood and Elementary Education Program and report directly to the program Chairperson. An annual evaluation of the Fellows will be completed by the Chairperson and shared with the participants, the Area Head of Curriculum and Instruction

Continued

FIGURE 7–3   *Continued*

and the LEA Superintendents. The school systems will meet annually with the Fellows to go over the reports and to assess the quality of the program.

Advantages
    The advantages of this program are numerous. The Fellows have the opportunity to experience new, invigorating roles. Mrs. Schweer has observed, "I anticipated the University staff being cautious about my participating; but in reality, I experienced complete cooperation and acceptance." Both Mrs. Schweer and Mrs. Nancy Rogers have expressed their interest in gaining a firsthand understanding of the program philosophy, objectives, and sequencing. Additionally, they have the satisfaction of directly influencing future teachers. Mrs. Rogers observed, "I believe that because of my everyday classroom teaching experiences, I can personalize and bring to life methods and procedures that might otherwise seem only theory.
    Upon completion of the program, the school systems gain teachers who have had experiences which will be invaluable in helping them to plan and institutionalize inservice programs. Both school systems employ many University of Alabama graduates. Having their own teachers directly participating in the preparation program significantly increases the sense of joint ownership in the task of preparing new teachers for the profession.

Buttery, T. J., and Henson, K. T. "Partnership in teacher education: The teacher in residence model," *The Professional Educator* (1987) Vol. 10, pp. 21–23.

This sample article has encouraged other school systems in other college towns to develop similar partnerships. Notice that much of the article focuses on the how-to process rather than on the characters involved.

In your own profession you may have discovered a way to overcome a major problem that confronts all people in your type of business. Figure 7–4 illustrates such a discovery. Notice that this article also focuses on the process involved. The *Physics Teacher* printed this article because it addresses a critical problem that every state in the country currently faces, and it offers the readers a step-by-step way to resolve similar problems. Notice that the authors of this article tell the readers precisely how they can use this process to provide more qualified physics teachers in their respective states.

Recommendation: Review Your Manuscript

Before sending your manuscript, take time to check it thoroughly. One editor advises, "Prior to submitting any manuscript, anywhere, have at least

FIGURE 7–4   Expanding the relevance of information.

The University of Alabama Summer Institute for Physics
Teachers: A Response to a Critical Shortage
Kenneth T. Henson, College of Education, University of Alabama
Philip W. Coulter, Department of Physics and Astronomy
J. W. Harrell, College of Arts and Sciences

For several years, the state of Alabama, like most other states, has had a severe shortage of qualified physics teachers.[1,2] Responding to this need, three years ago the Head of Curriculum and Instruction in the College of Education joined with an Assistant Dean in the College of Arts and Sciences to write a cooperative grant. The result was a rigorous, 10-week summer institute for uncertified physics teachers, funded by the State Department of Education. The proposal has since been revised twice by the Head of Curriculum and Instruction and by faculty in the Department of Physics and Astronomy. Both revisions have been funded, providing a second and third summer institute.

All three institutes have received excellent evaluations from the participants and from representatives from the State Department of Education. Several features have enabled this institute to complete successfully with other universities for funding for three consecutive years.

First, all teachers selected for participation in the institute are inadequately prepared to teach physics and do not hold teacher certificates in physics. Though unqualified, all participants are selected to teach physics next year. Therefore, they arrive motivated, wanting to learn everything they possibly can about physics. This sense of purpose and the inquiring attitude that it promotes are essential to the endurance and the success of the participants in the institute.

Second, the University of Alabama Physics Teachers Institute is very rigorous. It runs for 10 full weeks, all participants take 12 credit hours of physics courses, and all courses must be taken for credit. The intensity of this program draws serious teachers who come determined to succeed.

> *This article was easy to write. I just described the program, step-by-step. The first draft took about two hours to write.*

Third, the University of Alabama Physics Teachers Institute is practical. Most of the laboratory experiments chosen complement the high school textbook and require inexpensive equipment. (A special course uses the state's most frequently used high school textbook, examines applicable software, and emphasizes classroom demonstrations).

Fourth, a weekly seminar utilizes the resources of a major research university. Faculty from throughout the University campus give lectures and demonstrations on such topics as lasers, quasars, robotics, and biophysics.

The University of Alabama Physics Teachers Institute has one goal—to enable every participant to be more effective next fall, and it has ways to

Continued

FIGURE 7–4 *Continued*

assure that this happens. Following the institute, co-directors will make a follow-up visit to all teachers' schools. The purposes are: (1) to determine which aspects of the institute the teacher has found most useful and (2) to determine further ways to improve the quality of the institute for another year (in hopes that the institute will be funded the coming year).

Each summer, adjustments have been made to improve the institute. First, a special section of introductory physics was created for these teachers alone, providing them freedom to ask questions that concern teachers and eliminating the initial anxiety that comes from competing with regular University students. Second, a first-year attempt to use a high school physics teacher to teach the high school text was not successful. Although the teacher was truly a master teacher, the participants did not give her the respect that is automatically afforded a university professor. Therefore, a high school teacher was replaced by a university physics professor. Finally, the third summer, teachers were provided opportunities to have their demonstrations and experiments videotaped to take back with them and use in their classes.

Because of the high degree of success of these institutes, and because of the help that they are giving to small, rural schools throughout the state, the Alabama Coalition of CItizens for Excellence in Small Schools has funded an Advanced Physics Institute at the University. The first advanced institute was held during the early 1986 summer term. Six teachers who had attended either the 1984 or the 1985 institute attended the advanced institute.

References
1. R. L. Stanford and W. S. Zoellner, "Alabama teacher supply and demand for 1984–85," *The Professional Educator, 7,* (2), 31–36, (1984).
2. R. L. Stanford and W. S. Zoellner, "Alabama teacher supply and demand for 1986–87," Unpublished study, The University of Alabama, (1986).

---

two or three colleagues read (the) text for critical commentary." This is good advice because we often make the same mistakes repeatedly, and we are prone to overlook some mistakes again and again. *The Social Studies* editor advises, "Have a naive reader read and comment on the article before sending it for review."

The coeditors of *Psychological Reports* and *Perceptual Motor Skills* take a different perspective but a very good one. They say "Be of good cheer. Take time to do the job correctly, and check everything yourself. Consult with an expert when you need to." Remember that time spent clearing out errors is a very economical investment. Once the manuscript is in the mail, it is impossible to make corrections.

All of these citicisms and suggestions are both sound and necessary. Their credibility is assured by the fact that they come from experienced, professional editors. Their absolute necessity is reflected in the fact that these editors reject four out of every five manuscripts they receive.

I am going to end this chapter with the recommendation (which captures my own advice to writers) offered by one of the responding editors. "Think!"

RECAPPING THE MAJOR POINTS

Many errors never seem to go out of style. Through the years, they continue to trip authors. You can escape the damage these errors do if you remember to:

- Identify a few journals that you wish to publish your manuscripts. Consider journals in your specific content field, general journals, and journals in related fields.
- Familiarize yourself with those journals to which you submit your manuscripts. Very carefully read a few recent copies of each journal, paying close attention to its level of complexity, article length, types of topics, and documentation style.
- Check your manuscript for errors. Then ask an impartial colleague to critique it. If your typewriter or computer provides a spell check, use it. Finally, put the manuscript aside for a few days and proofread it again.
- Be sure that each of your manuscripts offers substance. Put simply, be sure you have something worthwhile to say. You can begin by selecting topics that you really know about; then use the library to add more substance. You may also wish to consider using a questionnaire to collect data to report in your articles. Finally, check the title and the lead sentence to see that both reflect the article's main message.
- Write simply and clearly. Begin by knowing your main message, then structure your articles to make sure that this substance stands out to even the most casual reader. Avoid jargon, cliches, and unnecessarily complex and lengthy words, sentences, and paragraphs.
- Having selected your target journals in advance and having read a few recent issues of each, adapt your manuscripts to fit each journal.
- Give each manuscript a captivating title that reflects the main message in the manuscript; then give it a lead sentence and lead paragraph explaining what the article is going to communicate about this topic.
- Because your chances of acceptance by a journal are three or four times as great in themed issues as in general issues, know when

theme issues are coming in your target journal, and time your manuscripts to coincide with the deadlines set for these themes.
- Explain how your manuscript content can be applied to programs throughout the country.

REFERENCES

Cole, R. "Professional Journal Writing." Videotape. Raleigh, NC: University of North Carolina at Raleigh, 1986.

Dunn, R. "Writing for Professional Journals." Videotape. New York: St. John's University, 1986.

Henson, K. T. *Writing for Professional Publication.* Fastback No. 262. Bloomington, IN: Phi Delta Kappan, Inc., 1987.

Henson, K. T. "Writing for Education Journals." *Phi Delta Kappan.* June 1988, 69, 752–754.

Kilpatrick, J. J. *The Writer's Art.* New York: Andrews, McMeel, & Parker, 1984.

Raymond, J. C. *Writing (Is an Unnatural Act).* New York: Harper and Row, 1986.

Strunk, W., Jr., and White, E. B. *The Elements of Style,* 3rd ed. New York: Macmillan, 1979.

Zinsser, W. *On Writing Well,* 3rd ed. New York: Harper and Row, 1988.

8

Communicating with Journal Editors

THE AUTHOR/EDITOR RELATIONSHIP

Successful writing for publication has two requirements. First, authors must learn how to write correctly and they must discipline themselves to do just that in order to produce a quality manuscript. Second, writers must learn how to communicate with editors. Just as good manuscript writing involves mastering certain techniques, *learning to communicate with editors requires mastering specific skills.* Basic to mastering those skills needed to communicate effectively with editors is understanding the editor's role and the relationship between writers and editors.

Beginning writers often perceive editors as their adversaries. Only a few rejection letters are needed to convince many aspiring writers that the editor's main job is to pass negative judgment on the author's work. A few more rejection letters may convince the beginning author that editors are really sick people who derive their life's pleasure from rejecting and putting down writers. Some successful novices, however, pick themselves up, shake themselves off, and conclude that this is really a competition between the author and editors. To these individuals, the editor becomes the major opponent, and this sense of competition is all they need to succeed.

But you can do better. Begin by accepting the fact that *all editors would rather receive good manuscripts than poor ones.* Most editors get no pleasure from rejecting manuscripts but they get much satisfaction from the time they spend accepting manuscripts. Realize that editors and writers are not natural enemies. On the contrary, *the successful author/editor relationship is symbiotic. When authors succeed, editors succeed.* Authors and editors share the same goal. That goal is to produce a high-quality article for the readers on a topic the readers find relevant. The article must give the readers something they need and want, and it must present this information so that the readers can easily understand the author's message. There are many possible channels of communication between the author and editor; some of these are much more effective than others. The choice of communication channel should be based on knowledge about the editor's preferences and knowledge about the advantages that each communication channel offers the writer.

The Telephone

Some beginning writers go directly to the telephone and call the editors of those journals to which they wish to submit manuscripts. Some editors welcome and actually prefer this channel of communication even for use by unknown writers. Other editors prefer not to get phone calls. Should you choose to call, remember that editors are very busy. Keep your call brief and to the point. Think through your conversation *before* you call, and know exactly what questions you wish to ask. Be able to describe your manuscript clearly and specifically.

Successful writers determine the preferences of the editors of their target journals. They often research their journals to learn the editors' preferences. Sometimes journal articles tell the requirements and preferences of their editors. For example, a recent issue of *Training and Development Journal* contains an article that gives the communication channel preferences for several business journals. Appendix A contains a chart which lists the preferences of these journals—information that was derived from a questionnaire the authors sent to the editors of these journals.

You can gather many important facts about these business journals. First, notice the key at the bottom of the chart. Identifying the journals in terms of these nine categories can prove useful to authors. For example, suppose you want to write for journals that publish experimental results. A quick glance down the column under Types of Research lets you quickly identify all of the journals that publish your kind of writing.

Scanning the column headings you will quickly learn such important facts about each journal as its acceptance rate, whether it is refereed, the number of subscribers, and how long it is likely to take to get a response from your query letter or your manuscript. You will also learn a lot about the journal's requirements, which will be a great help in preparing a better manuscript. Using this chart can help you significantly improve your acceptance rates in these journals.

Also included in Appendix A is similar information about education journals which appears periodically in the *Phi Delta Kappan* (December 1984; April 1986; April 1988; June 1990; June 1993). The most recent results of a biannual survey of some 50 education journals shows that there is a lot of disparity among the preferences and requirements of the editors of these journals. You should learn the requirements of those particular journals to which you wish to submit manuscripts.

The most interesting and important information found in this article includes:

- Two-thirds of the journals have circulations of 5,000 and fewer.
- Nearly all of the journals report on research of some kind.
- Ninety-three percent of the journals are at least partially refereed; 52 percent are fully refereed.
- The acceptance rates among these journals range from 5 percent to 90 percent; two-thirds of these journals reject two-thirds of the manuscripts they receive.
- One-fifth of the journals reject at least 90 percent of the manuscripts received, but one-fifth accept at least half of the manuscripts received.
- Annually, four-fifths of these journals dedicate one or more issues to a theme.
- Writing for theme issues increases a manuscript's likelihood of acceptance by 300 percent.
- The average time required to accept or reject a manuscript is 2.5 months; the average time for acceptance to publishing is about 8 months.
- Three times as many journal editors prefer query letters as prefer phone calls.
- When authors revise at the request of editors, the resulting manuscript is accepted 85 percent of the time.

The same survey was sent to journals of allied health and nursing, behavioral and social sciences, and library science. Those results are also shown in the charts in Appendix A.

Another way to learn about the preferences of journals in your own field is to go to the reference room of the local library and consult such reference books as those listed in Chapter 1. Most of these books are quite comprehensive and give information about preferences and requirements of their journals.

Perhaps you noticed that the editors of some of these journals prefer that writers use letters to inquire about their preferences and requirements. Actually, four-fifths of the editors of the education journals prefer not to receive letters from prospective authors. But, before dismissing the query letter as a tool to use to communicate with editors, consider what letters can do for you.

The Query Letter

A query letter asks for permission to send in your manuscript. A well-structured query letter provides the author a chance to:

- Accurately describe the purpose of your article.
- Stimulate the editor's interest in your article.
- Establish your credibility as someone qualified to write on this topic.
- Establish timelines of your topic.
- Show how the information can be applied in various settings.

To ensure the full benefits from your query letters, follow these 10 steps:

1. Address the editor personally, accurately.
2. Use the editor's correct title.
3. Make sure that you have the name of the current editor.
4. Type the exact title of the journal in UPPER CASE letters.
5. Explain the subject.
6. Establish credibility.
7. Establish currency.
8. Show application (tell how the reader can use it).
9. Obligate the editor to respond.
10. Be concise.

Most editors have extremely demanding jobs. Like our high school English teachers, the only reason most editors could offer to explain why they work so hard is their total commitment to their jobs. One editor was so involved in his desire to have people communicate clearly and accurately that, when the owners of a nearby laundry misspelled a word on their marquee, he went to the shop and asked them to correct the error. To many editors, grammatical errors, spelling errors, and punctuation errors are virtually obscene. (This should tell us something about our need to avoid such errors in our query letters!) Because of such high levels of commitment to high standards, editors are often accused of being picky, cranky, and idiosyncratic. For instance, they may get angry—and rightfully so—if correspondence is addressed to a former editor. The query letter shown in Figure 8–1 was actually sent to a journal editor. The handwritten comments show the editor's reaction. This editor, like most, is protective of his journal. Should this author follow up by sending the manuscript, it undoubtedly will be met with hostility, putting the novice author at a distinct disadvantage.

Another common and equally damaging mistake is any error in the journal title. The letter in Figure 8–2 shows that the editor in this case was greatly offended by the author's failure to recognize that "The" is part of the journal's title.

Too often, editors receive outdated manuscripts written by individuals who haven't the expertise to contribute to the reader's understanding of the topics. The query letter offers an opportunity to convince the editor that your manuscript is current and that you have the expertise to write such a

FIGURE 8–1 **A poorly received query letter.**

_____ ,Editor

_____ Journal

University of_____

City_____ , State_____   00000

Wrong editor.
Always get latest issue
of journal to get the
proper name. He
hasn't been editor
for 6 years!

Dear Sir:

Last year, a colleague and I conducted an experimental program in a high school setting. Using a speaker telephone system, our students were able to engage in direct conversation with nationally prominent figures. I have enclosed a list of the individuals who participated in this program.

Briefly, my class wrote to national figures with whom they wished to speak. If a positive response was received, a committee of five students was appointed which scheduled a time for the interview, conducted indepth research, and developed informed questions. This committee was then responsible for conducting the conversation, but the entire class (and on occasion several classes) could hear and participate in the conversation. On the average, the interview lasted eighteen minutes.

The cost of this program was minimal; the technology was readily available from the local telephone company for an installation fee of less than $50 and a monthly rental of $12. Usually, the program participant used his WATS line and placed the call to us, negating the long distance charge. For the sixteen telephone conversations I have listed, the total per pupil expenditure (including the equipment installation and rental) was 19¢.

Obviously, a program of this type has many other exciting possibilities. While our program was designed for a social studies unit, other

This letter is much too long, tells far too much, and only serves to tell us that the article will be as poorly written as the letter.

manuscript. Use it to achieve these goals. Whenever possible, you should let the editor know that your manuscript will explain how the reader can apply the information found in your article. Figure 8–3 shows a successful query letter. Use the 10 steps described earlier as guidelines to examine the query letter in Figure 8–3. Does this letter adequately explain the subject? Yes, "The purpose is to identify recent changes in school law. . . ." Does it establish credibility? If so, how? (Here is where most beginning authors

---

FIGURE 8–2   **Another poorly received query letter.**

Editor, The Journal of _____
University of _____
City _____ , State _____ 00000 _____

Gentlemen:

I would The appreciate receiving a copy of the guidelines for authors to follow if they wish to submit a manuscript for review and possible later publication in Journal of _____ .

A current area of interest with me is student educational self-evaluation as it relates to self-directed learning. What I hope to submit is a manuscript that will show classroom teachers how they can design and use a student self-evaluation tool with their learners.

Cordially,   Why tell us this if he doesn't ask whether we are interested in it?

---

trip.) The most common response is that the author's title (such as dean, senior architect, civil engineer, D.M.D., or Ph.D.) establishes credibility for the author. In fact, titles and degrees are very weak evidence that the author is qualified to write the article. Being told that this article "will report the results of a study" is much better assurance that the author is qualified to write the article. Direct experience is also a good source of credibility. For example, an author of an article titled "Baking Christmas Cookies" might begin the query letter by saying, "As the head chef at a major bakery for the past 12 years, . . ." or an article on "Interstate Auto Repair Rip-offs" might be signed by Robert Grimes, Mechanic.

Which part of the letter in Figure 8–3 establishes that the article content is current? One word removes any suspicion that this article might be a two-year-old manuscript that has been rejected by 20 other journals. The key word is *"underway."*

This letter also tells that readers of the article will be able to apply and use the information in it. It will "identify changes in school law" and will "give explicit examples of how the American middle school administrators should adjust school discipline codes to better comply with the new laws." What do you think about the relevance of this topic to the audience, school administrators? With the recent rise in lawsuits aimed at high school

---

FIGURE 8–3 Sample of a successful query letter.

_____ , Editor

Journal of _____

Street Address

City, State 00000

Dear _____ :

I would like to share with you a manuscript which will report the results of a study underway at Eastern Kentucky University. The purpose of the study is to identify recent changes in school law that affect middle school administrators. The manuscript will give explicit examples of how the American middle school administrator should adjust school discipline codes to better comply with the new laws.

    I shall look forward to hearing whether you are interested in this work. Thank you.

Sincerely yours,

---

administrators, it is likely that this topic would capture the interest of even the most confident administrators.

    The letter ends by asking the editor to respond: "I shall look forward to hearing whether you are interested in this work." Without this specific request, the editor may assume that the manuscript is already in the mail and might not respond to the author's query. Notice that all of these goals were achieved in only three sentences. Because editors are so busy, and because they receive so many manuscripts, a good guideline is to *always limit your query letter to one page or less.*

The Cover Letter

Most authors believe it is to their advantage to include a cover (or covering) letter with their manuscripts. Correctly written, the cover letter can achieve at least three important purposes. It can:

1. Remind editors of their prior expression of interest in this manuscript.
2. Reacquaint the editor with the title of the manuscript.
3. Reestablish the author's credibility.

The cover letter should be limited to just a few sentences. Its purpose is to "sell" the manuscript, not to repeat it. Figure 8–4 shows a sample cover letter. Examine it to see if you can identify the specific parts that achieve the three objectives. It reminds the editor of his prior expression of interest ("which you asked to see in your letter of January 3, 1994"). It reacquaints the editor with the manuscript by mentioning the manuscript's title. Finally, it reestablishes the author's credibility ("our research which culminated in the writing of this manuscript").

FIGURE 8–4   Sample cover letter.

_____ Editor

Journal of _____

Street Address

City, State 00000

Dear _____ :

Enclosed please find the manuscript "New Discipline Laws and the Middle School Principal" which you asked to see in your letter of January 3, 1985. Thank you for your interest in our research which has culminated in the writing of this manuscript.

I look forward to hearing your response.

Sincerely yours,

GUEST EDITING

One avenue for establishing yourself in the writing profession is guest editing. Because this effective method is used by a relatively few writers, you will do well to consider this approach. Here is how I learned about the tremendous power of guest editing.

At the time, I had served as guest editor of a special theme issue of the journal *Contemporary Education,* a journal published by my own employer at that time, Indiana State University. I mention this because the chances are excellent that either your current employer publishes one or more journals, or you have an alma mater that does.

I simply went to the editor of this journal and asked to plan and edit a special issue on earth science, because I received my master's degree in this field. Having participated in a National Science Foundation Academic Year Institute, I knew some 20 other people in the field who had returned to their own universities throughout the country.

My next opportunity to guest edit—the one which taught me the most— came totally by accident. I had always wanted to publish in *Theory Into Practice,* a scholarly journal written for professors and graduate students. So, I sent a query letter to its editor, Charles M. Galloway, describing my manuscript. A few days later the phone rang, and it was none other than Dr. Galloway who said, "You know, Ken, we don't accept unsolicited manuscripts." Actually, I didn't know that. This was some time ago, and at that time I knew very little about the vast differences among journals. In fact, I was as ignorant as a rock concerning their procedures, but I didn't let a little obstacle like that stand in my way. "However," he continued, "We like your topic and we wondered if you might wish to put together such an issue."

He said there were two ways that they let their guest editors work. I could choose to title all articles and identify some good authors, then let the in-house editorial staff do the rest. Or I could do that plus have all manuscripts sent to me for my editing. Either way, I knew that I already knew one of the authors—me. That was my first benefit.

Then I looked for the best known experts inside and outside the United States. I learned that, because of the journal's reputation, I could get an article from almost anyone I asked, so I chose the most highly acclaimed experts. This put me in a one-on-one working relationship with these renowned scholars. This was my second benefit.

In about three months, I received another phone call from the editor. This time, he asked me to consider planning and editing a subsequent issue of this journal. I gladly obliged and have since planned and edited several issues. Each experience provided additional benefits.

When the journal was approaching its twenty-fifth anniversary, I was asked to review 25 years of articles in my field, choose the three best articles, and use them to write an article for a Silver Anniversary Issue. This benefit was topped off by a distinguished service award given jointly by the journal and The Ohio State University.

From conducting surveys to editors of journals in the disciplines of Business, Behavioral and Social Sciences, and Nursing, I learned that over half of all articles in these journals are part of a theme. This means, that, whatever your field, you probably have journals that plan themed issues. I suggest that you consider planning a theme issue on an exciting topic. If the first editor you choose declines, go to another one.

Perhaps the greatest benefit from my experience—and certainly yours, too, should you choose to do this—was that all this required editing, and editing was the best writing teacher I've ever had. Good editing is good writing and vice versa.

RECAPPING THE MAJOR POINTS

As you prepare to communicate with editors in the future, remember:

- Authors and editors share the same goal, to produce an article that is relevant and helpful to the readers.
- Several communication channels are available to authors.
- Many editors prefer not to receive query letters.
- Correctly designed, the query letter and the cover letter work for the author.
- Editors are very busy; therefore, all phone calls and letters should be kept short.
- To work, query letters and cover letters must be correctly written.
- Authors should never miss an opportunity to tactfully establish their credibility with editors.
- Guest editing is a little used but highly rewarding entree into the publishing world.

9

Questions Writers Ask

All beginning writers can be put into two categories: those who ask questions and those who want to ask questions, if only they were brave enough to do so. All writers—beginners and experienced writers alike—have questions to ask. *Successful writers are bold.* This does not imply that they are pompous, arrogant, or egotistical. Boldness in successful writers means that they are confident, determined, and persistent. Those who ask questions are likely to grow much faster than those who have questions to ask, but wait, hoping that someone else will ask their questions for them.

In previous chapters we have addressed some of the most frequently asked questions" How do you find the time to write? What tools do writers use? Should I use query letters? When is the best time to write? Where is the best place to write? and How do you identify topics? In this chapter, I will ask—and answer—some of the remaining questions you may have.

WHY DO YOU WRITE?

All writers have their own reasons for writing. Many successful writers offer two reasons for writing. First, they are compelled to write. Apart from any tangible benefits—and far more important—they have a personal need to write. A psychology professor and practicing psychologist told the following story to impress on his students the importance of an individual's perceptions and the way these perceptions determine the individual's world.

> *I walked into the private ward of the hospital to see a patient. Mr. Jones was screaming at the top of his lungs. I asked him what was wrong.*
> *He shouted, "They're killing me! They're killing me!*
> *I said, "Mr. Jones, Who's killing you?"*

"Those little devils on my chest! They're stabbing me with pitch forks! Can't you see them?"

I responded, "No, but I can see that they are hurting you."

As workshop participants talk about their reasons for writing, sometimes their reasons sound so bizarre that they are almost unbelievable; then I remember the patient and the pitch forks. To him the devils were real. *People have different reasons for writing, and they have a right to these reasons— whatever they are.* Some people write only because their job requires them to publish; these people may never understand how others could ever feel compelled to write. The fact remains that this compulsion is the major force that motivates many people to write.

Most successful writers also say that they write because they immensely enjoy writing. Given the choice between writing or watching television or going to a movie, they will take writing every time. Perhaps it's a combination of creating something, completing a task, and knowing that someday it will be read by others.

Recently, I was attending a workshop conducted by Kurt Vonnigut, and someone asked him: Why do you write? Vonnigut answered that there is only one justifiable reason to write. He said that some people have a burning desire to be published, and, although this is getting close, this is not an acceptable reason for writing. Vonnigut said the only justifiable reason for writing is because you have something that is so compelling that it must be said. Certainly, such passion provides the internal motivation that writers must have to hone their manuscripts while honing their writing skills.

WHAT SUGGESTIONS CAN YOU GIVE TO ASPIRING WRITERS?

First, write. If you want to become a *successful* writer you must become a *good* writer. The best way to do this is to write. Write often and much. Make mistakes. Don't worry about it. First, get your ideas on paper. That's what counts. Then edit your work, and rewrite it. Set some goals; then set yourself a schedule. Give your goals some deadlines. Then watch your writing activities move forward.

Second, if for some reason you forget or choose to ignore all that you have read in this book, remember this one thing; you can succeed as a writer *only* if you think you can. I have yet to hear anyone say that for years they have really tried to learn how to write well but have failed to reach any of their writing goals, but I do receive many letters containing passages like this one:

I can't believe it. Once I finally took that first bold step and learned a few basic techniques, then I learned how easy it really is. I've had an article accepted in that journal that I always wanted to have publish my materials. Not only have I had one article published in it, I've since had others accepted and it's easy.

One way to learn the basics and then continue to expand your ability is to attend writing workshops. Appendix K contains detailed information about workshops.

HAVE YOU A FAVORITE SUCCESS STORY?

Yes. My favorite story happened to a friend. It's full of coincidences. In fact, it has all the earmarks of a fisherman's lie; I can understand if you don't believe it.

I walked into a trophy store in a large mall. There on display was a desktop nameplate with the name of an old army buddy. Let's call him Rey (Wayne) Washam. It is such an unusual name that I decided to check the phone directory to verify my discovery. I found the number and dialed it. For the first time in 25 years, I heard my friend's voice. I asked him to have lunch with me at a local club. We set a date. As I drove up to the club, I noticed that my friend (who hails from a background that rivals my own for being humble and unknown) stepped out of a new limousine. As we ate, we reminisced about our experiences as enlisted men in Uncle Sam's army. Wayne was the outdoors person who actually enjoyed bivouacking and sleeping on the ground, eating K-rations, and, in short, roughing it. In school Wayne was never considered a star pupil. By his own admission, he was lucky to get through freshman English composition. Although he did well in his major (wildlife), his writing skills were so limited that he had to repeat freshman composition. Twice!

As we ate, Wayne told me that he was sitting at home one day bored because the rain was keeping him inside. To cope with his boredom, he decided to write an article to share some of his personal experiences in the out-of-doors. He modeled his article after those in a leading national wildlife journal. To his utter amazement, the journal accepted his article, and with his letter of acceptance he received a substantial check. This whetted his appetite; so he wrote a second article, then a third, and fourth. In summary, this person who, in his own words, was lucky to ever pass freshman composition wrote a string of 15 articles for wildlife magazines—and, with the acceptance of the 15 articles, he had never received a rejection!

Equally amazing, Wayne began to write books, experiencing the same degree of success. He disclosed that he had just signed a contract for his eleventh book, a cookbook for campers, for which he received an advance of $85,000. He and his wife had been conducting writing workshops, but even for an enormous fee he could no longer afford to take time from his writing to conduct the workshops. With their writing and workshop earnings, Wayne and his wife had purchased their own publishing company and two hunting and fishing lodges. They had recently bought a summer house in Montana and a winter house in Georgia.

Several lessons can be learned from the experiences of this writer. Even with his bleak school record, Wayne was able to succeed; nevertheless, Wayne would be the first to agree that better composition skills would have made his writing much easier. What contributed most to his success? Wayne loved the out-of-doors. Since childhood, he nurtured a passion for hunting, fishing, and trapping. As he grew older, this passion gradually shifted from killing animals to preservation and conservation. He even took a job as a wildlife ranger on a national game reserve, a job which he loved from the first moment and grew to love even more.

Wayne was fortunate in that he was a modest person who was able to see his weaknesses and even admit them to others. He explained that he was astonished by the acceptance of his articles. "I just wrote about what I enjoyed doing. My articles were nonfiction, focusing on my own experiences." *A key to success for many writers is writing about a subject for which they care passionately.*

HOW DO YOU HANDLE REJECTION?

As an experienced writer and teacher of writing, I always want to respond to this question with fatherly advice and say something like, "I view rejections as evidence of growth." But to the novice, such fatherly advice may sound like "Eat your spinach; it's good for you." Well, as many parents will attest, spinach is good for you—but only if it doesn't cause you to throw up. Similarly, getting rejections may be good for you, but only if they don't cause you to give up.

Perhaps a better response is that *all successful authors get rejections.* Successful writers grow as a result of rejections because they learn from experience. Some aggressive novices ask the editors for advice. They ask the editors of referred journals for copies of the reviewers' evaluations of their manuscript. With this feedback in hand, rejections can become painful blessings.

Perhaps the best advice for dealing with rejections is to *study the rejections immediately, make the necessary improvements, and promptly send the manuscript to another publisher.* If no feedback is received, either ask for it, or quickly examine your returned manuscript for editorial marks. Then make the needed corrections, put the manuscript and a self-addressed stamped envelope in an envelope and send it to another publisher. Remember, *sometimes the reasons behind rejections are unrelated to the quality of the manuscript.*

There are two reasons for handling rejections hastily. If you leave the rejection on your desk, you will dwell on it—even if only in your subconscious—and it seems to grow. Second, by promptly sending the manuscript out again, you decrease the time between acceptances, and this increases your number of publications. If your manuscript has any value at all, there is likely to be some correlation between your number of acceptances and the time that your manuscript spends on an editor's desk.

After 20 years of writing, I still get rejections, and each one has a little sting. But each rejection brings a smile as I think, "That's ok. I've been rejected before, and I can take pride in knowing that I've been rejected by the very best."

Experienced authors know that some of their time is better spent planning to avoid rejections. Jesus Garcia uses an approach that is both preventive and objective. He has worked out a method to reduce rejections and a method to deal with rejections objectively.

Rejection should not be the most difficult part of writing, but it is. I suspect potential authors do not write for publication because they do not wish to deal with rejection. I learned early in my writing career that I would need to develop my own mechanism for addressing rejection. After a few rejections, I sat down and developed a process.

First, *I always attempt to develop quality manuscripts. Usually, when I have a manuscript rejected, it is not because it is poorly written or poorly put together. Nor is it because my idea was not well thought out.*

Second, *I target the manuscript for at least two journals. If one rejects it, I send it to the other.*

Third, *when I receive a rejection I read the cover letter and file the manuscript for a week.*

Fourth, *after the hurt has subsided, I return to the manuscript and read the cover letter and the constructive criticism provided on a rating sheet or on the manuscript. (If no constructive comments are provided, I send the manuscript to the second journal).*

Fifth, *when constructive criticism is provided, I weigh the comments and make those changes I feel are warranted. I then send the manuscript to the second journal.*

Individuals wishing to write for publication should not copy my approach but develop a mechanism that is reflective of their own personalities.

Garcia's effort to develop a quality manuscript before sending it to an editor saves time and disappointment. His process of carefully scrutinizing and using criticisms to improve the manuscript is wise. This may be difficult when readers are unkind, but remember that, left unchanged the manuscript might affect others in equally negative ways. Garcia's concluding advice is the voice of experience; individual authors must develop their own systems for dealing with rejection.

WHAT DISTINGUISHES HIGHLY SUCCESSFUL WRITERS FROM LESS SUCCESSFUL WRITERS?

Apart from their degree of commitment to learning the basics of good writing and applying them with diligence, *highly successful writers usually have several projects going simultaneously.* At any time, highly successful writers have a couple of investigations underway, two or more manuscripts partially completed, and several manuscripts being considered by editors. In contrast, the novice writer often uses a linear approach to writing, writing one draft, then correcting and revising the draft, then polishing it, then sending a query letter, then waiting for a response, then sending the manuscript, and then waiting for months or years for a response. For this type of writer, the highest success rate possible is one or two acceptances a year.

IS IT OK TO SEND A MANUSCRIPT TO MULTIPLE PUBLISHERS?

Simultaneous submission of article manuscripts to multiple publishers is nothing short of Russian roulette. The desperate writer who plays this game never considers the possible adverse consequences. Put simply, multiple submissions can produce multiple acceptances. Then, the writer must decide which journal to reject. Editors like rejections even less than writers do—for editors invest not only their own time but also their reviewers' time evaluating manuscripts. Editors also plan issues so that manuscripts complement each other. When one of these manuscripts is abruptly withdrawn, a unique piece of the jigsaw puzzle is missing. Because most journals operate on a tight schedule and may operate behind schedule, there simply isn't time to locate a satisfactory replacement for a withdrawn manuscript.

Despite the problems created, multiple submissions is a frequent occurrence. It has caused such a problem that some publishers and societies have written codes forbidding this practice. For example, the American Sociological Society has a written policy published in its journals to remedy the situation (see Figure 9–1).

An author who refuses to let a publisher print an accepted manuscript should be prepared to have this door of opportunity closed in the future,

---

FIGURE 9–1   Statement of ASA policy on multiple submission.

Submission of manuscripts to a professional journal clearly implies commitment to publish in that journal. The competition for journal space requires a great deal of time and effort on the part of editorial readers whose main compensation for this service is the opportunity to read papers prior to publication and the gratification associated with discharge of professional obligations. For these reasons the ASA regards submission of a manuscript to a professional journal while that paper is under review by another journal as unacceptable.

Section II, B4, ASA Code of Ethics

---

and no serious writers can afford to shut out any possible markets for their manuscripts. The alternative is even worse; allowing publishers to publish the same manuscript would be professional suicide. The bottom line for writers is: *don't make simultaneous submissions to journals.*

This advice applies to journal manuscripts only. For books, multiple submissions are acceptable and they are recommended but only when used according to the process described in Chapter 10.

ARE THERE ADVANTAGES IN COLLABORATING?

If you find the right partner, collaborating can offer several advantages. *The most important quality to seek in a partnership is similar personality.* For example, if you have a Type-A personality and feel compelled to get your work done on time, you should never work with a Type-B who thinks a deadline is the sign that it's time to start working on the job. Such an arrangement is equally painful for both partners.

When personalities are compatible, collaborating can bring out the best in all. Each partner stimulates the other. The unique expertise of each writer complements that of the others. For academicians who are required to publish, collaborating can accelerate the rate of publishing of all partners. But, even under the best of circumstances, all writers should go solo part of the time; otherwise, they become vulnerable to the criticism that they let others write for them. A few articles of your own can nullify such a charge.

Should you decide to collaborate, you will need to produce a product that is consistent and coherent. A good method to achieve these goals is to have each collaborator edit the entire manuscript. Each edit will remove some incoherence and inconsistency.

I asked Tom Good if he would share some of his insights on collaborating. Here is his response:

> *I have had the pleasure of publishing a lot of my work with coauthors. This experience, although sometimes awkward (why must my coauthor be in Tibet or at the condo when page proofs arrive?) has provided an important context for learning. Differences of opinion (theoretical values; what constitutes a good example; what represents valid evidence) have to be seriously confronted and negotiated successfully. Hence, issues one might "conveniently avoid" become opportunities for new learning. For example, I have learned much about Piagetian theory from Jere Brophy, my long-time coauthor who teaches at Michigan State University, and I have learned much about socially situated learning and Vygotskian theory from Mary McCaslin, who teaches at Arizona University.*

SHOULD I COLLABORATE LONG DISTANCE?

Some special advantages and limitations can be realized when authors collaborate over long distances. Perhaps the limitations are more obvious. For example, there is the delay in sending manuscripts through the mail. Facsimile machines and electronic mail are improving these conditions and making long distance collaboration more feasible. But in some fashion collaborators should read, edit, and rewrite their partners' work. Otherwise, the manuscript is likely to lack a uniform tone and consistent style.

A second limitation of collaborating long distance is the increased likelihood of miscommunication. As an author who has collaborated long distance on about a dozen books, I will share an example of this limitation. On one of my book projects, one of the coauthors wrote a chapter and sent it to the others as a model. Receiving the chapter, one of the authors took great care to assure that his drafted chapters had the same pedagogical subheadings. Later, when we met to go over their chapters, the coauthor who sent the sample chapter explained that the subheadings were optional and perhaps should differ according to content. His purpose for sending the sample chapter had been to show the other authors the length that his chapter set for certain parts—a feature that some authors had not thought important.

But, with care, these difficulties can be handled. An advantage of collaborating long distance is that it brings to the work a broader range of perspectives, which improves the product and allows each collaborator to develop awareness and insight that can only be gained through long-distance collaboration. Whether the advantages outweigh the disadvantages depends on the collaborators, their differences in expertise, and the topic of the book. A look at the number of textbook authors who collaborate over a long distance is testimony that for many the process does work, and for many it works extremely well. Hal Blythe and Charlie Sweet offer further advice on collaboration in Chapter 13.

SHOULD I WRITE ARTICLES BEFORE WRITING SHORT STORIES OR BOOKS?

The best answer to this question is probably, "yes." Article writing is excellent preparation for writing nonfiction books, and writing short stories is good preparation for writing fiction books. Article writing provides the opportunity to develop important writing skills. For those who wish to strengthen their ability to get a new job and for those who need to fill their resumes to earn merit pay, promotion, or tenure, article writing is usually a far better investment of their time than book writing.

WHAT IS A REFEREED JOURNAL?

At institutions of higher education, no term is more common among faculty members than "*refereed* journal". The extent of its use is exceeded, however, only by the degree to which it is misunderstood. Although to everyone the word *refereed* reflects scholarship, when cornered, even among those who so readily use the term, few could accurately define it.

Although the academic world disagrees on the many definitions of a refereed journal, most academicians would readily agree that journal refereeing has three common characteristics: *where, how,* and *by whom* the refereeing occurs.

Generally, the jurors or referees are considered to be peers in the profession. (See Figure 9–2.) At some journals, referees are carefully chosen for their reputations and because they are recognized throughout their field as experts. Some journal editors who claim refereed status for their journals would argue that they themselves are qualified referees. Another aspect of refereeing is location. Some people think that all refereed processes must be nationwide because it assures a national viewpoint as opposed to a provincial perspective; others consider the location of little consequence. Many professional journals are published on large university campuses. Some of the editors of these journals send each manuscript to a colleague in the appropriate department on their campus. Others would even argue that refereeing can and does occur in the editor's office.

Perhaps a more important criterion than either *who* evaluates the manuscripts or *where* the manuscripts are reviewed is *how* the manuscripts are evaluated. The most loosely conducted evaluations consist merely of

	Criteria
Third Degree meets all three criteria	Is refereed by experts throughout the country. Editor provides a rating instrument. Referee process is conducted anonymously.
Second Degree meets two of the three criteria	Is refereed by experts throughout the country. Editor provides a rating instrument. Referee process is conducted anonymously.
First Degree meets only one of the criteria	Is refereed by experts throughout the country. Editor provides a rating instrument. Referee process is conducted anonymously.

FIGURE 9–2   Refereeing occurs in degrees.

the reviewers' subjective opinions. Some evaluators use rating scales to make their judgments. The most rigid evaluators provide evaluation instruments to referees across the country and conduct the reviews anonymously.

IS IT WISE TO USE VANITY PUBLISHERS?

Vanity publishers are those who require their authors to pay all or part of the publishing costs. Sometimes this type of publisher may be a good choice; usually it is not. Suppose you have something important to say in a book, and you have tried several commercial publishers but all of these publishers have declined to publish your work. Suppose the content is accurate but the market for the book is too small to make it profitable. So, you cannot get a contract from a commercial publisher. One alternative is to turn to a vanity publisher. (You could also choose to publish it yourself). But suppose you don't have the money that is required to pay for the printing and materials; and suppose the vanity press requires only that you use the book in your classes. Vanity publishing might provide your only option.

Under most circumstances a vanity publisher would be a poor choice. For example, suppose your main motive for having a book published is to accrue academic prestige or academic rewards. Most academic institutions place far less value on works that are published by vanity presses. Some colleges even refuse to recognize vanity publications. The reason is clear;

unlike other publishers, vanity publishers seldom send the manuscript off to be evaluated anonymously by experts, and, for a fee, some vanity publishers will publish almost anything. Likewise, if your goal is to produce a very successful book, one that is recognized as a leading textbook or a leading professional book, many vanity publishers would not have the marketing capabilities needed to make their books highly competitive with those published by other publishers. Indeed, most vanity presses provide very little marketing support for their authors' books.

WHAT ABOUT SELF-PUBLISHING?

Like vanity publishing, the self-published author must bear the expenses—and like vanity books they seldom prove to be a route to professional recognition, fortune, or fame.

Some authors, however, have been successful at self-publishing. Hanoch McCarty is one such author with extensive experience in this method, and he gives the following advice:

Self-publishing has some big advantages and some very big disadvantages. On the positive side:

- *Your potential profit on book sales is much larger. My first book was a college text published by a major house. With three authors dividing the royalties, my per-copy earnings were about $.55. Each of my current self-published books earns me about $4.00 per copy. Sounds great, doesn't it? The real question is: Who is likely to sell more, you or the publisher? If you believe that your platform and other sales will be substantial, then self-publish. After all, you eliminate the middleman.*
- *No compromise. You decide everything. No one intervenes in your creation. This is delightful for an independent soul such as I. Yet, those times that I've had an editor, I've gained far more than I've lost. A good editor brings fresh insight, new ideas, courageous feedback for improvement (which your best friends may not have the courage to tell you).*

The negatives are very significant. As I indicated, you'll miss the feedback and fresh ideas an editor brings. In addition:

- *You must find the printer, graphic designer, photographer, etc., yourself. We publish a number of my books, and we get competitive price quotes from at least six printers every time we have a print run. Prices vary widely, and you save big if you shop. This is very time con-consuming. You also have to do all the other details such as copyright, photo and quote clearances, etc.*

- *You don't have the distribution network that a decent publisher will have. (Note: if you're choosing a publisher, this is one of the most important questions you should explore!)*
- *You must take a large financial risk in the initial publication and may be left with hundreds or thousands of unsold copies.*
- *You have to spend much time marketing and promoting the book. You must store a large inventory, become familiar with UPS, parcel post, Federal Express, and collection agencies (for customers who don't pay).*
- *Academic institutions don't give much credence to self-published material. Therefore, if publication is important for promotion and tenure, don't self-publish.*
- *Finally, you must do all the record keeping for tax purposes.*

In spite of all this, I self-published six of my own books, tapes and video programs. In addition, I write under contract to several publishers. My contract with them allows me to buy large quantities of my own books for platform and catalog sales. (This is a very good idea. It allows me to gain larger profit than a royalty alone would, but I don't have to worry about all the other details I've discussed). I have also produced a video program as a partner with a small video production company which gave me some relief from the financial risk and from all the many headaches and details necessary to complete that project.

One of my most valued colleagues has written books comparable to mine. She has a contract with a publisher. They send her books ahead to her speaking engagements for platform sales and take care of all the details. The company does all the artwork and design. She simply flies from place to place and gives her speeches. The publisher does all the rest. While she makes much less per copy than I do, she has much more time to devote to her next project than I have. With the wisdom of hindsight, I'd advise most people not to self-publish.

The self-published author is always subject to suspicion. This suspicion may or may not be warranted. For example, suppose Professor Jones writes a book and later discovers that she cannot find a recognized publisher who is willing to publish it. Many colleagues will conclude that it is because the book is shallow or that it is full of errors. This could be true, but there are other reasons for rejections. For example, the decision to reject a book proposal is often based solely on the publisher's perception of the market size.

Sometimes the publisher knows that the market for the book is so small that, even if the book were bought and used by *everyone* in this specialized field, the sales of the book would not be large enough to make it profitable for the publisher. This introduces my second favorite story.

In the late 1960s two professors at a midwestern university developed a prospectus for a book aimed at a new market. They contacted several publishers and were consistently told that such a market did not exist. Convinced otherwise, these authors went to a local press, designed a layout, and paid to have 2,000 copies of this new book printed. Using a small mailer which they also designed and paid a printer to produce, they quickly sold the 2,000 copies and immediately printed a second 2,000 copies. The success of the book prompted the authors to write and self-publish a second edition. The second edition was more successful than the first. As you might guess, the second edition led to a third edition. The book is now in its fifth edition and its sales have exceeded 40,000 copies, all mailed directly from the home of one of the authors. Obviously, these authors are pleased with their decision to self-publish. Such success stories make self-publishing sound attractive, yet such success may be more a product of the authors' own capabilities and commitment than of the merits of the self-publishing process itself.

The odds against a self-published book reaching this level of success are gigantic though there are always a few Davids with slingshots who are willing to tackle such giants. If you have a book inside you that must come out at any expense, self-publishing may be a viable option for you to consider.

Clearly, self-publishing provides an opportunity to get a book into print that otherwise might never be published. *What Color is Your Parachute?*, a guide for job seekers, by Richard N. Bolles was first self-published and later turned over to Ten Speed Press. This book has been on the *New York Times* Best-Seller List consistently for over a decade and has sold well over 3 million copies.

Peter McWilliams and John-Roger's *You Can't Afford the Luxury of a Negative Thought* has sold over a quarter of a million copies and still sells several thousand copies a month. McWilliams, a phenomenon in self-publishing, has been doing it for 20 years. He estimates that the sales of his books (including *Life 101* and *Do It: Let's Get Off our Buts*, both coauthored with John-Roger) have now passed 7 million copies. His book on self-publishing, *Self-Publishing, Self-Taught* was published by Prelude Press (which McWilliams named after his car). He spends about $1 a copy to advertise, another $1 a copy to promote through giveaways and press releases. Modern technology has made self-publishing affordable. Printing and binding 3,000 to 5,000 copies costs about $1.50 a book. The laser printer, personal computer, and software required to turn out a quality, camera ready product cost about $5,000.

IF ASKED, SHOULD I PAY A JOURNAL PUBLISHING EXPENSES?

For decades journals in some disciplines, particularly some of the sciences, have required their contributing authors to pay for certain publishing expenses such as the costs of graphs, charts, and page proofs. In recent years, additional disciplines (such as as education) have begun charging such costs to their contributors. Because some professional journals do not sell advertisements, charging expenses to contributors is often considered acceptable—but as an incentive to get faculty members to publish, many colleges and departments pay part or all of these expenses.

A few journals charge their contributors a reading fee. Many professionals find this practice unacceptable, unprofessional, and a contrivance to make money.

SHOULD I BE A SPECIALIST OR A GENERALIST?

As many aspiring authors think about their futures, they are uncertain whether they will benefit more from becoming a specialist or generalist. This decision is tough. It depends on the author's writing goals. If your purpose is to earn recognition in a particular field, the nature of the subject may restrict you to publishing in only one or two specific journals. If your field of expertise does not restrict your publishing so severely, there may be much benefit in your writing for a wide array of journals. The wider the range of your topics and audiences, the greater the number of outlets you will have for your manuscripts. Writing for a wide range of journals also enables you to reach more varied audiences and to indulge in different kinds of writing. You may have knowledge that can benefit groups outside your own academic major, and because they do not read your journals, the only way to reach them is through publishing in their journals.

Still another benefit of being a generalist is the opportunity it gives you to learn about the knowledge bases in other fields. This is important in that you can enrich your own knowledge base by studying several fields. For example, all administrators need to understand principles of leadership, and all fields have studies that contribute significantly to the understanding of leadership theory. Those who write for publication on this topic should at least review the leadership literature in other disciplines.

ARE COLLOQUIALISMS AND CLICHES ACCEPTABLE?

Colloquialisms offer skilled fiction authors a way to provide authentic descriptions of their characters. But for nonfiction authors, colloquialisms are like inside jokes. They invite miscommunication, leaving the outsider feeling estranged. A good rule for nonfiction writers is to avoid using colloquialisms.

Cliches seldom offer anything that brings quality to a manuscript. They are popular because they are convenient. Frequently, authors use cliches as substitutes when they cannot find the appropriate words to express their ideas. Because of their overuse, cliches soon become objects of boredom. They may identify you as a weak writer.

WHAT SHOULD I DO WHEN AN EDITOR KEEPS HOLDING MY MANUSCRIPT?

At one workshop I was conducting a participant said, "This editor has promised to give my coauthor and me a decision several times but always misses the deadlines. My coauthor wants to choke him. What should we do?"

My first advice was "Don't choke the editor." I realize that this editor has been unfair, and fairness is definitely a two-way street; yet, nothing would be gained from squaring off against the editor. On the contrary, something would be lost; you would eliminate one target journal for your future manuscripts. Perhaps one thing would be gained; you would have your manuscript back and would be free to go to another publisher. But you can do that without shutting off this one.

Calmly write a letter saying something like, "If I haven't heard from you by (include month and day), I will assume that you are no longer interested in this manuscript and will pursue this project with other publishers. Thank you for your continuing interest in this manuscript." This course of action should reclaim your manuscript and leave you on good terms with the editor. Should the editor fail to respond, soon after the designated deadline, go ahead and resubmit the manuscript to another publisher. Be careful to file a copy of this correspondence with your manuscript to be used as evidence of your innocence, should you end up with two acceptances.

WHOSE NAME COMES FIRST?

If your collaborators are colleagues, the person who initiated the manuscript should have the privilege of being listed first. If I asked you to join me in writing a manuscript, I would probably generate the first draft or at least an outline, and I would probably specify exactly what I considered your work role in this project. With your approval, I would even set deadline dates for the completion of the various stages of the project. These actions would make me the originator, organizer, and manager—and would entitle me to the placement as first author.

I have developed a system of collaboration that eliminates the possibility of conflict—I do not ask anyone to collaborate with me on just one article. When I initiate one idea, I make it clear that I expect the collaborator(s) to come up with an idea for a second article. For that article, the originator would be the first author. Remember, the sooner you specify what's expected of all parties, the fewer misunderstandings you will have.

WHO IS LISTED FIRST IF THE COLLABORATORS ARE PROFESSOR AND GRADUATE STUDENTS?

Some graduate advisors encourage their students to write for publication. Even more admirable, some professors collaborate with students. If an article reports a student's research performed in support of the thesis or dissertation (which of course, belongs to the student), fairness dictates that the first article generated from the study also belongs to the student. Therefore, I would insist that the student be listed as first author.

Many theses and dissertations have enough data for more than one article. Should the professor collaborate with this student on a second article, the professor would usually take the lead in writing the second article and should be listed as the first author.

IF I FURNISH MY DISSERTATION OR THESIS FOR A COLLABORATOR TO SHAPE INTO A MANUSCRIPT, IS THAT AN EQUITABLE EXCHANGE?

I don't believe I know anyone who would be willing to undertake the interpretation of someone else's work. I wouldn't feel competent to do the job unless perhaps I had served as the committee chair for the study. The first article from a study should be drafted by the student who conducted the study.

As to the question of equity, beginning authors often perceive the difference between a dissertation and an article to be small, only requiring a few adjustments here and there. I know this because as a guest editor I have received theses that have had only minor tinkering. But, these papers seldom, if ever, are accepted for publication. Actually, the task of converting a thesis into an article is tantamount to writing an article from scratch. The study provides the data; that's a lot, but it isn't enough to justify getting your name on an article.

IF I SHARE A BOOK IDEA WITH A PUBLISHER, HOW CAN I BE SURE IT WON'T BE TURNED OVER TO A MORE EXPERIENCED AUTHOR?

This suspicion raises its head in almost every workshop I teach. My first response is to share my own personal perception which is based on 20 years of submitting book prospectuses. Most editors are too honest to try such a stunt. Publishing houses need to retain credibility with authors, and the potential gain in such shady dealings would be outweighed over the long haul by loss of reputation with potential authors. Most publishing companies are in business for the long run.

But as I give this response I see that worried look on the questioner's face, and I remember how important this question is to an individual who wants to protect a really great idea, so I offer the following advice. If you are still worried that the editor might give your idea to an experienced author, before sharing your idea, go ahead and develop it. Begin working on some of the chapters so that when you do approach an editor you are far enough ahead in the project that you can finish it long before anyone else could write it.

WHAT DOES IT MEAN WHEN AN EDITOR ASKS THE AUTHOR TO REWRITE AND RESUBMIT A MANUSCRIPT? SHOULD I DO THAT?

Occasionally editors neither accept nor reject a manuscript. Instead, they write or phone the authors and ask them to revise the manuscript. Sometimes authors ask me how they should respond to such a request. I tell them: First, let's determine what this request means, or what it tells us about the editor's view of the manuscript; then, let's consider how rewriting and resubmitting a manuscript affects its chances of being accepted.

According to my latest questionnaire returns, professional journal editors receive about five times as many manuscripts as they have undesignated space in their journal. This means that most editors probably have enough good manuscripts to fill the next several issues of their journal. If that's so, why don't they just reject your manuscript instead of asking you to rewrite it? The answer is probably one of the following:

1. They see a good "fit" between the manuscript topic and the journal (which is to say that your topic is of interest to their readers).
2. The editor believes that your manuscript offers a worthwhile contribution (which is to say that the editor believes that you have something important to contribute).

The next essential consideration is how a resubmitted manuscript's chance for acceptance compares to that of an original submission. For that information let's consult the survey responses.

Contrary to some people's suspicions that a resubmitted manuscript will automatically be accepted, most editors indicate that they send the resubmitted manuscripts for review. Sometimes the author is asked to rewrite the manuscript a second or third time. But the good news is that 75 percent of all resubmitted manuscripts are eventually accepted, compared to a 15 percent acceptance rate for original submissions. This means that rewriting a manuscript to meet the requests of the editor improves its chances for acceptance by 500 percent. For me, the answer is clear; I usually honor the editor's request by making as many of the requested changes as I find comfortable. So my advice is: gladly accept this offer and give the rewrite close attention to meet all of the editor's requests.

One editor responding to the survey (Henson 1993) said, "A revise and resubmit recommendation indicates interest in eventual publication. If possible, look at recommended revisions as positive attempts to improve the manuscript. The most successful authors are those who revise well."

SHOULD I USE A COMPUTER?

This is a question that must be answered by each writer. Since I cannot think as freely and clearly with typing as I can while writing, I prefer to put the first draft in script. But, I have known individuals who, I am convinced, can think more clearly when they have their fingers on the keyboard. I suggest that you decide which system affords you the opportunity to think clearly, and then use that system.

I asked a couple of authors for their views on using computers. Robert Maddox, Associate Professor of Business at the University of Tennessee, says:

> There is, I believe, no way to write except by using a computer. Legal pad and pencil or typewriter just do not work. The ability to load tons of files of notes in the computer, to move around in these notes, and to switch from these notes to the document on which you are working (carrying some of the material with you) is invaluable as a time saver. I think that using a

computer also helps me to overcome the problem of having to discipline myself to write. I used to find it difficult to put words on paper when they had that permanent quality of going on paper. However, using a computer, I feel freer to get words down, knowing that poorly thought out or stated ideas can easily be deleted or changed.

PROFILE

Vance Wisenbaker earned bachelors and masters degrees at Florida State University and a Ph.D. from the University of Georgia. All three degrees are in sociology.

For the past seven years, he has served as Dean of Social and Behavioral Sciences and Professor of Sociology at Eastern Kentucky University where he served as chair of the Department of Anthropology, Sociology, and Social Work for 10 years before becoming dean.

His book, *Programming with Macintosh Pascal*, 2nd ed. (coauthored by Richard Rink and Richard Vance) was published in 1994 by Prentice Hall.

There are many small technical advantages to using a computer with word processing software to write. I could easily prepare an entire chapter for this book listing and explaining these individual advantages. The truth, however, is that the computer simply allows me to concentrate on the content and flow of my writing and forget the appearance and style. I need not worry about misspelled words or margins or formatting page numbers and footnotes. The computer can do all of these things later, after the rough draft has been committed to paper. Not only can it easily make such changes and corrections, it can do so swiftly and with a consistency that I otherwise could never achieve.

I have one bit of advice for anyone just getting started in the use of a word processor. Start out simple and let the word processor help with only a few things. Do not try to master its full features with your first book or article. Learn to do essential and simple things like margins, fonts, tabs, headings, and the spelling checker. Save some of the more difficult features for later projects. Some of us will use this software for years and never master its full range of features. It may be that you will never have an urgent need to do drop caps or circular text (to mention a few). Finally, do not hesitate to ask an experienced friend when you need help. Most computer "experts" are more than glad to share their knowledge with their friends.

WHAT SHOULD I LIST ON MY RESUME AS PUBLICATIONS?

Academic writers have a difficult job deciding what to list in their resumes under the heading Publications. Obviously, some find this decision very easy; they use the same process that many academicians use when applying for promotion or tenure. The rule seems to be, if it fits in a pickup truck, include it.

For those who are a bit more selective, several questions arise. A common question concerns "in press" publications. This is a great camouflage term. Some evaluators are willing to believe that, "in press" means the manuscript has been accepted and is sitting suspended on a launching pad about to blast off. But others are more skeptical. Professor Allen Berger (1985) of Miami University teaches Writing for Publication courses, and he says that to him "in press" means only that the person knows his way to the post office and is able to buy stamps.

Writers also ask if they should list meeting proceedings. The answer depends on the discipline. Some disciplines place considerable weight on meeting proceedings, but others do not. For example, in education, meeting proceedings have little meaning as evidence of scholarly achievement because usually they are not evaluated and therefore are not weighted heavily as evidence of scholarship.

My advice is, unless you know that it can significantly add to your credits, do not list it. By including questionable evidence, candidates run the risk of discrediting their complete resume.

A FEW OF MY COLLEAGUES AND I HAVE BEEN TALKING ABOUT GETTING TOGETHER ON A REGULAR BASIS TO DISCUSS OUR WRITING. DO YOU RECOMMEND THIS AND, IF SO, CAN YOU GIVE US SOME ADVICE?

I like this idea. In fact, when giving writing workshops on college campuses, I always recommend this to the audience. I call such a group of writers a "support group" because I believe that beginning writers need support, which is unlikely to come from outside. If conducted properly, other benefits can come from such an organization. Consider the following guidelines:

First, be systematic and set aside the same day(s) for such meetings, say the first Monday in every month. Second, keep the meetings short. Brown bag luncheons work well for most groups. Third, have a designated speaker and topic for each meeting. Some speakers can be members of the group but invited guests can also contribute significantly. For suggested topics, check the chapters of this book. You might ask a successful author from any department on campus to give a 20- to 30-minute presentation on "Why I write for publication" or "How I find topics" or "How I choose my target journals." Or you might ask a researcher to speak on developing and using questionnaires. A prolific English professor might be willing to speak for 20 to 30 minutes on "Writing lead sentences" or "Getting the Reader's Attention." Also, other departments on campus have some book authors. I would hold an occasional meeting aimed at motivating and reinforcing the desire to write.

RECAPPING THE MAJOR POINTS

Most questions that plague writers are perennial. For years these questions have baffled and impeded the success of writers, and they will continue to present problems for writers. Simply try to remember:

- Most successful writers immensely enjoy writing; they are compelled to write by a need to say something that they feel must be said.
- To become a successful writer, you must believe in your abilities, and you must write often.
- The best way to handle rejections is to repair the rejected manuscript and immediately send it to another publisher.
- Highly successful writers have two or three manuscripts underway while two or three others are being considered.
- Authors should never simultaneously submit a manuscript to multiple journals.
- Collaborating on writing projects with colleagues can provide needed motivation and opportunities to learn from your colleagues, while expediting your writing program. Such success depends on finding partners with similar personalities and work habits.
- Tables and graphs are more expensive to print than words and, therefore, should be used only when the journals to which you submit manuscripts use them and only when they communicate messages clearer than written comments.
- For the beginner, time is best invested in writing for national journals.
- There are several definitions of refereed journals. To make your writing program pay off, learn how your institution defines "refereed," and act accordingly.
- Vanity publishing is seldom a good choice for authors.

- Self-publishing is usually a better choice than vanity publishing—but only if you can both afford it and tolerate the risk involved.

REFERENCE

Berger, A. Perish the thought. *The Baltimore (Maryland) Sun.* 3 April 1985.

10

Getting Book Contracts

For most people, the act of getting a contract for a book has always been a chore; it's getting harder. Before the economic recession of the 1970s, many editors couldn't seem to find enough authors. Although in some fields, editors still vigorously pursue authors to write specific nonfiction books, such as college textbooks, an aspiring textbook author should not wait for an editor's knock on the door. The economics of publishing has made acquisitions editors cautious. If you have an idea for a book, carefully plan a strategy to pursue the publishers, rather than hoping they will pursue you. Writing a book is enormously time consuming, with no success guaranteed. If you still are determined to write a book, take the time needed to do it right. You can do it.

CHOOSING THE RIGHT BOOK
TO WRITE

Some people decide to write books but go no further than making the decision. Others write complete manuscripts and never succeed in getting them published. Some of the major obstacles include procrastination, striving for perfection, and ignorance about the roles of authors, editors, and agents.

Before putting pen to paper or fingers to keyboard, take a moment to reflect on the type of book you wish to write. Is it fiction or nonfiction? Is it a how-to book or a self-help book? Is its major function to inform or to entertain? Is it a professional book or a textbook? If it's a textbook, for what grade level is it intended? Generally, the larger the general market for a book, the harder the writer must work to beat out the competition.

WRITING PROFESSIONAL BOOKS

An overlooked market that is available to all professionals, regardless of profession or content expertise, is the professional book market. Usually written by individuals who have considerable experience in the workplace (although the length of experience varies), these books are often written by scholars of scholars and leaders of leaders. In psychology, Joyce Brothers is a leading author. In business, one readily thinks of Tom Peters, or in pediatric medicine one thinks of T. Berry Brazelton. All of these authors have been exceptionally successful. Most writers of professional books do not gain such recognition, yet, those authors did not win success overnight. Nobody should be discouraged from writing professional books. Those who succeed in getting contracts in this market usually combine the expertise gained from coursework with new insights gathered from research, surveys, or on-the-job experience.

In a sense, writing professional books is an extension of writing for professional journals. Both outlets provide opportunities to advance the profession while establishing professional credibility for the author. Like writing for university presses, the professional market offers opportunities for reaching particular markets that are difficult or impossible for other publishers to reach.

Before choosing a publisher for your professional book manuscript, be aware that only a few publishers can reach this specialized market. For example, university professors and business people write many professional books. One might assume that college textbook publishers would be a good choice for targeting these manuscripts, but usually they are not. Textbooks are sold in multiple adoptions. A professor might use 10 copies for one section of a course that has a small enrollment, while a committee may adopt several hundred copies for multiple sections of an introductory course.

In contrast, professional books are marketed for single copy sales. Since very few textbook companies can afford to advertise for single sales, you should be sure your intended publisher publishes and sells to a single adoption audience. *The Writer's Market* is an excellent source for identifying publishers of professional books and other particular types of books.

WRITING BOOKS FOR UNIVERSITY PRESSES

University presses can be an excellent outlet for certain books—but you must take time to learn the nature of these institutions. First, the royalties earned on these books are generally less than on commercially published books. Although the royalty rates of some of these books may equal that of their commercial counterparts, the dollars received do not. At least three factors work together to make this so.

First, university presses publish for specialized markets that are usually smaller than the markets for trade and other nonfiction books. Second, most university presses do not have the financial support needed to market books as extensively as do commercial publishers. Most university presses do not have full-time sales representatives in the field nor do they depend on sales profits for all of their funds. When commercial publishers fall short on sales, they have no alternative sources of funds on which to draw. Third, although many university presses are not insensitive to sales earnings, most have other sources of support; therefore, they are not forced to sell large numbers of books.

The fledging author may ask, "Then why do authors ever seek to have their works published by university presses?" This question has more than one good answer. Because some authors' topics are so specific, the university press is their only hope of getting their book manuscripts published. With small markets, even self-publishing is seldom a good alternative. For example, a professor who wishes to publish a book on the history of native Americans could not find a more likely publisher for this work than the University of Oklahoma Press. For publishing a book on gambling and gaming, the University of Nevada Press would be an excellent choice. For a manuscript on archeology, a writer might query the University of Michigan Press or the University of Pittsburgh Press.

For a book on anthropology, an author might contact the University of Arizona Press, the University of Iowa Press, the University of New Mexico Press, or the University of Pittsburgh Press. Many of the university presses focus on books that are of interest to their own geographic region. Several publish books on Americans. Appendix L contains a listing of university presses and the subject areas in which they specialize.

The point here is to avoid sending a manuscript or query to a university press until you first know the topic on which the particular press generally publishes. In addition to finding the university presses your best chance for some topics, professors and other professional scholars often prefer these presses because most of them stress scholarship. Some have as their main mission the advancement of particular academic fields of study.

PROFILE

Hanoch McCarty received a B.A. degree in English/Education at Queens College of the City University of New York, an M.S. degree in Educational Administration from Southern University, and the Ed.D. from the University of Massachusetts. He taught for almost 20 years at Cleveland State University in Cleveland, Ohio. Now he lives in Galt, California where he is president of his own consulting firm, Hanoch McCarty and Associates, Inc. He conducts workshops on "Stress and Energy in the Learning Process," "Teaching as a Performing Art," and "Gifted Kids Have Feelings, Too."

When I was working on my doctorate at the University of Massachusetts, I was confronted by Professor Peter Wagschal, a member of my doctoral committee, with a challenge: learn to write personally. I had submitted a paper to him filled with the usual impersonal jargon of academia: "one cannot conclude . . . , "the author finds that . . . ," and lots of impersonal pronouns. Pete asked me, "What do *you* believe? What do *you* find? What do *you* conclude?" He insisted that I take a position; personalize my work for him. I found it very difficult to do, since I had spent so many years succeeding at learning the academic style of writing. I resisted his challenge; I squirmed and argued. But, in the end, because I wanted to succeed in this new environment, I surrendered. Pete insisted that I rewrite in a personalized manner all the work I had submitted. It was a huge task but filled with learning for me. If you want to enter the commercial market and write for popular rather than professional audiences, you must learn Pete Wagschal's lesson: personalize.

Avoid scholarly trappings like footnotes, citations, long quotes. Non-academic readers aren't impressed by the strength of your bibliography or the erudition implied by your elevated polysyllabic vocabulary. In fact, they will be turned off rapidly and completely by that sort of language. Can you say it succinctly

and in plain talk? Tell it as a story. These are the keys to writing which move people to purchase books at the newstand and the mass market bookstore. As an experiment, compare any psychology textbook (even an elementary one) with the writing in any successful book found in the self-help/psychology section of your local book store. They may even both have the same concepts, but the style will be miles apart. The text will be dry, straightforward, with lots of quotes, references, and much unselfconscious use of technical jargon. The mass market book will have lots of stories. Every concept will be illustrated with one or more down-to-earth stories. If there are quotes, it's likely they'll be inspirational ones.

Begin with a story. Just as I did. Make it personal. Tell how you felt and what you learned from the experience. Then draw your moral. Use the word "I" as often as seems necessary. Don't obey my high school English teacher's dictum to never use I more than once in a paragraph. Keep your integrity by making sure that anything which is more opinion than fact is clearly identified as such, but don't shy away from "I." As John Cassavetes, the great film director, once said, "Don't be afraid to express an ego. It means self in Greek. If you don't have a self, who are you anyway?" Your audience in this market wants your experience, your opinions, your expertise. They are not usually seeking impartiality or neutrality.

Be concrete. Give examples, paint word-pictures, use colorful descriptive adjectives. Jean Piaget described the stages of cognitive development pointing out that most children become concrete operational thinkers in mid-childhood and become able to think abstractly, on what he called "formal-operational" level, at the onset of early adolescence. You might think, therefore, that most adult readers are comfortable with high level abstractions most of the time. Recently I read about an experiment at a university which showed that, more than 80 percent of the time, adults were thinking on the concrete level while professors talk more than 90 percent of the time on the formal-operational level! This means there's a rather big communications gap. Why do most textbooks seem dry and boring and most trade books seem easy to read, light, interesting? I think it's because they're written in these two different "languages." If you want to attract and keep the mass market audience, write to them directly. (Please note that I didn't say, "write *down* to them." They are intelligent but often not as committed as you are to your subject).

Think of your target audience. What turns them on? What concerns them, scares them, bothers them the most? Find some stories which speak to those issues and you're on the right track.

Speak in the active voice. One idea: tell your story, aloud, into a tape recorder. Pretend you're speaking to a friend. Be conversational. Do your editing later. Many writers lose the strength of their writing by what I call editing in advance. They try to get the words into finished form as they write them. This slows the writing process down and removes any chance that it will sound conversational and natural. Each word is too carefully chosen and crafted. Write (speak) first, and edit later. To edit more effectively, read it aloud, especially to a live person. As you read aloud, you'll hear where it sounds forced.

Think visually: collect good pictures, cartoons, illustrations for your book. Don't expect the publisher to do this for you. Start an illustration file with subsections for each of the topic areas you'll cover. Read newspapers and magazines with a scissor in hand. Ask friends for help in finding appropriate illustrations. Good visuals make a book successful.

Think visually: plenty of white space will make your book more inviting to the general audience; dense masses of print will seem forbidding and difficult. Open your book up. If you are self-publishing, spend the extra money to hire a graphic designer. This will improve the final product markedly. The designer should help with the total book from cover design (a strong graphic, a photo, the use of color and typography) all the way to the choice of type styles and page organization.

Think non-linearly: organize your book around interests and high points, not ploddingly obvious

"Harvard Outline" logic. Use "sidebars" to explore issues more deeply when the exploration would make your narrative drag. One of the key differences between academic text writing and writing for the mass market is that your reader isn't *required* to read your book. You've got to get them interested enough to buy it on a quick skim of the pages and keep them interested enough to finish it and recommend it to friends. This means that you must be marketing the book from beginning to end.

DEVELOPING A PROSPECTUS

Having decided to write a book, the next decision that confronts you is whether to first write the book and then seek a publisher or to begin by seeking a publisher. Writing a book requires an enormous investment of time and energy. To avoid the risk of having the investment result in an unpublishable manuscript, a plausible alternative is to develop a prospectus. Because it also saves time for the editors, most publishers require a prospectus. A good prospectus contains the following parts:

1. Contents outline
2. Sample chapters
3. Book description
4. Market description
5. Competition description
6. Author description

Content Outline

Moving from the would-be-book-writer category to that of a published author begins with getting an overall mental picture of the book you want to write. Begin by making a list of all the major topics (chapters) you plan to include. Then fill in the subtopics you intend to cover within each chapter. How-to books and self-help books might require only tables of contents because of the degree of detail and structure. Chapter outlines are usually much more detailed than tables of contents, and therefore more appropriate in some cases.

For example, Figure 10–1 shows the contents page in James J. Kilpatrick's book, *The Writer's Art*. Notice that some of these titles give clues about the contents. We might suppose that Chapter One will offer some analysis and criticism of the English language and that Chapter Two will emphasize the need for clarity in writing, but only the author knows what Chapter Three

---

FIGURE 10–1   Sample chapter outline for a how-to book.

Contents

Foreword

Introduction

1. How Fares the English Language?
2. Faith, Hope, and Clarity
3. Beyond the Toothpaste Tube
4. The Things We Ought Not to Do
5. The Things We Ought to Be Doing
6. The Tools We Live By
7. My Crotchets and Your Crotchets
8. The Games We Play

---

is about. Because most of these titles just sort of make the reader feel good, they are inviting and functional. But the acquisitions editor will want more. Some acquisitions editors ask to see the entire manuscript.

Compare Kilpatrick's contents section (Figure 10–1) to Dale Baughman's Contents page for *Baughman's Handbook of Humor* shown in Figure 10–2.

As you can see, even the contents section for nonfiction *how-to* and *self-help* books can be detailed and descriptive, each entry is succinct. Robert Hochheiser achieves the art of entertaining while informing the reader with the Contents page in *How to Work for a Jerk* (see Figure 10–3).

Other types of nonfiction books such as textbooks or professional books have formal chapters. These books demand a more detailed chapter outline. Figure 10–4 shows one chapter outline from each of two college textbooks.

When you consider that the education textbook has 20 chapters and 510 pages, and some other books have well over 1,000 pages, the need for detailed chapter outlines becomes obvious. Detailed chapter outlines help writers conceptualize and organize the vast amount of content in these books so that the enormous quantity of information in them is comprehensible to their readers. They also help acquisitions editors understand the overall purpose and nature of the book in addition to assuring the editor that the author has fully conceptualized the project.

Sample Chapters

The first chapter serves as a foundation for the following chapters, thus, many publishers specifically ask to see the first chapter. So you should begin

---

FIGURE 10–2 More detailed content outline for a how-to book.

The Practical Value of Humor in Education

SECTION 1: Types of Humor and Application in Education
The pun • The limerick • Comic verse • The gag • The joke • The anecdote • Rustic humor • One-liners • Riddles • Boners • The tongue twister • Publication bloopers • Fun with words • Report-card-day shock • Seasonal and holiday humor • Communications humor • Teacher dilemmas • Adolescent dilemmas • Kindergarten kapers • Student masterpieces • Examination humor • The double blunder • Parent perplexities • PTA humor • The fable • Satire • Plain nonsense

SECTION 2: How, When and Where to Use Humor in Education

The Nature of Humor

The Functions of Humor
Social lubricant • Safety valve • Therapy • Tonic • Sixth sense • Survival kit • MOtivation and cognitive challenge

The Phenomenon of Laughter

Laughter and Learning

Laughing at One's Self

Joy in the Schools

Sources of Humor

The Many Ways to use Humor in Education
Diagnosis • Humanizing • Democratic living • Variety and unpredictability • Tension reducer • Openers • Preoccupied minds • To make a point • Holidays and vacations • The mischief of language

References

---

by writing Chapter One. Then peruse your content outline and choose another chapter or two you think will be the best and most representative of the whole book. When you have written and polished Chapter One and one or two additional chapters, they will become the significant part of your prospectus.

Book Description

You must describe your book clearly and succinctly. For example, "This is a general secondary and middle school methods textbook for undergraduate

---

FIGURE 10–3 Contents section that both entertains and informs.

CONTENTS

1. THEY DO IT ON PURPOSE
Why bosses act like jerks, and how they get away with it.

2. THE CAST OF CHARACTERS
Identifying the type of boss you have and determining how to deal with him.

3. DILETTANTES, FOPS, EXPERTS, AND OTHER MEATHEADS
Assorted losers do reach the top. Here's how to get the upper hand with them.

4. CORPORATE DINOSAURS
Entrepreneurs as they evolve from fearless to fearful.

5. INHUMAN RESOURCEFULNESS
How jerks get hired. The schemes bosses use to avoid rewarding us. Counterattacking those schemes.

6. POLITICS
An assortment of unprincipled principles for dealing with uncooperative bosses, colleagues, and subordinates.

7. IF YOU'RE ALSO A BOSS
Motivating your people to work for you, not against you. Mutual indispensability and how it works. The importance of compatibility. How to hire good people.

8. IT'S ONLY A JOB
Putting your job in perspective as a means to an end. Controlling your ego. Dealing with egocentric bosses. Creative selfishness. When and how to be assertive. Setting goals. What to do when nothing works.

---

classes." Then tell the major features of the product. I used the following strengths to "sell" a book that is now in its fourth edition, *Methods and Strategies for Teaching in Secondary and Middle Schools:*

> *It is comprehensive [it has all of those chapters commonly found in secondary and middle school-methods texts]. It is timely [it has those new chapters that are not commonly found in methods texts]. For example, it contains a chapter on educational reform, a chapter on educational technology, an annotated bibliography on simulations and games (complete with addresses of sources), and a resource list for teaching thinking skills.*

FIGURE 10–4   Detailed chapter outlines for textbooks.

Chapter 7: Effective Schools
    Objectives
    Pretest
    Introduction
    Defining Effective Schools
    School Climate
    Positive Discipline and Control
    The Role of the School Principal
    Providing for Staff Development
    Monitoring of Clearly Established Goals & Objectives
    The Importance of Autonomy
    Parent Involvement
    Recapitulation of Major Ideas
    Summary
    References

From Armstrong, Henson, and Savage, *Education: An Introduction,* 3rd ed. Macmillan, 1989.

Chapter 8: Helping People Change
    Objectives
    Regional University EEC Case
    Leadership
    Resistance to Change
    Barriers to Change
        Failure to Use Research
        Teachers are Classroom Bound
    A Need for Involvement
    Ways of Involving Teachers
    The Use of Incentives
    Teachers as Researchers
    Staff Development
    NCSIE
    Consortia
    School Culture and Climate
    Forces that Promote and Impede Change
    Group Leadership
    Using Power
    The Future of Educational Leadership
    Summary
    Questions
    Suggested Further Activities
    Bibliography

From Kenneth T. Henson, *Curriculum Development for School Reform.* HarperCollins, 1994.

Since evaluation has become a topic of great reform interest, the prospectus for the next revision of this book will announce that it has two separate chapters on evaluation and testing.

Because I thoroughly update all the chapters and cite the latest research studies with each revision of this book, I am careful to say so. For example, "This book reports the findings of over 300 research studies." If your book is a textbook, pay close attention to pedagogy, and stress this strength in your prospectus. For example, In the *Methods and Strategies* book prospectus I say:

> Each chapter has a list of objectives, a pre-test, a post-test, a recap of major ideas, suggested further activities, and suggested further readings. Throughout each chapter, "Let's Ponder" sections cause the reader to interact with the dialogue. An "Experiences" (or case study) section at the end of each chapter shows the major principles being applied.

To determine the expenses or capital needed to publish a book, the acquisitions editor will need some information about the book's physical characteristics. For example: "The book length will be approximately 450 pages (or 750 manuscript pages). The book will contain about 25 photos and approximately 25 line drawings. Present plans include a Teacher's Manual of approximately 64 book pages. Present plans do not include supplementary aids for students."

Market Description

Of paramount interest to the editor is the market for which your work is intended. This market must be large enough to support the project, and it must be attainable, which means that it must be specific. Although authors may be tempted to think of their work as having application to many markets, editors know that few works are used by multiple audiences. An old adage expresses the dilemma: "The only thing that is wrong with a book that is written for everybody is that it is used by nobody."

In addition to being specific, the market description should provide examples of specific contexts in which the book might be required. For a college textbook prospectus, examples of particular university courses that would use this book should be provided. Most university libraries have college catalogs; it takes only a few minutes to look up the courses and jot down their names, numbers, and descriptions.

Description of the Competition

The worst mistake a military commander can make, they say, is to underestimate the potential of the enemy. Equally so, authors who fail to know and acknowledge the strength of the competition assure their own defeat. Because you are writing a textbook and it is in your field of study, you will have expertise on the subject, and you will be aware of some of the competition. But you may fall short unless you are aware of all of the viable competing texts. Furthermore, you must be more than aware of these books; you must be closely familiar with each competing book. Only then, can you use their strengths and weaknesses to improve the design of your own product.

All editors want assurance that your book will contain those chapters that professors who teach the course expect to cover. Also, they want your book to be superior to, not equally good, but *superior to* the competitors'. Two items are needed to communicate these features. First, you should submit a very detailed and very comprehensive chapter outline of competing titles—detailed enough to contain all of the major topics in each chapter. Second, you should create a content comparison chart that clearly demonstrates the superiority of your book. A sample content comparison chart is shown in Figure 10–5.

Such a chart allows the editor to readily identify those chapter topics that are common among the major textbooks used in the targeted course. In Figure 10–5, your book is in Column H. About two-thirds down the chart are those chapters that you chose to delete in favor of other chapters (listed at the bottom of the figure). The content comparison chart can help *you* design a superior book by helping you identify the chapter topics that you must cover, by helping you identify important and relevant topics for new chapters, and by helping you communicate these coverages to your editors.

Author Description

Finally, include a brief statement that clearly establishes your competence in writing this work. If your credibility emerges from your own research, say so. If you have had unique experiences that contribute to the quality of this work, the editor should know this. Also include a statement about your previous, relevant publications.

Contrary to popular belief, an author's degrees and titles are of little importance unless they assure that the contributor has the expertise needed to write a superior book. For example, "department chair" is a significant title only if you are writing a book on leadership or administration. Much more convincing would be your experience in conducting research, surveys, or other investigations on the subject of this book.

FIGURE 10–5   **Content comparison chart.**

Chapter Topics	Book A	Book B	Book C	Book D	Book E	Book F	Book G	Book H
Adolescence & Learning	X	X	X	X	X			X
Planning	X	X	X	X	X	X	X	X
Classroom Management	X	X	X	X	X	X	X	X
Evaluation	X	X	X	X	X	X	X	X
Teaching Styles	X	X	X	X	X			X
Motivation	X	X						X
Multicultures of Disadvantaged		X		X	X			X
History & Aims		X						X
Audio-Visuals		X		X				X
Teaching Special Pupils		X	X					X
Communications			X					X
The Professional Teacher/Getting a job		X	X					
Student Teaching		X	X					
Educational Reform								X
Effective teaching								X
Using technology								X

SELECTING A PUBLISHER

Once the prospectus is complete, it is time to approach a publisher. You will want to *choose only publishers publishing books in your subject area.* For example, if you send your textbook prospectus to a publisher who does not publish textbooks in your field, you have wasted valuable time. This can be avoided by checking your own professional materials to see who published them, or better yet by making a trip to the library. At the library, check the current reference book, *Books in Print.* In the "Subjects" volume of *Books in Print,* you will see listed all of the books according to particular subjects. Make a list of the publishers of these books. Then check the current *Literary Market Place* and the current *Writer's Market* for a detailed description of each publisher. You may wish to develop a chart such as the one in Figure 10–6, which was designed to help me identify the best possible publishers for a book on reading. A column heading was included for collecting each type of information that I believed important for this type of book and what I wanted to accomplish by writing this book.

Royalty Rate: Most academic projects provide 10 to 15 percent of the net sales to the author(s). For further information, please see Appendix B.

Number of Titles: The number of titles this publisher publishes per year tells you the size of the company.

Size of initial printing: Large initial printings give some assurance that the publisher will work hard to market the book to avoid being stuck with unsold copies.

Hardcover/paperback: The number of charts in this book makes a hardcover book much preferable, but if the company also publishes paperbacks, this may mean that instead of having a short life, the book might be reprinted in paperback at a later date and sold in mass at a lower price.

Advance: A large non-returnable advance can help assure the author that the publisher will not back out on the agreement and can assure that the publisher will work hard to sell enough copies to cover the advance.

Report Time: Helps the author track multiple submissions of the manuscript.

Publishing Time: is important if the author needs the book for merit pay, promotion, or tenure.

The next two columns, How-to and Self-help are important to this book because it falls under these categories. The final column is left open to write in any peculiar features of these publishers important to the author.

Send Query Letters

After you have identified several good prospective publishers, select five or six of the most appropriate ones and simultaneously send them query letters

FIGURE 10-6 Publishers chart.

PUBLISHER	Royalty	Titles/Year	Printing	Hard/Paper	Advance	Report Time	Pub Time	How-to	Self-Help	Other Important Features
Andrew, McMeel and Parker	R	30		H, P				X		4-1-89 Rejected 4-15-89
Arbor House	S	55		H, P			9 mos	X	X	
Avon		300		P	Y	2 mos		X	X	
Donning	7–15%	38		H, P	2,000	2 mos	1 yr	X	X	
Berkley	6–10%	900		P	Y		18 mos	X		
Little, Brown	10–15%	100		H, P	Y	3 mos	8 mos	X	X	4-5-89 Rejected 4-15-89
P-H	10–15%	150		H, P	3–5K	3 wks	8 mos	X	X	4-1-89
WW Norton	15–20%	213			Y		1 yr		X	4-5-89
Prima	15–20%	30+		H, P	Y	1 mo	6–9 mos	X	X	
Ten Speed Press		40	5,000 / 10,000	P	Y	1 mo	10 mos	X	X	
Ashley	10–15%	30		H, P	1,000	2 mos	20 mos	X		
Menasha Ridge	10%W	13	4,000	H, P	Y	1 mo	8 mos			
Jeremy Tarcher	10–15%	30		H, P		2 wks	1 yr	X	X	
Wadsworth	5–15%	600		H, P		2 mos			X	Speech & Communications
Writer's Digest	10%	45					1 yr			4-1-89
Dodd, Meade	10–15%	200			Y	6 wks	9 mos		X	4-5-89
Crown		250		H, P		2 mos		X		
Random House		120				3–6 wks				
Ballantine	8–10%	20		H, P		6 wks	1 yr	X	X	4-5-89
Contemporary	6–15%	100		H, P			10 mos	X	X	
Fearon Education		110				1 mo				
Fucal Press	10–17%	45		H, P	1,500	3 mos	1 yr	X	X	Communications
Stephen Green		30		H, P		3 mos		X	X	College of Ed. graduates
Metamorphous	10%+	10	2,000 / 5,000	H, P	N		8 mos	X	X	Query letter sent
PAR, Inc.	5–10%	8		H, P		1 mo	1 yr		X	Developing Writing Skills / Community College

asking whether they are interested in seeing a prospectus for a book of this type. Give them a brief description of your project, but no more than one page. Be direct, letting each editor know that you are contacting other editors. This will avoid the possible embarrassment of having two or more editors accept your work and then having to turn down one or more editors. It will also encourage editors to respond to your letter without unnecessary delay. Figure 10–7 contains a sample query letter to book publishers. (See also suggestions given in Chapter 8.)

NEGOTIATING THE CONTRACT

Once you succeed in getting a publisher to offer you a contract, it is time to negotiate. But if this is your first book, don't overplay your hand. My advice is to ask for a fixed percentage of the sales. I recently read in a local newspaper that a professor at a midwestern university wrote a book for which he received a flat fee of $200. The book has now sold at least 35 million copies. It doesn't take a mathematician to figure that this professor made a big mistake.

You can do better. Avoid commercial publishers offering straight fees. I make exceptions for non-profit professional associations in which I hold memberships. For example, I received a nominal fee for writing a monograph for *Phi Delta Kappan*. Phi Delta Kappa offers a standard fee for its monograph authors. Although the fee itself is nominal, many other benefits can come from such writing. For example, national associations offer tremendously large exposure. Your association with these organizations can boost your reputation. When strangers say, "I know your name. You work for *Phi Delta Kappan*, don't you?," then I know that my investment of time and energy was well directed.

In an article published by *The Chronicle of Higher Education* (see Appendix B), I advised authors to ask for an advance, but I warned against feeling disappointed if the publisher refuses to pay in advance. I also said that you should read the contract carefully and look for hidden expenses to the author such as costs of photos and permissions. If the publisher says that their authors always bear these expenses, then ask for a ceiling to be set on these expenses. Otherwise, you could write a book that is highly profitable to the publisher but one that brings no income at all to you.

RECAPPING THE MAJOR POINTS

This chapter is included to help you in your search for a publisher to produce your future books. Remember:

FIGURE 10–7 Sample query letter to book publishers.

_____ Editor

_____ , Inc.

Street Address

City, State 00000

Dear _____ :

Would you be interested in reviewing a prospectus for an under-graduate secondary and middle school methods text? This book will have those chapters commonly found in methods texts.

> *You might want to list those essential chapters that are found in existing texts.*

As a former junior high school teacher, I find that other chapters are needed which are not found in current texts. This book will fill that gap. Three of the chapters that are unique to this book are "Using Microcomputers," "School Reform," and "Effective Teaching Research."

> *This answers that paramount question that editors always ask: "How is your book superior to the existing texts?"*

Since I am contacting other publishers, I hope that you will respond at your earliest convenience and that you will specify if you require additional information beyond the chapter outline, the prospectus, and two sample chapters. Thank you.

> *This tastefully tells the editors that they can't put you on the back burner.*

Sincerely yours,

- Getting book contracts is highly competitive.
- A well-prepared prospectus can save you considerable time should publishers consider the target market for your proposed text too small.
- Each book prospectus should contain information about the book, the market, the competing books, and the author.
- When submitting a prospectus, include content outline, Chapter One, and at least one additional chapter.
- Multiple submissions of a book prospectus are acceptable, provided the author notifies each editor that the prospectus is being shared with other publishers.
- To succeed, your prospectus must convince the publisher that your book will be superior to other books on that topic already on the market.

REFERENCES

Armstrong, D. G.; Henson, K. T.; and Savage, T. V. *Education: An Introduction.* New York: Macmillan, 1989.

Baughman, M. D. *Baughman's Handbook of Humor in Education.* New York: Parker Publishers, 1974.

Henson, K. T. "When signing book contracts, scholars should be sure to read the fine print." *The Chronicle of Higher Education.* Oct. 1990, 132–133.

Henson, K. T. *Methods and Strategies for Teaching in Secondary and Middle Schools.* New York: Longman, 1988.

Henson, K. T. (1993). A study of the requirements of education journals, Richmond, KY. For details of the results of this study, see "Writing for successful publication: Advice from editors." *Phi Delta Kappan, 74*(10), June 1993, 799–802.

Hochheiser, R. *How To Work For a Jerk.* New York: Random House, 1987.

Kilpatrick, J. J. *The Writer's Art.* New York: Andrew's, McNeel, and Parker, 1984.

Thompson, A., and Strickland, L. *Strategic Management: Concepts and Cases,* 4th ed. New York: Macmillan, 1987.

11

Planning for Success

Many variables work collectively to determine an author's degree of success. Among these variables is—no doubt about it—luck. For example, at times editors receive several manuscripts that are so good that they want to select more than one; yet, these manuscripts are so similar that only one can be used. Those authors whose manuscripts are rejected just because they happen to arrive when similar, equally good (but not better) manuscripts arrived were unlucky.

There are also times when writers have *good* luck. For example, often an editor has more than enough excellent manuscripts to fill an issue, but to make the desired journal size, the editor needs one very short manuscript. These editors may be forced to reject some superior manuscripts because they are a little too long to "finish out" this issue. An author who submitted a very short, mediocre manuscript may find the article accepted when the longer but better manuscripts are rejected. This author is lucky.

One of my colleagues says this of a seasoned author, on his early writing efforts:

> *I remember when, as a junior faculty member at a major university, I wanted desperately to have an article appear in a particular journal. My college had a wonderful media center and an equally wonderful laboratory school. I asked the director of the media center for photos taken of teachers and students at our laboratory school, promising to give the university and the media center credit for any photos used in the article.*
>
> *The media center director led me to three file cabinet drawers filled with glossy black and white photos, offering me my choice and as many as I could use. I chose a couple of good close-ups that showed teachers and students actively involved in projects. As I closed the drawers, I thought,*

"If a couple of good photos would help get my manuscript accepted, four or five good photos should do twice as well." Then, I thought, "If four or five would help, a couple of dozen should make my article a shoe-in." After an hour of searching, I left the center taking about two dozen excellent photos with me. I then sent all of them along with my very short manuscript to my favorite journal.

A few weeks later as I checked my mail, I noticed a package from this journal. This wasn't uncommon; I'd received many returned manuscripts from the editor, each accompanied with a letter complimenting the manuscript but saying that it didn't meet the journal's current needs. But this package was thicker. A message flashed—complimentary copies! Sure. My manuscript had been accepted, and as with most professional journals this one paid the author by giving a few free copies of the journal carrying the author's article.

My hunch was correct. I quickly checked the contents section. Sure enough, there was my name. I immediately understood why actors fight over top billing. This table of contents was like a Las Vegas marquee. I quickly turned to my article and read it. It read well. Yet, it was very brief, and it didn't report any research. Rather, it reported some observations that I had made while living abroad, identifying some characteristics of American schools that seem to work against minority students.

Then it dawned on me that there were other articles in this issue; I wondered who wrote them. Maybe there were some well-known authors. Quickly checking the table of contents, I found several former presidents of the national association that published this journal. Here I was, a junior, assistant professor listed with some of the biggest names in my field. My chest swelled. But as I scanned through the other articles, I sensed a familiar déjà vu. Then I realized why. Each of those manuscripts had one or two of my photos. They still carried our media center's name. Then a disturbing idea struck. I realized that my manuscript wasn't accepted on the basis of its merits at all! It was accepted because the editor wanted to use all of these photos. But that was ok. I had made the big-time journal, and at that moment anything else paled in importance. I knew I was lucky, but I was also very pleased."

Good luck is always welcomed. But it is an overrated variable in writing for publication. Successful authors do not depend on good luck to bring them success; nor do they use bad luck to explain or excuse their lack of success. Successful authors plan for success. This chapter is written to help you plan a systematic writing program. Use it wisely, and you won't need to rely so heavily on luck to make your writing program succeed.

MANAGING EACH MANUSCRIPT

The chances of writers reaching their goals can be dramatically increased when they not only have a understanding of their goals but also have a sense of the relative importance of each goal. Only then can the most appropriate journal for reaching each goal be identified.

In Chapter 8, I described the wide variance in journal characteristics. For example, some journals are read primarily by researchers while others are read almost exclusively by practitioners. Some journals have audiences of only a few hundred; other journals are circulated to hundreds of thousands of readers. You need to search out your own major reasons (goals) for writing and then select those journals that can best help you reach these goals. You can use Figure 11-1 to: (1) list and order your reasons for writing,

---

FIGURE 11–1 Journal profile.

Reasons for Writing: Rank Ordered
    Most Important:
    Second Most Important:
    Third Most Important:
    Others:

Journal Criteria: Rank Ordered
    Most Important:
    Second Most Important:
    Third Most Important:
    Others:

Journals that Score the Highest

Name of Journal	Refereed	Acceptance Rate	Months required for Decision	Number or Readers	Prestige (High, Average, Low)	Other	Other	Other

.
.
.
etc.

(2) list and order those journals in which you would most like your work to appear, and (3) develop a profile for these journals.

Sometimes writers are unsure of which journals they want to publish their manuscript. You can use the following steps to identify and order your preferred journals:

1. Identify several topics that you enjoy.
2. Identify two sets of journals—specialized and general.
3. Match these journals to these goals.
4. Prioritize your list of journals.
5. Refine your list (delete all unsatisfactory journals).

Now, let's take a closer look at each of these steps:

Step 1: Identify Topic Areas

You should identify several topic areas that appeal to you, areas on which you would like to write. Consider those areas that you know best. As explained in Chapter 2, you can use a reference book such as *Reader's Guide* or *Education Index* to quickly identify those journals that are publishing articles on this topic. Following are six hints you can use to identify good topics:

1. Consider your undergraduate majors/minors.
2. Examine your dissertation or theses *carefully.*

   a. Examine the content.
   b. Who would be interested?

3. Consider other theses and reports.
4. Examine your job.

   a. Your major role as a teacher, administrator, supervisor, etc?
   b. Your grants.
   c. Other accomplishments.

5. Examine your life.

   a. Unusual experiences.
   b. Interests or expertise in other fields.

6. Examine your future.

   a. What kind of job would you like to have in five years? In 10 years?
   b. What are your retirement plans?

Step 2: Identify Two Sets of Journals—Specialized and General

Many beginning writers insist that there are only one or two journals in their subject field. It's true that some fields are much more limited than others. Generally, the more highly specialized the field, the fewer the journals in that field. For example, a marine biologist would find fewer marine biology journals than a general biologist would find biology journals. But just because your field is limited *you* don't have to be limited. A good solution for many subject areas is to identify a set of journals with general emphasis. For example, a marine biologist might have a list of one or two marine biology journals as well as a list of general biology journals.

Step 3: Assign Priorities to the Journals You Listed

Because your goals continuously change, you should re-rank your journal list periodically. You may find it necessary occasionally to delete some of the journals and add new ones. When ranking your list of journals:

1. Consider your employer's expectations.

    a. Level of journal accepted: Does your employer recognize journals whose circulations are national? Regional? State? Local?
    b. Refereed? Non-refereed? (Many employers, particularly higher education institutions, give credit only for referred journals.)
    c. Research based? (Some employers recognize only articles that report the author's research.)

2. Consider the journal's own characteristics.

    a. Acceptance rate. (Would several short articles appearing in practitioners' journals serve you better than, say, one scholarly article placed in a more prestigious research journal?)
    b. Preferred topics?
    c. Costs to author. (Does the journal charge the author a reading fee? Page fees? Would your employer pay these fees for you?)

3. Consider your own needs.

    a. Prestige.
    b. Uses in classes you teach.
    c. Promotion, tenure, merit pay.
    d. Other needs.

4. Plan your publications to achieve other goals.

    a. Grant writing.
    b. Books.
    c. Workshops.
    d. Others.

Each time you have an article accepted, immediately add it to your resume, and always attach a copy of your resume when applying for a grant. This way, the articles give support and credibility to the grant proposals. (It works! So far, my grant proposals have generated over $2 million).

PROFILE

Bonnidell Clouse was born to missionary parents in Costa Rica, and she grew up in California and Arizona. She received her B.A. degree in Psychology at Wheaton College, M.A. degree in Psychology at Boston College, and Ph.D. in Educational Psychology at Indiana University. Her first professorship was at Bryan College in Dayton, Tennessee. Since the 1960s, she has taught educational psychology at Indiana State University.

Writing for publication is a tool that all professors can use to reach important professional goals, but for some individuals writing for publication becomes an extension of their personalities and souls.

It began with the doctoral dissertation. After months of wondering what topic you will write on, you come up with what turns out to be the most interesting and important of all subjects known to humankind. You must, of course, share this with the world. It is your contribution to society and a way of paying back, at least in part, what others have contributed to your education. So, you write and rewrite until the dissertation is but a shadow of its former self and becomes one of the hundreds of articles to appear in academic journals the following year.

With that out of the way you begin teaching. You think you are free, only to be told that if you wish to be considered for promotion or for tenure or for merit or for membership on the graduate faculty or for whatever, you must put pen to paper (or fingers to the keys). So, you're off and running again, this time with new insights and new data and a prayer that it will be accepted by someone, somewhere. And sure enough, several rejection letters later, there it is, in print and absolutely beautiful.

So great is your joy that you begin the same painful process all over again—and again—and again. You watch the list of publications grow longer and longer. You update your vita twice a year instead of once. You get the promotion and the tenure and the merit and a place on the graduate faculty. You have found your place in the sun. Now you can relax and watch the rest of the world from your ivory tower.

But then the unexpected happens. You begin getting invitations to write for this journal or that magazine or the other book. No longer do you have to go begging for someone to notice your work. Someone has noticed and is asking for more. Publication is assured and may be accompanied by a check in the mail. Your resolve to "just say no" weakens as the prospect of thinking through anaother idea or doing another piece of research stimulates your senses, and your brain starts outlining and sorting it all out. Again, you are off and running, thanking the powers that be that you have something that occupies your time that is far more intriguing than the soaps or a shopping spree.

But far more important than getting the dissertation in print, and far more important than being pro-

moted, and far more important than keeping your brain in gear is being able to fulfill a long standing ambition. In my case, what I wanted to do was to integrate Christianity and psychology. This could best be done by writing for publication. Fortunately, this area is popular with many other scholars as well, as is seen in such publications as *Journal of Psychology and Theology* and *Journal of Psychology and Christianity,* and other journals and magazines that carry articles on the same subject.

My area of expertise is that of moral development and moral education. My latest book is *Teaching for Moral Growth: A Guide for the Christian Community* (Victor, 1993). Will I stop with this? As I tell my students, "The best predictor of future behavior is past behavior."

So, it appears I will continue writing. I know that through the printed page I will reach a larger audience than those who sit in my classes each day. And perhaps God in His grace will see fit to use what I write to encourage others in truth and justice.

Step 4: Refine Your Journal List

Some of your old goals give way to new ones. You may find that those journals that match the obsolete goals may no longer be appropriate for you. Don't be reluctant to delete these journals from each of your lists.

DEVELOP A TRACKING SYSTEM

The absolute necessity of getting several manuscripts in the mail was clearly emphasized in Chapter 9: "What distinguishes highly successful writers from less successful writers?" The answer is that highly successful writers write more, and they keep their manuscripts in the mail.

As you increase your number of manuscripts, two things will happen that can complicate your life. At any point, you may find it difficult to remember which journal is currently considering one of your manuscripts, and you may have trouble remembering the location and status of a particular manuscript. Have you sent a query letter? To whom? When? Has the editor responded? Was the response negative or positive? If positive, did you send the manuscript? When? Has the publisher acknowledged receipt of the manuscript? The life of each manuscript has many stages.

All prolific authors have several manuscripts under consideration at any one time, and the logistics of tracking a half-dozen can become quite complex. What if you were to forget that you had already sent a particular manuscript to a publisher and then sent a second manuscript to that same publisher? You may raise suspicion that you have tried all of the other publishers and that no other journals will accept your manuscripts. No editors want their journals to be used as dumping grounds, so you should try to avoid sending manuscripts to an editor who is already considering another of your manuscripts. Worse yet, think of the embarrassment of sending an older manuscript that was rejected once back to the same editor—or of sending the same manuscript to be considered simultaneously by two different journals.

To avoid these unpleasant and damaging situations, you need two types of tracking systems. First, for each of your manuscripts, create a file folder. This folder provides a convenient place to keep early drafts and the notes used during the writing process. In addition to providing a way of locating your latest copy of the manuscript and all related information, the file folder can become an excellent system for tracking the manuscript through its publication life.

On the inside of each folder, begin the tracking form recommended in Figure 11–2. Enter the names of those journals to which you plan to send this manuscript, listing them in order of preference. Because the manuscript is now fresher in your memory than it will be at a later time, making a ranked list of appropriate journals for this manuscript will be easier now than later. Should the manuscript be rejected by the first choice, knowing immediately where to send it next will save much time and will decrease the amount of time that the manuscript stays on your desk.

Now that you have a method of tracking each manuscript individually, you must develop a way of tracking all of your manuscripts simultaneously.

Upon completion of each manuscript, I immediately send a query letter, recording the date sent on a chart as shown in Figure 11–3. When a response is received (assuming that it is positive because most responses to query letters are positive), I immediately send the manuscript, recording

FIGURE 11–2   Sample individual manuscript tracking form.

Article Sent to:	Date	R/A*	Query Letter Sent	MS Sent
The Clearing House	12/1/85	R	7/15/85	7/21/85
Contemporary Ed	4/2/86	A	12/2/85	12/18/85
Educational Horizons				
College & University Teaching				
The High School Journal				

*Rejected/Accepted

the date sent. The names of the journals are listed in the far right column so that, at a glance, I can see if I already have a manuscript at a particular journal.

In Chapter 6 I recommended that you identify a few journals in your area and become familiar with each. In time, that list will grow. A list of your manuscripts, such as the one in Figure 11–3, will enable you to see at a glance which of your manuscripts you have pending at each of your target journals.

For example, the practical benefit of this list and the ease with which it can be used are readily obvious. Just a quick glance reveals some duplications at two of the journals. You will remember that generally this is a poor practice. But, both of these instances involve *invited* manuscripts. This makes a big difference; have no reluctance to send more than one manuscript to a publisher if the second manuscript is requested by the editor.

As manuscripts are rejected, mark through that journal title and, looking at the manuscript tracking form, query the next journal. If you receive a positive response from a query letter, then send the manuscript to the next journal.

GETTING MILEAGE

Once you've experienced the thrill of having a manuscript accepted for publication, you must choose between one-time success or ongoing success. I

FIGURE 11–3   Sample of multiple tracking system.

Author(s)	Manuscript	Date Query Letter Sent	Date of Response to Query Letter	Date Manuscript was Sent	Journal
Henson	Inquiry Learning: A New Look	11/1/86	1/7/86	1/8/86	Contemporary Ed.
Henson	Corporal Punish- ishment: Ten Myths	1/2/86	1/11/86	1/9/86	The High School Journal
Balantine & Henson	Back to Basics: Skills Needed	1/3/86	1/11/86	1/11/86	Contemporary Education
Henson/ Buttery/ Chissom	Middle Schl as Prevd by Cntmpry Tchrs	1/28/86	2/4/68	2/2/68	Middle School Jnl
Block & Henson	Mast Lng & Middle Sch Instruct	1/31/86	2/4/86	2/3/86	American Middle Jnl
Henson/ Chissom/ Riley	Impro. Instr in Middle Schools	1.31/86	2/4/86	2/5/86	AMSE
Henson	Publishing Textbooks & Monographs	2/25/86	3/2/86	3/3/86	Thresholds in Education
Henson & Morris	Prospectives, Insights & Direction	2/29/86	5/7/86	3/8/86	Thresholds in Education
Henson/ Coulter/ Harrell	The UA Summer Inst for Physics Tchrs	2/30/86	5/7/86	3/8/86	The Physics Teacher
Henson/ Saterfiel	How to Get Good Research Data	3/1/86	3.9/86	3/10/86	Amer Sch Board Jnl
Henson/ Buttery/ Chissom	Middle Schl Tchr as a Mbr of Cmty	3/27/86	4/2/86	4/2/86	Middle School Jnl

believe that spending some time to make the article serve you is a wise investment. Here are some ways to get more mileage from your work.

Maintain a Current Resume

To assure that an article acceptance is not a one-time success, you should immediately add this entry to your resume. Using the referencing style most commonly used in your discipline, add the title to your resume under a heading, "Publications." Each time you make a new entry you should also note the date on the resume.

Every new article on your resume enhances your credibility. Each article raises your level of expertise on the particular topic. By keeping your resume current, you can use it to further your career. It also serves in a variety of additional ways. For example, attach the resume to grant proposals to assure the judges that you have expertise that merits the trust that is involved each time a proposal is funded.

Also include your resume each time you submit a book prospectus. Getting book contracts is highly competitive in our current economic climate. I use my vita to convince the publisher that I have the expertise needed to write accurately on the subject. What better evidence could I offer than a nationally refereed article?

Write Book Chapters

Anyone who is capable of writing a published article is also capable of writing a publishable book chapter. I use articles to do this. Currently, I am writing a book titled *Curriculum Development for Educational Reform*. One chapter in this book begins with an article titled, "The Little School that Grew," which is a satire on curriculum development. Because satires don't age like other topics, I was able to go back in my resume and pull out this 15-year-old article. It sounds as though it were written to address current education reform practices.

In another current textbook, I used no fewer than a half dozen articles to write a heavily researched chapter. The articles supply the research and framework for the chapter, and they keep the chapter current. I have revised this 1974 book in 1981, 1988, and 1993. Each revision contains new articles. The book motivates me to write new articles on these same topics, and the new articles keep the book current.

Many authors write chapters for collaborative textbooks that are edited by others. Some authors are invited to write professional yearbook chapters. Invariably these authors use their articles when writing these larger works.

Apply to Daily Work

Many writers are professors who have heavy teaching responsibilities. I do not know of any professors who separate their writing and their teaching. On the contrary, most professors who write for publication use their articles and books in the classroom. This practice was mentioned as a reason for writing for publication; it gives a teacher the confidence and reassurance needed to deliver lessons that are meaningful and enjoyable to both the instructor and the students.

RECAPPING THE MAJOR POINTS

When carefully planned, writing for publication enables authors to reach many professional and personal goals that they could not otherwise reach. But the setting and reaching of these goals require careful planning. Whether or not each of your goals will be reached will be determined in part by the types of manuscripts you write, the topics you choose to write about, the journals to which you submit your manuscripts, and *especially* by how many manuscripts you write.

As your number of manuscripts increases, so does your need for a system to track them. Making a folder for each manuscript is a must. Equally important, you need a system to show you where all of your manuscripts reside at any one time. This chapter has presented and discussed the preparation of an example of each of these systems. These systems are simple to construct but very useful—they work! Your professional and personal goals are unique, so you should either modify these systems to work for you or develop your own personalized systems.

Success is achieved when you reach your goals. This chapter has provided information to help you use writing to reach these goals. The following points are worth remembering:

- Writing can help you reach professional and personal goals, but only if your goals are clear and your writing program is consistent with these goals.
- Success through writing requires extensive writing. As your number of manuscripts increase, your need for a system to track your manuscripts increases.
- A simple manila folder can provide a safe place for your manuscript and related information. A log sheet inside the folder provides an easy system for tracking that manuscript.
- You should use your goals as criteria for choosing article topics and for choosing the journals to which you send your manuscripts.

- Identifying several journals for a manuscript at the time it is written can save turnaround time should the journal that was your first choice reject the manuscript.
- Simultaneously placing two manuscripts at the same journal can jeopardize the acceptance of each; simultaneously placing copies of the same manuscript at two different publishers can destroy your relationship with one or both of these publishers.
- Luck can play an important part in an author's success, but without planning, *good* luck can be a stranger to a writer.

12

Grant Proposal Writing*

Economic constraints place severe limits on many businesses and other institutions—public and private, large and small. Organizations from small
colleges to major university systems, from small family-owned businesses
to major conglomerates, and from small county and town offices to major
city, state, and national governments can be severely affected by scarce resources.

"Do more with less" becomes the motto that expresses the economic
reality of such periods of recession but stretching resources can go only so
far. One alternative to doing more with less—or doing *less* with less or learning to do without—is grant proposal writing. Grants from foundations and
other institutions provide recipients with resources and opportunities that
otherwise would not be available.

But in a nation with free enterprise, the law of supply and demand is
always at work. The consequence is that with money in short supply there
are more people who are ready to work hard and creatively to take it. In
more practical terms, this means that grant money is getting much harder
to get. Yet, it is still there for the taking, and all that is required to get it is to
learn how to prepare a highly competitive grant proposal. This chapter is
designed to help you do just that. The examples given in this chapter, though
simplistic in tone, are tested and proven—they have earned over $2 million.
By following the guidelines that are set forth, you will be capable of producing a highly competitive proposal, one that will edge out 95 percent of the
competition.

*Credit is given to Dr. Donald Orlich, a professor from Washington State University, who
conducts grant proposal writing workshops. Much information in this chapter is taken from
these workshops. The material is used with permission. Valuable feedback on this chapter was
also provided by Dr. Steven Grubaugh of the University of Nevada Las Vegas

Robert Lewis Stevenson once said that, "[The essence of good writing] is not to write but to write what you mean, not to affect your reader but to affect him precisely as you wish." This is true of successful grant proposal writing. Money can and does buy accountability. Most people who have money to give away are astute enough to know this and will demand concrete evidence to assure that they will get their money's worth. For example, if one writer says, "There is a critical need for a safety project" and another applicant conducts a survey of the number of accidents over a given time, the data will be more convincing than words.

Money is an important reason for writing grant proposals, but it's not the only reason people choose to spend their professional time writing proposals. A few years ago I had the pleasure of meeting and working with a person who impressed me with her level of commitment to proposal writing.

Over the past eight years, Olga Ramirez, Associate Professor of Mathematics and Computer Science at the University of Texas–Pan American, has written 15 funded Eisenhower math and science education grants. When I asked her why she put so much time and energy into grant writing, she responded:

Writing these grants is my professional and personal contribution to a community where I was born and raised. These grants bring to elementary teachers necessary mathematics instruction and support materials; hence, the grants contribute greatly to enhancing mathematics instruction and in eliminating the shortage of qualified mathematics teachers.

Although grant projects involve extensive work, they afford some benefits that otherwise would not be as accessible or pronounced. These benefits include: (1) establishing public school and university education partnerships; (2) working side-by-side with colleagues; (3) implementing and discovering new and exciting teaching ideas with teacher in-service audiences; (4) visiting teachers and students in classrooms; (5) collecting data pertinent to teacher training research; and (6) gaining administrative and people skills.

Most important, I write these grants because the teacher audience makes me feel needed, wanted, and appreciated. I like to see and document their attitudinal and cognitive growth. Altogether, the grant-funded projects provide many fun opportunities and much room for my own professional and personal growth.

Perhaps you are ready to try your "luck" at proposal writing, or you may wish to improve your odds in the grant proposal writing game. Such repeated success as that experienced by Olga Ramirez involves more than luck; it requires learning how to do it right. In this time of economic recession, if you are to be successful you must produce proposals that are among the best 5 percent. And, in case you are wondering if you can reach this goal, the answer is yes; you can operate at this level of success, but only if you demand of yourself your very best. Following are some suggestions that can put you in the top 5 percent of proposal writers.

MAKE YOUR PROPOSAL TIMELY

To write a successful grant proposal, that is, one that will be funded, you must have a good, *timely* idea. A topic that was a good idea a few years or even a few months ago may be a very poor idea today. The power in acting on a good idea at the right time is shown in a single example. During the 1970s our nation experienced one of its greatest energy shortages, and a creative principal in Minnesota thought of a way to heat his school building at half the regular cost. This idea was received so enthusiastically that special efforts were taken to assure the proposal success.

LEARN HOW TO DEVELOP FRESH IDEAS

Sincere proposal writers usually start their work by asking where others get such good ideas. Unfortunately, most struggling proposal writers get their ideas from reading newspapers and magazines, watching television, or listening to the radio. What's wrong with that? After all, those are the main sources of news. There are two problems with these sources: (1) they belong to others and (2) they are old news. Even the next day, they are old hat. Such is the nature of news. So, you ask, how can I get ideas that are fresh? Ideas that are mine?

You can *learn* how to develop fresh ideas through a simple process that requires the same skills required to work a jigsaw puzzle. If you have ever spent any time working jigsaw puzzles, you know that the mind can train itself to look for patterns. Instead of going to your office and sitting down with a pencil and paper, or sitting at your computer just waiting for creative inspiration, pick up a newspaper, or better yet, a magazine or journal in your field. Notice the topics that are getting the attention. Now, see if you can relate two or more of these topics to form a new idea. The ability to generate an original idea does not require ignoring all existing ideas. Sometimes a highly successful idea is no more than seeing how to apply the parts of two or more existing successful ideas.

IDENTIFY AND USE YOUR ASSETS

Too often, grant proposal writers think that they must start with no existing knowledge and use only their imaginations to create grant proposals. But starting from zero places an unnecessary burden on the proposal writer. Exacerbating the problem, these proposal writers are afraid that they will break some type of copyright or patent laws or violate some professional ethics code if they use any existing information, which restricts their thinking even further. Successful grant proposal writers know better than to restrict themselves unnecessarily. They know that, so long as they use existing knowledge creatively, get written permission when necessary, and give credit where credit is due, they are not being dishonest.

For example, for economic reasons, most higher education institutions have increased their number of part-time faculty members. This has caused some grave concerns over the quality of instruction; many are worried that the use of too many part-timers will diminish the institution's quality of instruction so much that ultimately both the institution's reputation and quality will suffer. Virtually every higher education institution has a developmental program for helping tenure-track faculty members improve their teaching effectiveness. But how much is being done to develop and support the instruction of part-time faculty members? Probably far less than for tenure-track faculty. A grant proposal combining the two concepts—improved instruction and part-time faculty—would be timely and perhaps tempting to the right donor.

GATHER THE NECESSARY MATERIALS

A good way to start your grant proposal writing program is to gather the necessary materials. One document that many consider indispensable is the *Catalog of Federal Domestic Assistance* which is available for about $50 from:

Superintendent of Documents
U.S. Government Printing Office
Washington, DC 20402
Ask for stock #922–014–00000–1

Another useful document is the *Federal Register,* a booklet that is published daily giving deadlines for requests for proposals. A subscription to the *Federal Register* is too expensive for most writers, but this document is available at most libraries. Figure 12–1 shows a sample entry from the *Federal Register.* By studying these headings, you can become familiar with the nature of projects for which funding is available.

FIGURE 12–1   Sample entry from the *Federal Register*.

Federal Register
Monday, September 21

PART II: DEPARTMENT OF EDUCATION

Direct Grant Programs and Fellowship Programs; Notice Invititing Applications for New Awards for fiscal Year 1993.
    84.061C Planning, Pilot and Demonstration Projects for Indian Children (Planning Projects)

Purpose of Program: To provide grants for projects designed to plan effective educational approaches for Indian children.
    Eligible Applicants: State educational agencies: local educational agencies; Indian tribes; Indian organizations; Indian institutions; and federally supported elementary and secondary schools for Indian children.
    Applicable Regulations: (a) The Education Department General Administrative Regulations (EDGAR) in 34 CFR parts 74, 75, 77, 79, 80, 81, 82, 85, and 86; and (b) The regulations for this program in 34 CFR parts 250 and 254.

Note: The regulations in 34 CFR part 79 apply to all applicants except federally recognized Indian tribes.

Project Period: Up to 12 months.
    For Applications or Information Contact: U.S. Department of Education, 400 Maryland Avenue, SW., room 2177, Washington, DC 20202–6335. Telephone: (202) 401–1902.
    Program Authority: 25 U.S.C. 2621(a)(1), (b).

A particularly good source for identifying grant sources to fund small projects is the *National Data Book of Foundations*. Since the federal government requires anyone who gives money to file an IRS Form 990, you can look up any grant and learn what groups have been funded by a particular party and the amount of each grant.

MATCH YOUR STRENGTHS WITH THE FUNDERS' GOALS

Grant proposal writers can chose either a shotgun approach or a rifle approach to writing their proposals. Both approaches require the writer to understand the nature of the funder, the proposal writer's own strengths, and the strengths and needs of the writer's institution and community (see Figure 12–2). Using the shotgun approach, some writers prepare their proposals and then seek a funder or funders. (This approach is usually more effective when seeking small grants.) The rifle approach—tailoring the proposal to a particular request—is almost essential to capturing large awards.

Grant writing is like playing the stock market; there is seldom a guarantee that your efforts will be rewarded, but the more you know about the process and the more you use this knowledge, the greater the probability for success. So, if you see that a particular proposal request will result in only a small amount being awarded over the year, skip this request and select one with better odds. There is an exception to this advice, however. It's been said, "Most corporations fund only in the shadows of their smokestacks," so small local grants from religious institutions and other community oriented organizations represent a realistic opportunity for success.

Deadlines

Most requests for proposals (RFPs) specify deadlines. Suppose you learn about the opportunity just a week or two before the cutoff date. Many

---

FIGURE 12–2   Matching strengths with the funders' goals and practices.

The Funding Source
- What types of projects has it funded?
- What is the range of dollars given to projects?
- What types of subjects does it avoid?

KNOWLEDGE
NEEDED

Yourself
- What type(s) of expertise do you have?
- What limitations do you have?
- What personal characteristics make you especially well-suited for this project?

Your Institution & Community
- What special resources (including human resources) are available to support this project?
- What special needs does your institution/community have?

novice proposal writers panic and go for the deadline—which is tantamount to racing a train to the crossing; both can be disastrous. A last minute proposal is usually a poorly conceptualized proposal. You have an alternative. Go ahead and send the RFP, and start your draft for next year. Most RFPs change very little from year to year, so when the new request is available you will already have a first draft of your proposal.

Sometimes people ask how much lead time is required to respond adequately to an RFP. Time is needed to think through the project. Donald Orlich, a professor at Washington State University who has given many grant proposal writing workshops, says that 20 working days is a minimum; but he warns that you will probably need even more time for complex projects and for those projects that you have not already given thought to how you will organize your activities.

A Format for Proposals

The elements that are essential to every proposal are: (1) statement of need, (2) project objectives, (3) statement of procedures, (4) statement of strengths, and (5) a method for evaluating the effectiveness of the program. These basics and other components that enhance proposals are discussed here in detail.

1. **Statement of Need.** A good starting point for any proposal is establishing a need for funds or restating your understanding of the needs as described in the RFP. This need should be specific, not general. A good guideline to follow when establishing the need is to keep the statement narrow and precise. If you do not know the exact needs, you may wish to begin by designing and conducting a needs assessment using one or a combination of the following data sources: questionnaire or survey, test scores, committee reports, or literature reviews. Figure 12–3 (Orlich 1992) gives a checklist for evaluating a needs statement.

2. **Project Objectives.** Once your need for the funding has been established, you must outline the objectives of the project, describing exactly what you plan to accomplish. Like your needs statement, each objective should be specific. Your list should not exceed five objectives. Write each objective clearly, which usually means that each objective should be succinct and should have a specific, identifiable subject followed by a transitive verb. Each objective statement should be a complex sentence.

   When these few objectives are written, rank them in order of their relative importance. If your proposal is complex and you find that you need more than five objectives, consider writing two or three goals. If you do include goals, each goal should be paired with one or more objectives. This gives your proposal organization, a quality that counts in most evaluation schemes.

FIGURE 12–3   Sample evaluation of problem or needs statement.

Below is a series of criteria to be used in judging the needs or problem statement. Evaluate each criterion by circling the number to the right of the statement.

4	Very apparent
3	Somewhat apparent
2	Not readily apparent
1	Missing
NA	Not Applicable

1. Appropriate introduction is provided.   4   3   2   1

2. Logical lead to problem or need statement.   4   3   2   1

3. Problem or need is feasible to address.   4   3   2   1

4. Statistical data support statement.   4   3   2   1

5. If a training project, the "target" group has provided support to the need or problem.   4   3   2   1

6. Assumptions or hypotheses are clearly stated.   4   3   2   1

7. Need or problem appears to be credible.   4   3   2   1

8. Statement is clearly written.   4   3   2   1

9. The statement is presented in a logical order.   4   3   2   1

10. What is your overall impression of statement?

11. Strengths:

12. Comments for improvement:

3. **Statement of Procedures.** The statement of procedures tells how you will conduct this project. It should be brief and to the point, telling exactly what you and others will do to achieve the objectives. The statement of procedures answers those questions that reporters ask when conducting an investigation: Who? What? When? Where? and Why?
4. **Statement of Strengths.** Although this part is absent from many proposals, it is found in most of those proposals that receive funding. A statement of strengths is an opportunity for you to tell why you or your organization should be awarded this money. What qualifications do you have that will assure that you will succeed? If appropriate, examine your community, too. What resources does it have that could be used to achieve the proposal's objectives?
5. **Evaluation.** The purpose of the evaluation is to measure the degree to which your project accomplishes the objectives stated. For major projects, consider an external evaluation. Having someone outside your organization to design and conduct the evaluation gives the evaluation objectivity and credibility.

Once your proposal draft is complete, proof it for errors, and then ask a colleague to read it for clarity. If you think there isn't adequate time for this step, consider holding the proposal for a future RFP. A poorly written proposal can be worse than no proposal.

PROFILE

Donald C. Orlich is a Professor of Education and Science Instruction at Washington State University, Pullman. He has published very extensively and has authored or coauthored several books, including *Teaching Strategies: A Guide to Better Instruction,* 4th ed. (D.C. Heath, 1994) and *Staff Development: Enhancing Human Potential* (Allyn & Bacon, 1989). Orlich has written 81 funded proposals and has directed 30 funded in-service/staff development projects. He has coauthored two books on grant proposal writing, including *The Art of Writing Successful R & D Proposals* (distributed by Gordon and Breach Publishers, P.O. Box 786, Cooper Station, New York, NY 10276). He has given numerous proposal writing workshops throughout the United States and Canada.

Ken Henson's chapter on grant proposal writing is one of the most compact and useable statements written on the subject. His following 10-guidelines should be used as a checklist by anyone who wants to improve proposal writing skills. A major implication from the chapter is that one plays the probabilities of being funded. You gather valuable information when conducting the pre-proposal program officers. For example, in a recent issue of the *Federal Register* an announcement called for a planning, pilot, demonstration project for Indian children. Upon close scrutiny, it was observed that only one, o-n-e, award would be made in the U.S.A. Stay away from that one as the probabilities of funding are so slight.

Having a "unique angle" is important. Creativity is very much appreciated by peer review panels who must plow through dozens of mundane proposals. An important element is practicality. Provide some data on piloted work that hint of even more success. Remember, success is highly valued by foundations. Foundations are established by successful business people. They will shun dubious projects and risky adventures. But, unique approaches to old problems or even new problems are rewarded.

As you read this chapter, stop and reflect. Observe how clear, straightforward, and succinct each paragraph is. Funded proposals exhibit those good writing traits. Reviewers tend to rush through the reading. If you have long, clumsy, complex or choppy sentences, reviewers will tend to rate the proposal lower because it lacks "flow." Keep it concise and focused.

When preparing the budget, be certain that every person who is listed in the budget is also mentioned in the proposal's narrative. As the procedures are being discussed, answer the five Ws—who, what, when, where, and why. That simple scheme requires that you think about the details. Unfunded proposals tend to be overgeneralized and do not discuss the contributions of each person listed in the proposal.

Finally, when your proposal is fully crafted, be absolutely certain to check each section against the guidelines. Have you discussed every point that the guidelines address? Have you examined the evaluation criteria listed in the guidelines? Usually, the evaluative section will give specific criteria against which all proposals will be evaluated. Use the terminology found in the guidelines to gently guide the reviewers through your proposal. You might even consider using the headings of the guidelines and evaluative criteria as headings in your proposal.

No one can guarantee that any proposal will be funded. But you owe it to yourself to write the most technically sound proposal that you can. The *best written* proposals do get funded.

FOUNDATION PROPOSALS

Most foundations fund only small proposals ($5,000 or less). Yet, there are so many foundations that the number of funding opportunities they offer warrant attention as a potential source.

Suppose, like many professors, after having received your degree you wish to update your dissertation for publication. A very practical place to look for such resources is foundations. Another advantage of foundation grants is that having no staff to evaluate the proposals, most foundations require and prefer only a one- or two-page statement from the applicant. Figure 12–4 is a model proposal letter.

The following guidelines can be used to write effective proposals for any situation.

GUIDELINE 1: MATCH YOUR EXPERTISE WITH THE NEEDS OF VARIOUS AUDIENCES

Successful proposals don't always require the writer to have the answer in hand. Albert Einstein said that the ability to ask the right questions is more valuable than the ability to find the right answers. Indeed, if you can raise significant, timely questions you may be able to find a sponsor who will pay you or your assistant to research the correct answers.

So, how do you identify timely questions? The same process you use to identify article topics works well on grants. Begin by thinking of your audience. This time your audience is your prospective sponsor. What would this sponsor most want to know? This may be far from what you, yourself, find most interesting. But, if you want the benefits of a successful grant, you may be willing to identify and study a topic that has the only chance of being funded—one that the funder finds interesting.

Keeping the needs of your audience in mind, think about your own expertise—not just the knowledge you have gained from books and courses, but knowledge you've gained from direct experience as well. Don't overlook this valuable source; identify those things you do well, both on and off the job. Ask yourself what your audience wants and needs and then take an inventory of your own unique knowledge and skills.

For example, everybody wants to discover ways of cutting back on unnecessary expenses. A professor of applied arts and technology might have learned how to cut out patterns that will avoid unnecessary waste. Or a mathematics professor might collaborate with a woodworks professor to write a proposal with the purpose of discovering the most waste-free systems for cutting out patterns. If there are no donors who support woodworks, the same type of proposal might be applied to textiles or other materials.

FIGURE 12–4   A model proposal letter.

[Use appropriate letterhead.]

Statement of purpose: Provide an overview of the project including some general activities. (One brief paragraph)

Balance of letter: *Situation and Problem.* (One paragraph)

Capabilities. What your organization has done and its ability to carry out the project if support received. (One paragraph)

Program Methods and Operation. What you will do, how you will do it, who will be involved— community agencies, other organizations, donors? (Two paragraphs)

Impact. How will youth, schools, or the community benefit? (One paragraph)

Evaluation, Reporting, and Visibility. How will success be measured, how will the donor be informed, and what visibility will the donor receive? (One paragraph)

Budget. The amount being requested. Include when you need the pledge, when you need the contribution, and your IRS number. (Short answer)

Summary. A brief recap of the significance of this program for people, the community, and the donor. Add telephone number if not on the letterhead. (One paragraph)

Signatory: Someone needing *no* introduction (e.g., president of organization).

Length: Keep the entire letter to about two pages.

Best Use: Companies, businesses, plants, foundations, local family charities, community trusts, individuals.

GUIDELINE 2: ADD A UNIQUE ANGLE

Individuals who evaluate grant proposals are impressed by unique features. This is understandable in light of the dozens of proposals that are usually reviewed at a single sitting. Undoubtedly, many of the proposals are very similar, so evaluators are compelled to look for uniqueness among them.

An example illustrates the importance of uniqueness to grant proposals. Facing a national shortage of science, math, and foreign language teachers, the federal government issued a block grant to each state so that each could entice universities to develop summer institutes to prepare qualified teachers in these critical disciplines. More exactly, the purpose of this program was to take teachers who were teaching out of their field (for example, biology teachers who were teaching physics or chemistry, or physical education teachers who were teaching mathematics) and better prepare them to teach in the needed fields. Summer teacher training institutes would be used to lead these teachers toward full certification in the target disciplines. Each state would be granted only one summer teacher training institute in each subject.

In all states, the winning proposals had unique features. For example, in one state the winning physics grant had a feature that received more attention from the proposal evaluators than any other of its features. This unique feature was a course that brought a "master" teacher (i.e., a teacher recognized by colleagues and administrators for expert teaching ability) from a high school classroom onto the university campus to teach a special course. Using the most popular *high school* physics textbook in the state, chapter-by-chapter, this master high school teacher worked all of the problems for her fellow teachers.

The critical questions are: How did the authors of this proposal hit upon the idea for such a course; and, of all unlikely approaches, why did they propose to use a high school teacher to teach this course when any member of the university physics faculty could have easily worked these problems? The proposal writers anticipated that the grant proposal evaluation team would be excited over this feature because master teachers were the focus of many education reform reports of the day. The writers knew that the team of evaluators would be educators who worked in the state department of education. These people would be familiar with the school reform reports.

A second unique feature in this proposal was a weekly seminar which brought in special guest speakers. The guests included a retired physics professor who continued to research the private lives of physicists, an astronomer who specialized in galaxies, and a robotics professor who brought his self-assembled robot to the seminar for demonstration.

This special course taught by a master high school teacher, and this seminar which tapped unique expertise in the community (expertise which, incidentally, was cost-free to the funding agency) undoubtedly caught the eyes of the evaluators. During the first year this grant money was available, 11 institutions in this state submitted proposals to a team of eight independent evaluators. This particular proposal was selected as the best of the 11 proposals by all eight evaluators.

GUIDELINE 3:
MAKE A CONVINCING COMMITMENT

Many grants are made on a matching basis. Some RFPs require the recipient to make a dollar-for-dollar matched contribution. Many RFPs that do not specify this requirement outright nevertheless will restrict recipients to those whose proposals show a heavy contribution.

Granting agencies usually have several good reasons for requiring proposal writers to make a commitment of their own resources. Two reasons always prevail. Despite many misconceptions, funding agencies do not have unlimited resources. By getting the recipients to commit their own resources, the funding agency can fund more grants, thus attaining more of its goals. A second reason that agencies require a heavy commitment by the recipient is to assure the funding agency that the resources will be managed judiciously. Even the most wealthy sponsors of grants don't want their money squandered, and a heavy commitment by the recipient guarantees good stewardship and good management.

Many grant proposal writers and their employers cannot afford to make a cash contribution to the project, so they offer an "in-kind" contribution. For example, the company or institution may offer the use of buildings, rooms, equipment, and personnel. Proposal writers may even offer their time as a contribution. The author of the winning proposal in our example offered to codirect the summer institutes at no cost to the funding agency. Furthermore, he offered to drive throughout the state *after each summer institute ended* to visit each participant and see what parts of the institute each teacher was applying in class. By contributing his own time, this proposal writer was able to persuade his institution to supply a car and gasoline. While visiting each participant, the writer conducted a follow-up evaluation of the summer institute, asking what the teacher had found most useful and what else might have been done to benefit the participants.

The evaluators were obviously impressed with this heavy, personal commitment by the proposal writer and with the almost 50 percent in-kind contribution from the grant writer's institution. This proposal outperformed the other 10 competing proposals not once but several consecutive summers. See Appendix M.

GUIDELINE 4: BE FLEXIBLE

Abraham Lincoln said that when planning for a debate, he spent about one-third of his preparation time thinking about what he was going to say and about two-thirds of his time thinking about what his opponent was going to say. This principle will apply well to grant proposal writing. The writer must spend some time thinking about what the prospective funder wants and how to deliver in full—not what the *writer* wants to happen but—what the prospective funder wants to happen.

Many proposals fail because the authors refuse to shape their proposals to meet the expectations of the prospective grantor. Sold on the greatness of their ideas, these proposal writers think they can stand firm and make demands on the funding agency. This seldom works, and rightfully so. If these unsuccessful proposal writers were paying for services, they, too, would insist on getting what they wanted for their money. The following example illustrates this point.

An education professor at a midwestern university wanted to create a competency-based teacher education program. The state had no available money to create innovative teacher education programs; however, the state did have money designated for use by its K–12 schools to develop innovative programs. Hearing this, the professor wrote a program that had two goals: to create a competency-based teacher education program (a higher education goal for which there were no available funds) *and* to solve a teacher burnout problem which was a timely topic and much in the news (a K–12 level goal which qualified for proposal funding).

By being flexible, this professor succeeded with this grant and received $385,000 to fund his innovative program, which eventually was recognized with an award from the national Association of Teacher Educators.

GUIDELINE 5: USE EVERY OPPORTUNITY TO GATHER INFORMATION ABOUT AVAILABLE MONEY

The imbalance in supply and demand assures a wealth of proposals for most announced grant opportunities. Usually, among these many proposals are several excellently written proposals. So, what determines which proposals are funded? Many grants owe their funding to a tip from someone on the inside of the funding agency. The tip may or may not be intentional. For example, the author of the grant for the innovative competency-based teacher education program owes its success to a casual comment overheard in a coffee room. Someone mentioned that the state department of education had funds to support innovative public school programs. The conveyor of this information vaguely remembered that the RFP for these funds said something about teacher burnout. Overhearing this comment, the proposal writer drove to the capitol city and met with officials who were in charge of the funding. By talking to them, he was able to get a true sense of what they wanted for their money. Upon his return home, the proposal for Project ESCAPE (Elementary and Secondary Competency Approach to Teacher Education_ retained its title but was altered to focus on teacher burnout.

Another grant that owes its funding to the flexibility of its authors was a technology grant written to the American Telephone & Telegraph Company (AT&T). The writer wanted to acquire a computer network program that would link the education programs in three buildings. An attempt was made to include some benefits for each department in the college and for other colleges at the university. By talking to some of the representatives, the writer learned that the company was highly interested in some of the topics and *dis*interested in others.

The grant proposal writer was keenly interested in two goals; implementing a model distance learning program and providing computers in the offices of all instructors in the college. But the AT&T representatives showed no enthusiasm for these subjects. So, rather than trying their patience by trying to sell them on ideas which held little or no interest for them, the writer refocused his attention on the potential funders to learn what they wanted, quickly tossing out a half dozen other timely ideas.

One of the topics that the writer mentioned was a state-of-the-art computer network system for the college's nursery through twelfth grade laboratory school. Since the company officials seemed intrigued with the institution's large laboratory school, the grant proposal was immediately modified to focus heavily on the lab school. The writer's initiative and willingness to explore several possible areas of interest were rewarded; the grant was funded for the largest amount of any AT&T grant proposal funded during the year.

GUIDELINE 6: MAKE YOUR REQUEST ECONOMICALLY RESPONSIBLE

One of the greatest temptations that face grant proposal writers is the desire to get too much individual gain from the grant. Such attempts seldom succeed. When grant writers get greedy, their greed becomes immediately obvious to most proposal evaluators. Experienced proposal evaluators have a refined ability to sense greed quickly. One of the most common mistakes—perhaps *the* most common mistake—contemporary writers make is throwing in a computer or two, thinking that at the end of the project there will be something permanent to show for all this work.

Because so many writers include a surperfulous computer or two, you would be wise to avoid this temptation. Even if the grant activities require a computer and you do not have one available for this purpose, a wise alternative is to rent or lease a computer and build the rental cost into the proposal's budget. This alternative provides you with the use of the computer and it tells the funder that you are not trying to give yourself a gift at their expense. Although you may think yourself beyond reproach, remember that nobody, regardless how innocent their intentions may be, can afford to have others question their integrity, especially prospective funders.

GUIDELINE 7:
MAKE THE PROPOSAL EASY TO READ

Good proposal writing, like any other good writing for publication, is simple and clear. Use the same advice given in Chapter 4 on writing for journals—avoid jargon, complex paragraphs, and complex sentences. Avoid unfamiliar words. Some experts say that successful proposals must use the "in vogue" words of the day, and sprinkling a few of these words at appropriate places in the proposal might help. Still, it is better to place the goal of clarity above any felt need to juggle the right jargon.

Before submitting your proposal, give it a viewing from a distance. Look at the overall structure and ask yourself how you can alter your proposal to make it clearer and easier to read. Following are three ways to clarify that always work.

First, having written the proposal, now **write an abstract.** Some proposals specifically require an abstract. If your request for proposals requires an abstract, note the length and make your abstract comply. Even if the RFP does not ask for an abstract, make one anyway. If the evaluators don't want it, they can ignore it. But the chances that they will read the abstract are good. Often evaluators are so busy that they just quickly skim over the proposals. A good abstract can focus the evaluators' attention on the major strengths of the proposal. Figure 12–5 shows the abstract that was submitted with the physics proposal.

Second, make a **table of contents.** A succinct table of contents tells the reviewers at a glance what this proposal is all about and helps the evaluators quickly survey the entire proposal or locate any specific part.

Third, write some **objectives.** These objectives should be clear. A simple, short, numbered list works best, leaving a sense that these authors are serious; they know exactly what they wish to achieve; and they know how to conduct the activities specified in this proposal to achieve these goals. Remember that you are asking to be trusted to manage and protect this money as if it belonged to you. It's no wonder that potential funders demand clarity. It's no wonder that they choose to fund those proposals

---

FIGURE 12–5   Sample proposal abstract.

Responding to the critical shortage of high school physics teachers, the University of _____ proposes a 10-week summer institute which will better prepare secondary teachers who are now teaching physics or who anticipate teaching physics this fall but who lack certification in the area of physics. Each participant will be given a total of 266 contact hours of physics courses, laboratory experiences, tutorials, and seminars, providing students the opportunity to earn 12 semester credit hours.

During the fall semester, each participant will be visited at his or her own school and provided opportunity to ask further questions and share successes and criticisms of the materials developed in the institute.

---

that have clear objectives and logical procedures for attaining these objectives.

GUIDELINE 8:
FOLLOW THE RFP GUIDELINES PRECISELY

The RFP is the best single source of information available to most writers; yet, few use it to its full advantage. If you are fortunate enough to have an RFP, follow it to the letter. The RFP is usually written by a team. Often, some or all of the RFP developers are also assigned the task of evaluating the proposals. Each makes sure that the RFP contains some of his or her personal needs or interests. So, by carefully responding to *each part* of the RFP, proposal writers help to ensure support from all of the evaluators. Unlike the sample physics proposal, which received a 11 to 0 vote, most grant decisions are based on a very narrow margin. Points are carefully counted and added for each part of each proposal. Often the winner is identified by only a few votes, sometimes by only a fraction of one percent.

Proposal evaluators are usually provided a rating form. By examining a sample rating form you can begin to see the proposals from the evaluators' perspective. Appendix N shows the actual rating form used to evaluate the physical proposals. Do not be reluctant to ask the funding source for an evaluation form.

GUIDELINE 9:
DEVELOP A PROJECT EVALUATION PROCESS

Most RFPs require a project evaluation process as part of every proposal. To provide impartiality, most RFPs require that such evaluations be conducted by outside evaluators who have expertise in conducting evaluations and who are positioned to conduct the evaluation impartially and objectively. The purpose of this requirement is to assure representatives of the funding agency that they are getting complete value from their investment.

When correctly designed, the project evaluation can serve the proposal writer, too. For this reason, you should always include an evaluation component in your proposals, even when it is not required. By doing so, you give the funding agency an assurance that most of the competing proposals won't offer. This, alone, gives your proposal some advantage. Perhaps even more important, the evaluation can help your proposal remain competitive when you apply for repeats if you address the weaknesses identified by the evaluation. The follow-up visits with the built-in evaluations undoubtedly played a significant role in the physics proposals which beat all of the competition for several consecutive years. The more closely you follow the RFP, the more support you garner.

Project evaluations should appraise both the process by which the study was conducted and the product or outcome. For example, the hypothetical proposal (mentioned earlier) to improve instruction skills of part-time faculty members would be evaluated by focusing on the steps used and by assessing how smoothly and exactly each step was implemented. The product evaluation might measure the performance of students in a control group of part-time teachers' classes and the performance of a similar group of part-timers who participated in the program.

GUIDELINE 10:
TEST THE BUDGET AGAINST THE NARRATIVE

When you have finished writing your proposal and have developed a budget, test this budget against the narrative part of the proposal. A sensible budget must include costs associated with personnel, equipment, and travel.

When complete, the budget should mirror the narrative. This means that the major objectives and the major parts of the project should incur the largest expenses. This happens best when you write your budget last. An imbalance between your proposal narrative and budget can be corrected by adjusting the budget so that it will reflect the narrative. (See Section VI of the physics teachers institute proposal contained in Appendix M.)

The two largest items in the budget for the physics teacher institute were support for the participants and the coursework that the participants take. Together, these two items account for a significant percent of the total budget for this proposal. This parallels the importance of these two elements. Suppose that the combined budget for these two items had totaled only 20 percent or 30 percent of the total budget. The proper way to correct this imbalance is not to change the text, nor is it to compromise and tone down the importance of these items. Rather, the correct way to adjust for this discrepancy is to change the budget, increasing the amounts allocated to these two major goals until their allotments accurately reflect the relative importance of these two goals to the importance of the total projects.

RECAPPING THE MAJOR POINTS

In summary, grant writing offers a way to obtain resources and opportunities for your organization or institution—resources and opportunities that otherwise would not be available, especially during an economic recession. But the competition is getting stronger all the time, and this means that you must develop and refine your grant proposal writing skills so that you can produce the best proposal submitted. The following elements are essential:

- **Excellent timing:** Combine two or more highly popular ideas. If needed, consult the research.
- **Unique Angle:** Give your proposal a quality of its own, but be practical.
- **Heavy Commitment:** Get your organization to make a strong in-kind contribution. Match this with a personal commitment of your own time and expertise.
- **Flexibility:** As a proposal writer, your job is to please the funder. If you are very lucky you can please yourself, too; however, the importance of your own desires must be a distant second to those of the funder. Use inside information when you can get it, but never give up hope just because you don't have an inside source.
- **Responsibility:** Don't ask for too much, and never use the grant to get individual gifts for yourself or your own office.
- **Clarity:** Write simply. Include an abstract, a list of clear objectives, and a table of contents.
- **Attention to the Guidelines:** If an RFP is available, follow it precisely and completely.
- **Evaluation:** Always develop a method to evaluate your proposal. Include both processes and product appraisals and have them conducted by external evaluators.

Perhaps the best guideline you can follow when writing a grant proposal is to think of yourself as the potential funder. Knowing that you would want to get the most possible for your money, design every part of the proposal, especially the budget, accordingly.

13

Professional Writing

As was evidenced through the personal responses given to the question "Why write?" in Chapter 1, many professionals—especially professors and college administrators—find that writing fulfills a professional need. These writers seek to maintain a balance among their professional activities. They teach, serve on committees, consult, advise students, conduct research, give papers and speeches, and write—mostly for journals in their discipline. Their research and writing often enriches their other roles because they research and write about topics they teach. Most writers are pleased that their writing can improve their thinking and their teaching.

But other writers want more; these writers are unable to control their lust for writing. To them, writing is even more than a way to improve their teaching, much more. Rita Dunn once said that for her "writing is like breathing." These zealous authors break the common boundaries. Some write textbooks for which they receive additional satisfaction *and* royalties. The royalties further whet their appetites. Some become successful enough to significantly increase their annual incomes. A few eventually become trade book writers and writers for newspapers and trade magazines. These broader markets often enable these writers to reach other goals. For example, some academicians write to alter the behavior of their legislators; others write to affect immensely large audiences such as parents. Some write to inform, some to entertain, and some to inform while entertaining.

My experience with giving workshops has shown that in any group of 20 or more writers, at least one or two aspire to enter this group. They no longer can settle for the status of professionals who write; they will settle for nothing less than being professional writers. Because of his writing success, a psychologist friend in San Diego has taken early retirement. An avid golfer, he writes every morning and, weather permitting (and in San Diego it usually does), he plays golf every afternoon.

When a search of the literature failed to locate information to help writing professionals become professional writers, I called on some successful writers to tell how they became successful. First, let's hear from a lawyer/professor of police studies whose expertise is writing newspaper book reviews.

PROFILE

Richard E. Givan received his A.B. and M.A. degrees in English at Eastern Kentucky University and his J.D. degree at the University of Louisville. As a Professor of Police Studies in the College of Law Enforcement at Eastern Kentucky University, he began his professional writing with articles for professional journals, followed by writing chapters for professional books. For the past two years he has been writing reviews of mystery crime novels, and in the following short essay he describes his transition to writing reviews (and books?).

About 30 times over the past two years I have had the pleasurable experience of opening the Sunday paper, turning to the book pages, and seeing my name attached to one of the reviews. Imagine, my words circulated to a pool of readers far more numerous than any stuffy academic journal I've ever graced.

It gets better: the newspaper actually pays me! One final bonus—for each review actually written I get two or three free hardbound books, usually before they are even published.

A recommendation by a mutual friend to Art Jester, the book editor of the *Lexington Herald-Leader,* started me in the reviewing business. Art said that my being a lawyer and teacher of criminal law on the university level and an amateur pop fiction writer were adequate credentials to review a crime novel.

I muddled through that first review, and Art must have been satisfied, because I've stayed busy ever since. Here's how I stay in my editor's grace.

Writing Skills

Lots of academicians are better at thinking and talking than writing. With an A.B. in English and an M.S. in creative writing, I had a leg up.

If you feel you need a little help with your writing skills, you probably do. There's no substitute for practicing writing and having it criticized by a knowledgeable person. Take advantage of the writing classes offered at your institution.

The best writing is generally rewriting. I've never failed to improve a review by letting it rest a day or two, then reworking it. Reorganizing, compacting, clarifying—these all come easier with a fresh look.

Also, I'm blessed with a spouse

who, despite being a math teacher, has excellent writing instincts. I always run my reviews past her before shipping them off.

Know Your Genre

Since my first library card, I've haunted the thriller and crime fiction sections of nearby libraries. In my personal budget, book money comes behind food and medicine, but not far. In short, I've been unwittingly preparing for this job ever since my lips stopped moving when I read. Decide where your interests really lie and work to increase your depth of knowledge in that area.

Be Editor Friendly

Professors are notorious for procrastination. Don't. When the editor has a hole on a page that you've promised to fill, be sure to meet the deadline. If it should be utterly impossible to meet your deadline, inform your editor as early as possible.

Do tough reviews. It's hard (at least for me) to dismantle books written by local authors who will probably be upset at criticism. Some reviewers dodge such assignments. But, somebody's got to do them, and you will win your editor's gratitude for tackling these jobs.

Which leads to: be fair to the authors and honest to the audience. Remember that someone has labored long and hard over each book. Don't dismiss their work lightly. On the other hand, don't shill every book that comes along. I much prefer raving over a great novel to trashing a lousy one, but my ultimate obligation is to help potential readers spend their book money wisely.

So take a shot. Whatever field you teach, important books will come along aimed at the general market. Watch for them, then write or call the book editor of the paper for whom you are interested in writing. Pitch the book as a likely candidate for a review and yourself as the perfect person to write it. It could be the start of a beautiful relationship.

TRADE MAGAZINE ARTICLES AND BOOKS

Like Richard Givan, many academicians use the book review route to entering both academic and trade writing. Other academicians enter trade book publishing by first writing articles and short stories for general interest magazines. Hal Blythe and Charlie Sweet exemplify this approach. Permit me to introduce them as they were first introduced to me.

When I first moved to Richmond, Kentucky, the realtor ushered our family from house to house. By about 2:00 P.M., exhausted and famished, we were relieved when the realtor asked if we wanted to stop for lunch. Soon we found ourselves in the local McDonald's restaurant. Above the next table was a very large, professionally framed photo of two pleasant and friendly looking men. The realtor explained that the restaurant management had provided the picture and had dedicated that booth to these two local English professors who had earned the recognition by their frequent and regular use of the booth to write for publication. Now, having known these two authors for five years, I am even more impressed with their mastery of their own writing destiny. When people ask me how I find the time to write, I just wish that they could know Hal Blythe and Charlie Sweet.

PROFILE

Hal Blythe was born in Louisville, Kentucky. He received his B.A. from Kentucky Southern College, his M.A. from the University of Florida, and his Ph.D. from the University of Louisville. His doctoral dissertation was a critical study of the novels of Tobias Smollett. He has been at Eastern Kentucky University since 1972 and is currently a Foundation Professor with major teaching emphasis in literary theory and creative writing.

Charlie Sweet was born in Boston and grew up in central Connecticut. He took his B.A. from Washington and Lee and both his M.A. and Ph.D. from Florida State University. His dissertation dealt with Bernard Malamud. He is currently a Professor of English at Eastern Kentucky University, where he was recently made a Foundation Professor. His specialties include American literature—especially Edgar Allen Poe—and creative writing, but he has yet to teach a course on Malamud.

Since 1974, Blythe and Sweet have collaborated on over 500 pieces, both fiction and nonfiction. Their critical work has appeared in such journals as *Poe Studies, Studies in Short Fiction, Studies in Browning and His Circle,* and *The Hemingway Review.* The pedagogical articles have been published in journals ranging from *College English* to *Writer's Digest* and *The Writer.* Their fiction has appeared in *Ellery Queen's Mystery Magazine, Hardboiled, Woman's World* and a host of other publications running the gamut from family magazines to men's adventure magazines. For three years they ghosted the monthly Mike Shayne novella in *Mike Shayne Mystery Magazine.* Their *Private Eyes: A Writer's Guide to Private Investigators* was published in 1993 by Writer's Digest Books. Currently they are working on a domestic thriller novel. Here is what Blythe and Sweet say about trade writing.

Writing is one of the few full-time professions you can practice part-time—if you have a full-time professional attitude. Professionalism consists of a disciplined approach, a structured methodology, and a well developed sense of marketing. And talent.

So you want to be a writer? Here are some suggestions about everything but talent. That we can't help you with.

Becoming Disciplined

Find a specific time each day to write. The time can vary, but it's best to do it at the same time every day. Anthony Trollope wrote before work each day. We write from noon to 2:00. Two hours a day, five days a week, 50 weeks a year, most holidays.

Choose a specific place to write. Each of us has a study used only for writing at home. We also have an office, but truthfully we collaborate each day at our booth at the local McDonald's. Harlan Ellison can write in a department store window. John Cheever wrote in the nude in his basement. Neither where nor wear really matters—just writing does.

Set a word-count goal in the beginning. Many people call themselves writers even if they sit and stare at the word processor for two hours per day. A writer is one who writes, who produces a readable product. John Grisham tried to write five pages per day despite being a full-time attorney. We shoot for about 1,000 words—every day.

Establish a methodology. We write together on white lined paper, Charlie types up/revises the product on a word processor at the end of the day, and Hal acts as the collaboration's secretary. Every weekday's session begins with Hal reading out loud the writing from the previous day. This primes the pump while letting us know where we were. Hemingway always tried to stop just before an exciting part. The precise format you adopt is less important than the fact you adopt one.

Writing for the Trades

Read. Why would you try to write something that is not in an area of expertise/something that interests you? Even a computer needs input to produce output. On our way to and from McDonald's, we often discuss something relevant to the thing we are writing. This may be a newspaper story, a magazine piece, a critical article, a bestseller, the latest Parker novel.

Read in the area in which you intend to write. Don't try to write for *Playboy* unless you read *Playboy*. There are two schools of thought on writing something you wish to get published. School One says write what you want and then try to publish it; this works best for serious/literary writing. School Two says learn what your marketplace wants and write it. This methodology works best for popular markets. If you want to write *Playboy* fiction, familiarize yourself with the whole magazine. Even the ads tell you something about your potential audience. Know your readers.

Study your market. Don't read one Ellery Queen story, scream "Eureka!" and write. We read 12 consecutive issues. Then we charted the frequency of characters, plots, techniques, etc. We also researched secondary sources such as what then-editor Fred Dannay had to say about

EQMM fiction. After twenty-six rejections our twenty-seventh story to EQMM sold.

Learning How to Market

Send it off. Nothing ever got published sitting in your bottom desk drawer.

Look like a pro. Use proper manuscript conventions. Have professional letterhead stationery made. Include a self-addressed stamped envelope with every submission.

Use a cover letter. All of ours have three parts—a hook, a description of what we are submitting (including why the editor should accept it), and a quick close. All three parts have a common goal—establishing a rapport with the editor. It's hard to reject someone you like (even if you've never met them).

Keep records. With one story out, you can keep track in your head. At any one time we may have 40 items in circulation. We have a master chart that shows what, where, when, and disposition (including when and what we got paid). We love the chart almost as much as our accountant.

Keep it circulating. The biggest defense against "rejection-slip-itis" is to send the piece out again as fast as it came back. Study those rejection slips for clues to your rejection.

Don't Collaborate

We can do it. We know a few others who do. We know lots more who have failed at it. We've been teaching creative writing for a combined 50 years. In all those years, no pair of our students has successfully co-authored anything. One head is better than two.

The Ultimate Tip

Thoreau claimed it was to simplify, simplify, simplify. Henry James advised a young writer to dramatize, dramatize, dramatize.

We say, "Write! Write! Write!"

Writing Book Reviews: A Way to Break Into Trade Writing

Writing book reviews gives beginning writers an opportunity to closely analyze writing qualities. A further advantage in becoming involved with book reviews is that they help address the "I'm nobody" feeling that beginning writers often harbor. *Writing book reviews is an excellent entrée into writing articles and books.*

Most journal editors receive several times as many article manuscripts as they can use. Yet. those same editors often receive many more books from authors than they can find reviewers to review. By writing book reviews, you can polish your writing skills, keep abreast of the developments in your field, fill in blank spaces on your resume, get your name in front of your colleagues in the profession, and introduce yourself to the editors.

THE AGENT

Ninety percent of Blythe's and Sweet's success is due to a combination of their talent, organization, self-discipline, and hard work. Luck was also a factor in that their magazine editor became a book editor. If we could arrange for this to happen, we might not need an agent. Whether you should seek an agent or go directly to a publisher depends on you and your book. If your book is a professional guide or a textbook, you probably won't need an agent. In fact, because of the limited potential for many professional books and textbooks, few agents are willing to take on this type of property. If, however, your book is aimed at a very large market, you should familiarize yourself with the roles that a professional agent plays and the disadvantages and advantages of having your own agent.

Consider why many authors prefer not to use agents. There's a fee to be paid, usually 10 percent to 15 percent of the royalties, although this percentage may vary. Then there's the task of finding an agent who is willing to take on new clients. This is a strong deterrent for beginning authors because most agents require that their new clients have already successfully published similar works or that they have earned a set minimum amount from their royalties during the past year. Then there is always the possibility of getting tied to an agent who assigns your projects low priority. Paradoxically, although agents take a percentage, if they are good they may negotiate additional benefits for you that far outweigh their fee.

A good prospectus can help persuade an agent to accept an inexperienced writer. Most agents are honest business people who intend to earn their pay through providing quality service to the writer. Should you decide that your agent's goals and expertise do not match your own, he or she will probably recognize this and be willing to negotiate a release of obligation. Most authors agree that the agent who has spent time reading your product, writing letters, and making phone inquiries would be due some compensation. This could be settled as a reduced percentage fee for the first edition sales, or the author could offer a straight payment for the agent's time.

I asked Sally Wendkos Olds to share with us her writing experience along with her experience getting an agent.

PROFILE

Sally Wendkos Olds has written extensively about intimate relationships and about developmental issues throughout the life cycle and has won national awards for both her book and magaziane writing. She is the author or coauthor of nine books and more than 200 major national magazine articles. Her first book, *The Complete Book of Breastfeeding*, originally published in 1972 and revised in 1987, has become a classic, having sold well over 1 million copies. Her three college textbooks, *A Child's World*, *Human Development*, and *Psychology* (coauthored with Diane E. Papalia, Ph.D.), have been read by more than 2 million college students. Among her other books are *The Eternal Garden: Seasons of Our Sexuality* and *The Working Parents' Survival Guide*. A Phi Betta Kappa graduate of the University of Pennsylvania, she is a former president of the American Society of Journalists and Authors (ASJA) and is a coeditor of *The ASJA Handbook: A Writers' Guide to Ethical and Economic Issues*.

Do you need an agent? If so, how do you find one? This is often a catch-22 situation. An established agent will not want to represent you until you have been published—but it may be hard to have a book published without an agent. You don't need an agent, though, if you're writing only short pieces. This is how I got my start as a professional writer. I began by writing articles for magazines and newspapers, and over the next five years a number of them were published. Then I saw a need for a book on a topic I had written an article about, and I wanted to write that book. At that point I felt that I needed an agent.

If you're writing trade books (those written for general readers, rather than students or academics), having an agent is important. What does the agent do? She or he may give you guidance in writing a book proposal and will then submit the proposal to selected publishing houses. Many publishers these days will not even look at a book proposal unless it comes in from a reputable agent. Then, if a publisher wants to bring out your book, you need someone knowledgeable about publishing to read and modify your contract, to get you higher advances and better royalty terms than you might get on your own, and in general to protect your interests. Your agent may also work with you and your publisher in choosing your book's title and cover, and getting publicity for your work, and should mediate any author-publisher problems. Once you begin to collect royalties, your agent will monitor royalty statements, collect funds due you, and quickly send them your way.

I found my first agent by going through the directory of the American Society of Journalists and Authors, noting the names of members' agents. (I had joined the Society as soon as I had enough published work to make me eligible and have found it of immeasurable help over the past 25 years). I spoke to a few fellow members, and I followed up on one recommendation. This word-of-mouth route is probably the most common way of finding an agent.

Whether or not you have been

published, you can ask any writers you know who their agents are. If you don't know any writers, don't give up. Go to the reference room of your local library, find the book, *Literary Market Place* (LMP), and look up the names of literary agents. Or write to the Association of Authors' Representatives, 10 Astor Place, 3rd Floor, New York, NY 10003. Enclose a self-addressed stamped #10 envelope and request the association's pamphlet, "The Literary Agent." It explains the agent's role and lists current AAR membership.

The usual way to contact an agent is the route I took. First, I dropped a short note to the agent I wanted to represent me. I told him what I had published so far, said that I had an idea for a book, and asked whether we could meet. If you have not yet published any work, you would want to trot out your strongest credentials, making the case for you as the best author of the particular book you have in mind. In my case, both the agent and I were in New York, so a personal meeting was feasible; for people in different cities, a phone conference might be your initial get-together—or it might be worthwhile for you to plan a trip to meet in person. If your credentials are strong or you have an original idea for a wonderful book, you may want to interview two or three agents to see which one you can best work with.

Some agents require nothing more than a handshake to represent you and require a contract only after a book has been sold to a publisher. Others ask you to sign a contract as soon as the two of you agree to work together. Most agents today charge 15 percent of all monies you earn on works for which they represent you, and a good agent will more than earn this commission. The only thing no agent will do is write your book for you. Facing the blank page—or computer screen—is still the challenge reserved for the author!

I was teaching at the University of Alabama at the time. Having children in elementary and middle schools, my weekends were usually pulled in several directions: football, writing, and family responsibilities. Because this weekend was a road game, my sense of family responsibility won and I accompanied my family to the mall for some serious shopping—with the understanding that I could migrate to the Sears store to watch the Bama-Tennessee game.

Since our serious shopping was occurring in the opposite end of the mall, I ducked into the drugstore to listen to their radio, afraid I might miss the kickoff. Instead, I heard a familiar voice. The present of our country was addressing a new report titled, "A Nation At Risk." The message was clear. Our schools were awful, and all that was needed to correct them was to spend the resources in different ways, increase the length of the school day and year, and hold the teachers accountable.

Having served as a PTA president and having just marched the streets of Tuscaloosa to encourage support for an increase in school taxes and knowing that many schools throughout the country did not even have enough money for textbooks for all of their children, I was infuriated that the president would say that educators just needed to shift their money from one pocket to another. Knowing that the heavy workload of teachers is a mirror image of their poor pay, I was outraged at the idea of lengthening the school day.

I put my feelings in words. Since I wanted to reach a broader readership than my friends and also I wanted to be heard by non-educators, I sent my manuscript to the magazine *USA Today*. I was pleased but a little confused with the editor's response. "This is what we want, but it is too academic". My first thought was, "Sure, it's academic. I'm an academician and I work hard to be academic". When I collected my wits, I asked my wife who is not an educator, what this editor meant by "too academic." She pointed out the jargon, the long sentences and paragraphs, and the heavy documentation. I removed the jargon and references and shortened the paragraphs and sentences. The editor responded to my revision by saying, "yes, this is what we want."

Our next profiled authors, Suzanne and Sidney Simon, speak directly to the task of writing differently when addressing a trade audience.

PROFILE

Suzanne Simon is a teacher, counselor, workshop facilitator, and writer. She has conducted workshops throughout this country and in Germany, Greece, Canada, and Norway.

Suzanne worked as a public school educator for 10 years and then as the Assistant Program Coordinator in the Violence Against Women Program at the Everywoman's Center at the University of Massachusetts. She is a consultant in the area of child sexual abuse and has facilitated dozens of support groups for incest survivors.

Currently, Suzanne writes a monthly column called "Family Secrets," for *Change Magazine*. Her ongoing goal is to continue her own healing and encourage and empower others to continue on *their* healing journeys, too.

Sidney Simon, a Professor Emeritus at the University of Massachusetts, is an internationally known pioneer in psychological education. He conducts workshops all over the United States, Canada, Mexico, and Europe. He is one of the authors of the four classic books *Values and Teaching; Values Clarification: A Handbook of Practical Strategies; Clarifying Values through Subject Matter;* and *Meeting Yourself Halfway*. Combined, these books have sold close to 2 million copies.

Sid Simon is working to link his many professional and personal experiences into new theories for helping people live fuller, less fragmented lives. Part of this effort emerged in his books *Negative Criticism* and *Helping Your Child Find Values to Live By*. His more recent book, *Getting Unstuck*, landed him on the Oprah Winfrey Show!

The Simons coauthored their latest book, *Forgiveness: How to Make Peace with Your Past and Get on with Your Life*, which was published by Warner Books and adapted for television by Nebraska PBS (Public Broadcasting System).

So, you want to know something about how to make the leap from writing for the academic world and landing in the Trade Market. We have to make a quick disclaimer here. We never really wrote much for the academic market. We never wanted to.

I, Sid, was a teacher for 40 years, and somehow, perhaps through sheer cleverness, during all those years, I brilliantly avoided being an administrator *and* being an academic writer. No small achievement. I remember one colleague in particular who took great relish in trying to pillory me on the horns of his contention. He would say, "I see you have another article in one of those pop-u-lar magazines." Of course I did. It was what I valued.

I, Suzanne, never got caught up in the publish or perish juggernaut. I taught elementary school before getting training in counseling. I have somehow been spared the agonies of writing what I didn't want to write, or saying what I *had* to say. I cherish the freedom that has brought, both a freedom of thought and of expression.

Now, that you've gotten past the disclaimer, writing together and sharing our collective wisdom with you, we'll give you three crisp, insightful, and highly useful *pitfalls to avoid* and *three stars to reach for* if you'd like to taste the delights of writing for a popular audience.

Pitfall #1. You must struggle to avoid being all-inclusive. And we assure you it will be a struggle. You will have to fight the temptation to "say it all." You will be hounded by the demon that says you "must cover your bases." And haunted by the ghosts urging you to "leave no stone unturned." If you give in to demons, you give into dullness. If you want to be read by more than 20 other scholars (which I see as the destiny of academic writers), you just might have to be briefer. You may have to leave some things "out of the book." Eventually, the baby has to be born. Yes, you want it to have all of its limbs, but it doesn't have to have a mustache yet, to be desirable.

Pitfall #2. In order to write for the popular press, you have to build an ego strength that takes you outside of and well beyond the criticisms of your colleagues. Oh, no, another struggle? Yes, and an essential one.

Academicians don't like seeing other academicians "make it." Some of it is envy, and some of it is doubting their own capacities to do it, and some of it is the training almost all academicians get. Yes, the slavery years of their dissertations and the assistant professor groveling years have made some of them wounded birds.

Your joy in finding your own voice *and* an audience is, to put it gently, somewhat threatening to them. Their training has taught them to compulsively look for "flaws," and they will find them. (They find them in academic articles, too, of course.) Your new solid ego strength has to lift you above your colleagues' often petty criticisms.

You will have made some choices in what you want to say, and some choices in what you don't say. But they need to be your choices, not theirs. Yours.

Pitfall #3. This one we all will wrestle with until the last comma, question mark, and period. We call it, The Holier Than Thou pitfall.

You see, once we set out to tell people what they should do (like right now), we can lose our humility. We think we have the answers for everyone, for all situations, and for all time. People get turned off in the presence of people who think they have all the answers. Yet, here we are trying to tell you what to do. Do you see why it's a pitfall?

Now, the three Stars. These are easy.

Star #1, Keep it simple. Keep it honest. Keep in coming from the heart, and build into your article the utmost of practicality. Fill your articles and books with practical strategies. That focus on strategies is crucial to writing for a lay audience. They want to know "How to Do It." (Don't you? Isn't that why you've read this book?)

Sid's biggest success was a book that was nothing but strategies. Perhaps you know the book. More than likely you've used something from it—750,000 buyers have. The book was called *Values Clarification: A Handbook of Practical Strategies.* It was written with Howard Kirschenbaum and LeLand Howe.

Star #2. Use anecdotes, case studies, and examples out of your own life's search and story. Make what you write real. It's that simple. Speak your voice, tell it from your pain and from your joy, and always from your heart. Even if it gets soupy, occasionally sentimental, or simplistic. Clearly, Shakespeare and Dickens knew this, and today's best writers such as Maya Angelou know it too. Study these writers to see what you can learn about developing your own voice.

Star #3. Keep living your life fully so you have lots to write about. Maybe that's one of the saddest things about academic life. We begin to slice a specialty thinner and thinner and too our lives often get narrower and narrower.

Reach for the stars. What did Joseph Campbell say? "Follow your bliss." It worked for *that* academician. Follow yours. We're trying to do that.

If you're going to follow your bliss, it demands that you have some working acquaintance with bliss. In some of our workshops we ask people to make a list of three times when they have known bliss, bliss that has lasted longer than five days in a row. We ask them to put down the years when each of those vibrant memories happened and what was it that made them bliss-filled. Would you be surprised at the number of people who don't have three to list?

But, oh what bliss you will know when you get letters from real people saying that what you wrote touched them so deeply. Here are two sentences from two of these letters.

I've never written a letter like this but, I just want to thank you for your wonderful book, Forgiveness. I've just finished reading it and it has already helped me, or at least put some thoughts in my head with regards to what I have been going through for the past few years.

Writing a book like yours is a great thing, just to be able to to reach out and help someone like you do is a wonderous thing.

That's what lets you know you've avoided, for the most part, the three pitfalls we've talked about and that you've reached, really high for the stars. That's where bliss lives. It's there for the taking. You just have to value it enough.

RECAPPING THE MAJOR POINTS

Some academicians are unable to maintain a balance among their major responsibilities: teaching, service, and scholarly activities. To these individuals, writing becomes more than a tool; it becomes so much a part of them that they drive themselves to write far beyond that required or expected by their institutions. Many of these writers eventually give up their academic responsibilities, prior to or at the time they are scheduled to retire. This affords them the opportunity to increase their writing.

Most of these writers eventually enter the trade market, either through book reviewing or by writing for trade magazines and then trade books. Success in this market requires authors to read vociferously and to develop a thick skin.

Unlike academic writing, trade book writing requires an agent who may take about 15 percent of the project's royalties but who may increase the book's earnings far beyond that 15 percent. Getting agents is difficult because most agents insist that their new clients already have considerable financial success in writing and publishing.

The following points may be useful if you want to become a professional writer:

- Writing for the trade market is much more difficult to break into than writing for the professional or textbook market.
- Success in trade book writing requires many of the same management skills needed in journal and textbook writing.
- Writing book reviews is an excellent entree into trade writing.
- Successful trade authors specialize in genres with which they have a lot of expertise.
- Most textbook publishers do not require that the authors have agents; most trade publishers do.
- Writing magazine and newspaper articles can be an excellent way to break into trade book writing.

FINAL NOTE

There is much reason for optimism about your writing. Throughout this book, I have said that you can set your own goals and reach them. As I reflect on my two decades of writing for publication, my first thought is that I wouldn't trade a minute that I have spent writing for other activities. Having always been an avid fan of football, basketball, mysteries, and wildlife shows, I can't remember ever giving up an important game or show in order to write. I'm sure there were times when I was pressed to meet deadlines and did not see some of these things, yet I did not miss them because my writing projects brought me even more pleasure. Having always enjoyed the theater, museums, and travel, I have managed to use my writing to support these activities. I cannot remember ever missing church or daily exercise in order to write. By good planning, there is plenty of time for all those things that we really enjoy—and still plenty of time to write.

My second thought is that I remember times when I couldn't decide on a proper writing project. What article or book should I write next? Sometimes, I struggled just to identify a publishable topic. But sooner or later some ideas for topics always came. By reflecting on these ideas, good topics always surfaced and I knew when they were the right ones for me. Now, topics come at me like meteor showers—and I don't mean every 18 years—but rather in clusters. Writing becomes more exciting every day.

If I have succeeded in communicating the value writing has for me, then you will use writing to reach your own personal and professional goals. Oscar Wilde was right, "We are all lying in the gutter, but some of us are looking up at the stars."

Appendices

Appendix A

Preferences of Journals in Various Disciplines

Writing for Successful Publication: Advice from Editors
By Kenneth T. Henson

Since 1979 I have been holding workshops on writing for publication to help professors prepare manuscripts for journal articles and books. Each year I offer about a dozen such workshops on college campuses across the country. In addition to drawing on my own long experience as an academic writer, I derive much of the information for these workshops from a simple one-page questionnaire that I use to ask journal editors the questions that I think would-be contributors to their journals would most like to ask. The information that appears in Table 1 comes from a mailing to 59 journal editors; 54 of them responded, for a 91.5% rate of return.

Workshop participants often ask, How do I know to which journals to direct my manuscripts? My answer is really quite simple. I tell them first to decide what goal they wish to achieve and then choose a journal that matches their goals. Some people write to share their knowledge with as many people as possible; they need to publish in journals with large circulations. Some wish to write for university professors and researchers. These writers should not be writing for journals that are read primarily by practitioners.

The audiences for the journals I surveyed range from as few as 250 to as many as 165,000. Two-thirds of the journals have fewer than 10,000 readers, and most of those have circulations of 5,000 and under. Two-thirds of the contributors to the journals are university personnel.

Reprinted with permission from *Phi Delta Kappan* (June 1993), pp. 799–802.

TABLE 1 Characteristics of a Selected Sample of Education Journals

Journal	Number of Readers	Contributors Who Are University Personnel (%)	Refereed	Research Articles (%)	Theme Issues per Year (%)	Acceptance Rate (%)	Days to Answer Queries (Avg.)	Days to Acknowledge Receipt of Ms. (Avg.)	Weeks Required for Decision (Avg.)	Months Required for Publication (Avg.)	Preferred Length (in Ms. Pages)	Min./Max./ Pages	Number of Additional Copies	Style				
Action in Teacher Education	4,000	75	3	20	100	30	14	14	16	6	15	8–20	2	APA	None	Yes	Yes	L
American Biology Teacher	12,000	20	3	70	0	60	5	5	8	5	16	1–16	2	—	Possibly	Yes	Yes	L
American Secondary Education	3,400	20	2	12	8	40	4	4	5	5	—	8–15	1	Campbell	None	Yes	Yes	E
Child Development	9,000	98	2	100	5	20	1	3	12	8	25	1–60	3	APA	None	Yes	Yes	E
Clearing House	3,500	50	2	25	0	40	14	1	14	3	10	1–18	1	Chicago	Possibly	Yes	Yes	E
College Student Journal	400	90	2	70	25	75	10	10	3	8	11	10–12	3	APA	None	Yes	Yes	L
Comparative Education Review	2,300	95	2	90	10	15	3	3	10	10	30	20–40	3	Chicago	Possibly	Yes	Yes	E
Computing Teacher	12,523	13	3	10	90	59	9	9	10	10	8	3–12	2	APA	None	Yes	Yes	E
Contemporary Education	1,500	75	1	10	25	5	7	7	2	6	10	8–12	2	APA	Possibly	Yes	Yes	E
Creative Child & Adult Quarterly	—	70	1	75	0	60	7	7	6	6	10	7–15	3	APA	None	Yes	No	L
Current Issues in Middle Education	300	90	3	75	50	90	1	2	4	4	6	4–10	3	APA	None	Yes	Yes	P
Eastern Education Journal	1,045	10	—	30	40	30	14	5	12	12	10	3–15	3	APA	Likely	No	Yes	E
Education	3,500	85	2	15	40	50	60	60	5	10	7	—	2	APA	None	Yes	Yes	E
Educational Forum	60,000	13	3	15	100	35	7	14	12	6	15	1–30	4	Chicago	Definitely	Yes	Yes	L
Educational Horizons	15,000	50	3	20	90	5	30	21	12	12	15	3–20	1	Chicago	Possibly	No	No	L
Educational Leadership	165,000	15	2	40	0	90	5	3	4	11	9	1–25	2	Chicago	Definitely	No	No	P
Educational Perspectives	1,000	75	2	10	—	90	15	7	5	9	11	15–20	2	Chicago	Definitely	Yes	No	L
Educational Psychology Review	350	100	3	0	33	—	1	1	12	9	35	25–50	2	APA	None	Yes	Yes	L
Educational Record	8,000	100	2	10	80	15	7	3	6	6	12–15	5–20	1	Chicago	Possibly	Yes	Yes	L
EKU Educational Review	2,200	20	3	50	50	50	10	10	8	4	15	8–15	2	APA	None	Yes	Yes	P
Elementary School Journal	5,200	70	3	95	40	8	2	2	8	19	30	—	3	APA	None	Yes	Yes	E
High School Journal	2,300	75	2	90	25	25	15	15	9	6	14	8–25	2	APA	None	Yes	Yes	P
Intervention in School and Clinic	5,000	30	3	10	20	21	2	2	9	9	15	8–30	2	APA	None	Yes	Yes	L

Journal																		
Journal of Experimental Education	1,000	—	3	—	0	35	7	3	17	4	25	—	2	APA	None	Yes	Yes	P
Journal of Instructional Psychology	400	90	2	70	0	65	10	20	6	8	12–16	—	2	APA	None	Yes	No	L
Journal of Physical Ed. & Dance	30,000	25	3	20	30	65	5	2	10	10	10	5–20	3	APA	Possibly	Yes	Yes	L
Journal of Reading	18,000	20	3	15	12	20	3	3	10	7	20	—	3	APA	Possibly	No	No	N
Journal of Reading Behavior	1,500	95	3	95	0	20	5	5	13	5	—	—	4	APA	None	Yes	Yes	E
Journal of Res. in Science Teaching	1,200	90	3	75	10	35	5	2	11	12	15	1–24	3	APA	None	—	—	E
Journal of Teacher Education	8,000	95	3	50	100	10	5	5	10	7	15	5–20	3	APA	None	Yes	Yes	L
Kentucky Reading Journal	700	5	3	20	0	80	15	15	10	10	10	8–15	4	APA	None	Yes	Yes	P
Middle School Journal	16,000	3	3	5	18	20	15	2	16	6	12	—	1	APA	None	Yes	Yes	L
NASSP Bulletin	40,000	1	0	—	40	30	14	3	5	18	11	—	1	Chicago	None	Yes	Yes	E
Peabody Journal of Education	2,000	85	2	40	100	0	10	10	30	3	250	—	2	APA	None	Yes	Yes	E
Perceptual & Motor Skills	2,000	—	1	80	—	29	1	1	6	1	—	—	3	APA	Possibly	Yes	Yes	L
Phi Delta Kappan	150,000	18	0	50	30	5	5	1	8	9	15	1–25	0	Chicago	Possibly	Yes	Yes	P
Planning & Changing	558	100	2	80	25	10	14	2	5	24	—	—	—	APA	None	Yes	No	L
Principal	27,000	6	3	6	35	33	10	42	6	12	8	5–10	1	Chicago	Possibly	Yes	Yes	L
Professional Educator	250	90	1	80	—	75	2	3	7	3	25	12–30	2	APA	None	Yes	Yes	L
Psychological Reports	1,900	—	—	80	—	29	1	1	6	1	—	—	3	APA	Possibly	Yes	Yes	L
Reading Improvement	1,100	10	1	60	—	50	10	5	5	9	—	4–40	2	APA	Likely	Yes	—	L
Reading Research Quarterly	10,000	90	3	100	100	10	3	8	9	5	35	25–100	6	APA	Likely	Yes	Yes	L
Reading Teacher	66,000	7	3	33	11	10	5	2	10	7	18	—	4	APA	Possibly	Yes	Yes	L
Review of Educational Research	17,000	90	1	100	0	16	2	5	12	6	60	1–100	5	APA	None	No	No	N
School Administrator	19,000	10	1	20	33	31	14	7	8	10	4	1–14	0	Assoc. Press	None	Yes	Yes	L
School Science and Mathematics	3,500	80	3	25	0	50	10	10	25	18	10	3–18	4	APA	None	Yes	Yes	L
Social Studies	3,000	60	2	15	30	45	—	4	18	8	16	10–25	1	Chicago	Possibly	Yes	Yes	E
Teacher Education and Practice	1,000	90	3	10	0	10	3	3	15	9	—	—	3	APA	None	Yes	Yes	E
Teacher Educator	800	80	2	40	70	20	5	5	7	2	—	1–18	1	Chicago	None	Yes	Yes	E
Teachers College Record	3,000	15	1	33	25	15	10	2	7	7	25	20–30	2	Chicago or APA	None	No	No	N
Tech Trends	9,000	69	3	33	70	25	10	14	8	4	16	8–20	2	Chicago	Possibly	Yes	Yes	E
Theory Into Practice	4,000	70	2	—	100	90	20	1	8	8	15	10–18	2–3	APA	None	Yes	Yes	E
Training and Development	3,200	20	3	0	30	25	4	7	10	5	—	8–20	1	Chicago	None	Yes	Yes	L
Vocational Education Journal	42,500	30	3	10	80	20	14	14	14	4	8	—	1	Chicago	Likely	Yes	No	L

*All or most articles are by invitation only.

Nearly all of the journals in my survey publish at least some articles that report on research of some kind. For 20% of the journals, at least 89% of the published articles report on research. Clearly, the inclusion of some research data is an important aspect of most professional articles accepted for publication. However, when writing for journals whose audiences consist largely of practitioners, you should avoid the formal research article format.

The reward systems of some colleges and universities dictate that their faculty members publish in "refereed journals." Since what it means to be a refereed journal varies widely from journal to journal, I have devised a simple three-point scale to reduce the confusion. I assign one point to each of three criteria that I consider important in refereeing. If manuscripts are regularly sent out of the editorial offices for review by peers (or if an editor regularly uses a combination of in-house and field-based review), I assign the journal one point. If the reviewers do not know the name of the author or the institution with which the author is affiliated, I assign the journal one point. If the journal furnishes its reviewers with a rating instrument with which to evaluate manuscripts, I assign the journal one point. The total for each journal is the figure reported in Table 1 under the heading "Refereed."

Fifty-two percent of the journals in my survey scored a full three points on my refereeing scale; 80% scored at least two points. A full 93% reported some degree of refereed status. Since the previous survey two years ago, three formerly nonrefereed journals have become refereed journals. I should note that merely meeting these criteria does not insure quality. Moreover, an author whose purpose in writing is to pass on practical information might best meet this goal by publishing in a nonrefereed journal that is read by a great many practitioners, while a researcher who wishes to advance the basic knowledge in his or her discipline might better achieve this goal by publishing in a refereed journal with a smaller number of readers who are primarily researchers.

Perhaps the question that aspiring writers ask most frequently is, What is the acceptance rate of a particular journal? Acceptance rates among these journals range from 5% to 90%. Two-thirds of the journals reject at least two-thirds of the manuscripts they receive, and one-fifth reject at least 90%. Still, another one-fifth of the journals I surveyed accept at least half of the manuscripts submitted. The average acceptance rate for all of these journals is almost one-third (32.8%).

To help aspiring writers increase their personal acceptance rates, I asked the editors how many theme issues they plan each year. Four-fifths of the responding editors (80.4%) dedicate all or part of one or more issues a year to themes, and almost half of all the articles in the journals that publish theme issues (45%) are related to a theme. This figure is up 29% from 1990. By reading these journals regularly, writing on an upcoming theme, and timing the submission of a manuscript so that it reaches the editors before the announced deadline, you can significantly increase your chances of getting into print. One journal, on whose publications committee I have served for several years, plans both theme issues and general issues each year. The editors typically receive three times as many manuscripts for general issues as they receive for theme issues. The mathematics is simple: by writing for the theme issues, you have three times the chance of being published in this journal.

The promptness with which an editor evaluates a manuscript is an important concern for all potential contributors. The 54 editors who responded to my survey require from one day to two months to respond to query letters. As many as 60 days may be required merely to acknowledge receipt of the manuscript, though the average is a little over one week.

Such an average doesn't sound so bad. But once the manuscript has been received and acknowledged, the process of review slows down considerably. These editors take from two to 30 *weeks* to decide whether to accept or reject a manuscript. On the average, this decision takes about 2½ months (9.7) weeks—or 10 times as long as the average time required to respond to a query letter. This large disparity suggests that, when selecting journals to which to submit manuscripts, you might wish to query the editor about his or her interest before sending a manuscript. It also suggests that, unless you know that a particular journal has a shorter turnaround time, you should wait at least a couple of months before inquiring about the status of your manuscript. Once having accepted a manuscript, these journals take between one month and two years to publish it. The average delay is 7.9 months.

Do not be timid about contacting editors. Ninety-six percent of the editors who responded to my survey welcome inquiries, and most don't care whether you write or call. Of those who have a preference, about three-fourths prefer letters over phone calls. Remember that most editors face heavy workloads and deadlines, so all communication, whether by phone or mail, should be kept brief.

Few beginning writers realize the importance of making their manuscripts fit the requirements of the target journals. Put bluntly, the editors will not alter their journals to fit your manuscript. I know of one editor who won't even send a manuscript out for review if it violates any referencing rules. Some two-thirds of these journals require APA (American Psychological Association) style; about 30% use the University of Chicago style; one uses Campbell; and one uses Associated Press. Manuscripts should also correspond to a journal's length requirements. The acceptable length varies widely from one journal to the next, from as brief as one manuscript page to as long as 250 pages (though this is clearly an anomaly).

Do photos improve your chances of getting published and, if so, how much? Just over one-third of the editors (37%) said that photos could help get a manuscript published. If a writer wishes to submit photos, black-and-white glossy prints are preferred. The photos should show people engaged in activities related to the topic of the manuscript. It is also a good idea to obtain a signed "release" from every individual who can be identified in the photos.

Each time I mail this survey, I revise it to answer new questions that have been raised in my workshops. This year is no exception. Data reported in the following paragraphs are new and do not appear in Table 1, which lists only data on those topics about which I regularly survey editors.

Writers often wonder exactly who determines their fate once their manuscript is dropped into the mailbox. Is it the editor? A board of editors? A panel of referees? Or perhaps there is a high executioner whose life mission is to reject manuscripts.

For two-thirds of the journals in my survey, the editors make the final decision to accept or reject a manuscript. About one-fourth (26%) of the journals have an editorial board that makes such decisions. A couple of journals have an executive editor who decides the fate of each manuscript. For a couple of journals the editor and author use the referees' input to decide collectively whether to accept or reject.

A question that is seldom asked, yet should be raised by those who are not members of an organization that sponsors a journal is, Does acceptance of my manuscript require that I hold membership in the association? This question is becoming more important since the increased pressure to publish is forcing people to look at opportunities in journals in disciplines beyond their own. While 95% of these editors said that membership is *not* a prerequisite for acceptance, 5% said that it was. If a journal's guidelines to contributors do not specify whether membership is required, this is a question that you may wish to ask the editor directly.

Sometimes, when contributors hear that editors invite individuals to submit manuscripts, they conclude that the only way to publish in the journal is by special invitation. What these contributors fail to realize is that, even when writers are asked to contribute to a particular issue, the invited manuscripts may be subjected to the same rigorous evaluation process that faces uninvited manuscripts.

This survey found that inviting individuals to submit manuscripts is a common practice. Ninety-three percent of these editors do at times invite individuals to submit manuscripts to their journals. But about half (51%) of the manuscripts that are received as a result of an editor's invitation are submitted to the review process.

I often hear from workshop participants that editors ask them to revise their manuscripts. They ask whether I think they should do this. Before answering this question, let's examine the data. From time to time, all of these journal editors ask contributors to revise and resubmit their manuscripts. When this happens, 75% of the revised manuscripts are eventually accepted; however, some manuscripts must be revised several times. Thirty-five percent of these journals accept 90% or more of the revised manuscripts; about half (52%) accept 80% of the revisions; 71% accept 75% of the revisions.

A request for revision reveals that the editor considers your topic appropriate for the readers of the journal and believes that the manuscript can make a significant contribution. Most editors, given the surfeit of manuscripts they face, would not bother to pursue a manuscript that they perceive to be worthless. Remember, too, that revisions mean extra work for the editor as well. In essence, a revised manuscript has 2½ times the likelihood of being accepted as an original manuscript. So my advice is to say yes to editors who ask you to revise your manuscript.

The physical appearance of your manuscript is important and too often overlooked. The manuscript should be neat and free of errors. Send only the original manuscript and the required number of copies. For the journals in my survey, the number of copies in addition to the original varies from zero to six. Also remember to enclose a self-addressed, stamped envelope, and never submit a manuscript simultaneously to more than one journal without notifying the editors.

Before submitting your next manuscript, study Table 1.* Choose a journal with a readership and publication requirements that match your goals. Read several recent issues, and pay close attention to the style and tone of the articles.

Finally, most of us think we have good writing skills, but few of us do. Good writers edit and rewrite—again and again. Often they put a manuscript aside for a few days between revisions. Many writers also find it useful to ask a colleague to critique their writing, a practice I strongly recommend. Follow these suggestions, set yourself some deadlines, and never give up. You *can* succeed.

---

*Subsequent to publication of this article, I have compiled similar information on journals in other disciplines. This additional research appears in Tables 2 and 3.

TABLE 2 Characteristics of a Selected Sample of Other Journals

	Number of Readers	Contributors Who Are University Personnel (%)	Refereed	Research Articles (%)	Theme Issues per Year (%)	Acceptance Rate (%)	Days to Answer Queries (Avg.)	Days to Acknowledge Receipt of Ms. (Avg.)	Weeks Required for Decision (Avg.)	Months Required for Publication (Avg.)	Preferred Length (in Ms. Pages)	Min./Max./ Pages	Number of Additional Copies	Required Style	Effect of Photos on Acceptance (N=None, P=Possibly, D=Definitely, L=Likely)	Welcome Query Letters	Welcome Phone Calls	Prefer Letter (L), Phone Call (P), Either (E), or Neither (N)
HEALTH & NURSING																		
Adapted Physical Activity Quarterly	800	80	3	70	—	40	—	10	13	6	20–25	—	3	APA	N	Y	Y	E
American Journal of Physiology	—	99	2	99	—	60	7	3	8	4	6–8	3–12	3	APS	L	Y	Y	L
Journal of Allied Health	1,500	100	3	95	—	25	5	8	7	5	12	—	1	AMA	N	Y	Y	L
Journal of American College Health	3,000	99	3	60	20	25	7	3	14	5	20	4+35	1	AMA	N	Y	Y	L
Journal of Applied Communication Research	2,000	95	3	90	20	20	2	2	8	12	25	—	2	APA	N	Y	Y	N
Journal of Health Education	10,000	75	3	75	30	20	18	14	8	11	10	1–12	3	APA	P	Y	Y	L
LIBRARIANSHIP/ INFORMATION SCIENCE																		
Journal of Education for Library and Information Science	1,600	95	3	95	25	—	11	11	9	16	—	—	2	Chicago	N	—	—	—
Library and Information Science Research	1,500	80	3	80	—	60	4	2	5	2	20	—	3	MLA	N	Y	Y	L
Library Quarterly	2,000	90	3	85	20	30	3	3	8	6	—	—	2	—	N	Y	Y	L
Wilson Library Bulletin	12,000	25	0	—	—	20	10	10	8	5	8–10	3–12	1	Chicago	P	y	y	—

SOCIAL AND BEHAVIORAL SCIENCES

Journal																	
The Counseling Psychologist	2,300	60	3	10	100	—	0	0	6	—	—	—	3	APA	N	Y	Y	L
Economics and Business Education	3,500	11	3	—	—	—	14	14	12	5	—	—	2	—	N	Y	N	L
International Journal of Social Ed.	1,000	35	3	90	95	18	4	4	—	—	20–25	—	2	Chicago	P	Y	—	—
Journal for Specialists in Group Work	9,000	40	3	30	25	50	14	14	12	12	20	10–40	2	APA	N	Y	N	L
Journal of Child Psychology and Psychiatry	4,000	—	2	90	—	20	10	2	6	6	—	—	3	—	—	—	—	—
Journal of Counseling Psychology	4,000	—	3	90	—	25	7	7	6	6	20–30	—	4	APA	N	Y	Y	P
Journal of Humanistic Psychology	4,000	60	2	10	—	10	14	10	8	12	20	10–40	1	APA	N	N	N	L
Journal of Pediatric Psychology	1,000	—	3	95	15	20	3	2	6	9	25	—	3	APA	P	Y	Y	P
Journal of Youth and Adolescence	2,000	95	1	90	—	30	7	7	25	9	—	15–30	2	APA	N	Y	Y	L
Merrill-Palmer Quarterly	1,400	90	2	83	15	21	7	1	10	11	28	1–40	3	APA	—	Y	Y	L
Psychological Review	2,000	—	3	100	0	15	90	2	90	6	—	—	3	APA	N	N	N	N
Psychotherapy: Theory, Research, and Practice	7,000	—	3	98	—	20	7	7	14	11	15–20	1–20	3	APA	N	Y	Y	L
Social Education	26,000	10	3	10	15	18	3	3	9	7	3–8	3–20	4	Chicago	P	Y	N	L
Social Science Quarterly	3,600	—	3	—	0	14	0	0	8	9	23	1–30	3	Chicago	P	Y	N	L
The Social Studies	3,000	60	2	10	30	48	10	2	13	10	—	10–25	1	Chicago	P	Y	Y	L
Sociology of Education	2,500	90	3	100	25	10	7	2	12	9	30	1–50	3	ASA	N	N	Y	—
Theory and Research in Social Ed.	1,000	95	3	—	10	15	2	1	8	6	20	12+	4	APA	N	Y	Y	L

TABLE 3 Characteristics of a Selected Sample of Business Journals

	Acceptance Rate (%)	Refereed	Number of Subscribers	% of University Contributors	Prefer Query Letters	Welcome Phone Calls	Days to Answer Query Letters	Days to Ackn. Manuscript Receipt	Months Required for Publication	Preferred Length of MSS (# Pages)	Minimum/Maximum Pages	Theme Issues per Year (%)	Articles Reporting Research (%)	Types of Research (key below)	Number of Photocopies	Accept Letter-Quality Printouts	Accepty Dot-Matrix Printouts	Effect of Photos on Acceptance
BUSINESS																		
Academy of Management Journal	11	yes	8,900	95	no	yes	1	1	15	30	10/50	0	100	D, H, A, CC, Q, C, E	5	yes	yes	no
Academy of Management Review	12	yes	9,500	99	yes	yes	7	1	8	25	1/25	0	100	T	2	yes	no	—
California Management Review	15	yes	5,500	85	no	no	7	1	8	25	15/30	20	50	D, H, CC, C, E, T	3	—	yes	Psbl 8 x 10
Journal of Applied Behavioral Science	10	yes	3,000	80	yes	yes	7	7	11	20	10/30	25	95	D, H, A, CC, Q, V, C, E, T	5	yes	no	no
Journal of Human Resource	15	yes	3,000	90	no	yes	14	7	12	25	—	—	99	E, T, econ, emprcl	5	yes	yes	no
Journal of Instructional Development	35	yes	1,500	83	yes	yes	14	3	4	25	15/30	25	25	D, Q, V, T	4	yes	no	no
Journal of Management	3	yes	1,300	95	no	yes	5	1	12	23	15/25	0	90	D, H, CC, Q, C, E, T	3	yes	yes	Psbl 5 x 7
Journal of Management Development	35	yes	1,000	70	yes	yes	10	10	4	—	—	50	50	D, H, A, V, T	—	yes	—	no

Organizational Dynamics	12	yes	9,500	99	yes	yes	7	1	8	23	—	0	33	D, H, A, CC, V, T	2	yes	no	no
Personnel Administrator	15	yes	5,500	85	no	no	7	1	6	10	5/15	100	30	CC, V, C, T	3	yes	no	Lky 5 × 7
Personnel Journal	10	yes	3,000	80	yes	yes	7	7	11	12	8/25	0	1	—	1	yes	yes	no
Psychology Today	15	yes	3,000	90	no	yes	14	7	12	10	—	25	75	E	0	yes	yes	no
Training & Development Journal	35	yes	1,500	83	yes	yes	14	3	4	15	10/20	0	8	A, Q, E, T	1	yes	yes	no
Training	3	yes	1,300	95	no	yes	5	1	12	10	1/5	0	6	D, A, CC, E, T	1	yes	no	Lky 5 × 7

KEY: Descriptive: D   Action: A   Causal-Comparative: CC   Quasi-Experimental: Q   Developmental: V   Theoretical Model Building: T   Historical: H
Correlational: C   Experimental: E

Appendix B

When Signing Book Contracts, Scholars Should Be Sure to Read the Fine Print

By Kenneth Henson

It's happening everywhere, it's exciting, and it isn't even illegal. Authors on campuses around the country are joyfully signing book contracts with commercial publishers. But by this time next year, the joy of some of these authors will have faded when they realize that they have signed away many of the advantages that attracted them to writing in the first place.

When I recently received in the mail a contract for a forthcoming textbook, I realized that my reaction was far different from when I first began receiving contracts. A decade and a dozen books ago, I was elated by the arrival of each contract. But now, having been burned several times, I no longer rip open the envelope with passion and delight. Instead, using bomb-squad precautions, I slowly and carefully remove the contents.

Looking back, I'm embarrassed about the bad advice I once gave to novice authors who brought me their contracts for my "expert" opinion. After all, I had published several books, with commercial publishers as well as a university press. "Don't worry," I would say, "This is a reputable publishing company whose century-old reputation depends on its fairness."

Scanning the document without noting the details, I would continue: "Yes. It's the standard contract. No, you don't need an attorney. Just sign it."

I know better now. You should read every word, and you shouldn't assume fairness. But, by watching for a few simple traps, you can get yourself a decent contract.

Don't be afraid to negotiate. Most publishers are honest. But commercial publishers have only one means of survival—making a profit. Their need to make money often leads to losses for authors, intended or not. If you expect to make a profit by writing, you must learn to protect your own interests. Remembering that your relationship with a publisher is a business relationship can help you earn a fairer deal.

Recognize that royalty agreements can be complicated. Most beginning writers are obsessed with royalty rates. When new writers hand me their first contracts, they often ask first about the fairness of the royalty rate. Once my advice was: "Take anything. It's a beginning." But now my response has changed. Some basic facts about royalties should be understood.

The royalty rate quoted in contracts with commercial publishers is based on net sales receipts. This means that an author's earnings will be based on the money received from sales, *minus* certain publishing expenses. For example, if you sign a contract that pays a 15 percent royalty on a book that sells for $29.95, your share is not 15 percent of the $29.95 retail price, or $4.50. Instead, your profit is 15 percent of the retail price *minus* the bookstore's discount from the publisher (usually 20 percent), free samples, returns, transportation charges, taxes, and other publishing expenses. So instead of receiving $4.50 for each book sold, you will receive about $3.50.

Bookstores are given even larger discounts on trade books (usually 25 to 30 percent, sometimes 40 percent). The royalty rate paid to authors of trade books is usually considerably less than the 15 percent commonly paid to textbook authors. Most authors of trade books receive royalties of between 5 and 10 percent. You also can expect a lower royalty rate on books sold outside the United States. Books sold by mail order or through book clubs may earn even less.

Ask for a fixed royalty rate. Some contracts specify a fixed percentage of net receipts; other contracts offer a sliding scale. Sliding-scale contracts became popular with commercial publishers during the economic recession of the 1970s, because, I suspect, publishers wanted a hedge against rapid inflation and other economic constraints. A sliding scale can be advantageous to the author when the book's market is large and the book sells well. But publishing companies assess the potential sales of a given book and design variable scales that favor themselves. I therefore believe that beginning writers are far better off with a fixed rate.

Here's how the sliding scale works. Suppose that instead of offering you a straight 15 percent royalty rate, a company offers you a 12 percent rate on the first 5,000 copies of your book sold, 15 percent on the next 5,000 copies, and 18 percent on all copies sold in excess of 10,000. When computed on this sliding scale, a $30 book that sold 6,000 copies would earn its author $18,000, compared with $21,600 on a straight 15 percent scale, after deducting the retailers' 20 percent discount from the publisher.

If you do accept a sliding-scale contract, be aware that there are two basic types. One offers a fixed rate on the first group of copies sold, a higher fixed rate on the first group of copies sold, a higher fixed rate on the next volume sold, and an even higher fixed rate on the next volume sold. For example, a contract might specify 12 percent on the first 10,000 copies, 15 percent on the next 5,000 copies, and 18 percent on all additional copies. This means that if you sold 10,005 copies you would earn 15 percent on only 5 copies. Generally, this type of contract extends over the life of the edition. If the book is revised, a new contract must be issued.

The other type of sliding-scale contract provides increases that are contingent on the sale of a specified number of copies within a certain period of time. For example, using the same percentages, the royalty would increase to the higher rates only if 15,000 copies or more were sold within a calendar year. With this type of contract, you should know whether the rate increase covers all copies sold that year or just those exceeding the specified levels. In other words, using the same example, it is important to know whether a book that sells 11,000 copies in a year earns 15 percent on all 11,000 copies or earns 12 percent on the first 10,000 copies and 15 percent on the last 1,000 copies. If after examining the contract you are not sure, you should ask the acquisitions editor for clarification, and include the clarification in the contract.

Ask for a nonrefundable advance. In book contracts an advance is a stated amount of money given to the author at specified times before his or her work is published. But often the publisher's view of advances differs from the author's. The publisher considers an advance as a loan to authors to help defray research or typing expenses, but many beginning authors consider it just a windfall. Some publishers offer to give advances; others will give advances only at the author's request; and others never pay advances. Don't be afraid to ask for an advance, but don't be discouraged if your request is denied.

In asking for an advance, you should be sure the amount is proportional to the estimated size of the market for your book. For a book with anticipated sales of 5,000 or fewer units, a request for a $1,000 to $2,000 advance is reasonable. A book with anticipated first-year sales of 25,000 copies often commands an advance of $15,000 to $20,000.

One contract item that is well worth checking is whether the author is responsible for returning the advance if the publisher decides to cancel the contract. Commercial publishers can and often do cancel contracts at any point during the publishing process. To guard against this disappointment, you may wish to ask that the advance become a "kill fee" if the publisher decides to cancel. If the publisher agrees to your request, be sure that your contract is altered to include this condition.

Watch for hidden expenses that may be deducted from your royalties. An expense often charged entirely to the author is the cost of permissions to quote from other copyrighted works. Although most contracts specify that these costs will be charged to the author, you may wish to ask the publisher to pay. (Don't be disappointed if your request is denied.)

If you have to pay for the permissions, you can reduce these costs by carefully selecting your sources of material. For example, federal government documents can be quoted without cost. At the other extreme, the use fee for some quotations may be several hundred dollars for just a few words.

Some people advise writers that they have no choice but to pay the assessed permission fees. That's not true: You always have a choice. If a requested fee seems exorbitant, try to negotiate. If that fails, seek another source. I once asked Metro-Goldwyn-Mayer for permission to use the last two lines from the song "Somewhere Over the Rainbow." I couldn't afford the fee they specified, so I wrote a second letter explaining that my book was a professional book whose expected sales were very low. The company reduced its original fee by 50 percent. Since I still felt the fee was too high for the type of book I was writing, I chose another quotation—from a book—and was charged no fee at all. (Many book publishers do not charge for permission to use short quotations.)

Another hidden expense in some contracts is the cost of artwork and photographs. In the early 1980s I had a textbook published by a leading publisher. The book was a success in that, although written for a small market, its net receipts for the first year, exceeded $20,000. Normally my straight 15 percent royalty would have earned me $3,000. However, because of a misleading phrase in the contract concerning photographs, I received no royalties for the first-year period. In fact, at the end of the first year I owed the company $1,843.15 for use of photos and quotations.

In all fairness, I should admit that I did receive a grant of $350 from the publisher to cover photo costs. The contract included the brief statement, "The publisher agrees to pay the author a grant of up to $350 for manuscript preparation and photo costs upon written request." This was the only mention of photographs in the contract. I had assumed this grant would cover all photo costs. But what I thought was a "gift" cost me dearly. After writing to the editor for copies of the photo payment receipts, I was devastated to learn that in addition to the many photographs that I myself had taken for the book, more than additional ones had been purchased. The charges for each photo ranged from $50 to $150. I had had no idea that so many photographs would be used, photos that I would have to pay for. The grant paid for only a fraction of their cost.

You can do better. Ask the publisher to pay for photographs. Publishers often do, but if yours refuses, ask for a ceiling on the costs to be charged to you. Agreeing to pay for photographs without stipulating a maximum is tantamount to handing your publisher a blank check with your signature on it. Don't do it.

My final advice is: Don't let my warnings discourage you. I just signed my 12th book contract and, knowing that I heeded my own advice, I am excited about the prospect of having another book published. Book writing is a way to reach professional and personal goals that you could not otherwise reach. So stay alert, watch for pitfalls, and go for it!

Appendix C

Six Ways to Capture and Hold the Attention of Nonfiction Readers

By Kenneth T. Henson

In a way, good writing is like good fishing. Success begins with getting the audience's attention. You must either go after your audience or lure your audience to you. Often you get only one try, so you must give it your best. Like all modern consumers, nonfiction readers have a pretty good idea of what they are looking for. If you know what it is, you can provide an attractive lure.

Successful anglers know that the habits of a bass are unlike those of a trout, and they choose their bait accordingly. When choosing your next writing topic, stop and think about the reader. All nonfiction readers are looking for substance. But what is right for one audience is wrong for another. For example, if you are writing to managers of small businesses, you may wish to emphasize ways to make businesses more personal. But, this could be all wrong for many managers of large conglomerates who may prefer articles on international mergers or massive take-overs.

Having identified an area of interest to your potential consumer, you can choose a topic that will catch the reader's eye and lure the reader to your article or book. A quick look at modern life will explain why you have only one chance to catch your reader's attention. Since people are so busy, some read only a select few of the articles in any journal, choosing only those articles or books that promise to fill their needs. But, as an author, you are not powerless: you can use the following six steps to capture and hold your readers' attention.

STEP 1. Write Captivating Titles
STEP 2. Use Subheadings to Capture Attention

Reprinted by permission from *Writers' Journal* 14(1993): 19–20.

STEP 3. Write Fluidly
STEP 4. Write Simply
STEP 5. Write Assertively
STEP 6. Show Application

1) Write Captivating Titles. Since most readers begin their selection by looking at article, chapter, or book titles. You must make each title reach out and grab the reader's total attention. Consider the captivating power of a recent article title which appeared in Consumer's Digest, "How to Get 150,000 Miles Out of Your Car." Remember that these are times when most people are keeping their cars for several years. Or consider the power of the title "How to Reduce Your Chances of Being Sued." To appropriate audiences such as physicians, board members, or politicians, this article title would be most effective. It could become even more captivating if written so that it makes a definite promise to the reader. For example, "Six Ways Attorneys Can Avoid Litigation."

Your books or articles must deliver on the promises of their titles. Most of us can recall being disappointed over choosing and reading a book only to discover later that its contents failed to live up to its title.

In striving to make your writing true to your titles, don't let your titles become your master. First and foremost, say what you think is important to the readers. If necessary, after you finish writing your article or book, you can easily revise your title to make it fit your message.

2) Use Subheadings to Capture Attention. When prospective readers scan the titles of book chapters or articles (either in the contents list or hopping from article to article while fanning through the magazine), they make tentative selections and quickly verify each by scanning the article. This is your chance to set your hook. A few good subheadings can reassure the reader of the article's value, especially if you keep your subheadings simple and practical.

The full potential of subheadings can be appreciated with the realization that some magazines *require* authors to place subheadings *at specified intervals.* Subheadings are like the largest divisions in an outline. To the reader they are more; they assure the reader that the author is going to deliver on the promise made in the title. Correctly written, subheadings can also show the reader that several smaller but more concrete deliveries will be realized. Put bluntly, you can use subheadings to convince your readers that your article is substantive. This means a lot to nonfiction readers who read for information. You can get full use of your subheadings by using numerals. Either number each subheading or include under one or more headings a numbered list of items.

3) Write Fluidly (As Though Speaking Informally to the Audience). Having captured your readers' attention with an effective title and subheadings, you must hold their attention throughout the article. There is a way to do this. Begin by relaxing and writing as though you were talking to one of your readers. As all experienced writers know, the first law for all authors is that they need to be about their business—writing. Writers should write as quickly as the words will flow, not worrying about style, grammar, punctuation, spelling or anything else until all the words are on paper. Now that you have an audience in mind try reversing the roles. Imagine you are the audience. What would you want the author to tell you? What kind of questions would you want to ask if you could meet and talk to the expert? This is where your article should begin: answering those questions that the readers would most likely raise. As you write, keep your imaginary audience in mind. Your job is to serve this audience by providing the answers to *their* questions. Sometimes it means that you won't get to say what you want to say, at least not until you have satisfactorily answered the audience's questions. Many people desire to become writers because of the expert power authors have over the audience. Paradoxically, the most successful authors remain subservient listeners whose paramount goal is to serve their readers.

4) Write Simply. Nonfiction authors must keep in mind that their audience reads for understanding. They want concrete facts. They want to read something tonight and implement it tomorrow. Their reasons for reading are clear to them, and these reasons do not include making the author wealthy or famous, or providing the author and opportunity to impress others with arrogance and pomposity. To give your writing some punch, delete all the unnecessarily long words, paragraphs, and sentences. Each paragraph should be so brief that having just read it, the reader can remember all of the major concepts. Each sentence should be structured so that the subject is at the beginning of the sentence and is quickly followed by the verb. Remove all unnecessary long words. For example, the word *utilize* should be replaced with the word *use*, prioritize means to order or rank, effectuate means to change, and administrate isn't even a word although it is often found in "scholarly" writing. The deletion of unnecessary words, sentences, and paragraphs adds clarity and makes reading faster and easier (see figure 1).

Consider an entire article, or worse, a book that is written in the earlier form. Then consider the difference in how it reads after such practical editing occurs. The difference is the same as that which exists between good nonfiction writing and an erudite dissertation or thesis. When have you notice anyone reading a dissertation for pleasure or to gain practical information? Seldom or never. Unlike a dissertation, this simple style results from careful editing. It produces clear and powerful writing.

5) Write Assertively. Although readers do not read to provide authors a forum to espouse their wisdom, nonfiction readers must have confidence in their author's expertise. Convincing the readers that the author is indeed an expert on the topic is the author's responsibility. Force can be garnered

---

Figure 1

Writing Simply

<u>**"She is not the type of person who frequently stumbles forward before first considering some of the possible consequences."**</u>

1. The word *person* is unnecessary since this concept can be achieved without the word; so delete it. In fact, the entire phrase *is not the type of person* is unnecessary. Delete it. "Frequently stumbles forward" is a long way of saying that she acts.

2. The rest of the sentence says that she first considers the possible consequences. The word *possible* is totally unnecessary since these consequences are possible; else, how could she consider them?

With these deletions, the once long, awkward, and passive sentence now reads:

"She thinks before she acts."

---

by using positive language. Assertive writing results from a combination of simple words and positive statements. For example, sentences that begin with *not a few* could better begin with the word *several* or *many*. "Not all laws serve to protect citizens" could read "Some laws fail to protect citizens." Now remove all unnecessary conditions and disclaimer statements. Research reports and scholarly theses may demand these, but most magazines and books do not. Conditioners weaken your work. Expressions like "sometimes," "maybe," "possibly," and "under certain circumstances," dilute the reader's confidence in you. Get rid of them.

6) Show Application. Most nonfiction readers are serious practitioners who seek solutions to real problems. Nonfiction readers are always looking for specific ways to improve a process. They don't like long, pedantic treatises because they don't have time for them and because they want ideas they can use. You can win the nonfiction reader's support by offering specific ways to apply the information in your article or book. Give the readers specific examples and then explain how these are applicable to all potential readers of this material. You do this by first studying your audience and then selecting examples that can be used by everyone who reads the magazine or book. This means that if you offer an example with palm trees you'd better be sure that your readers in Kansas and Oregon can relate to it.

Likewise, make sure that your work represents all socio-economic levels and ethnic groups who regularly read it. Beginning writers tend to be too provincial and too restrictive, leaving to the readers the job of drawing meaning from their writing. This won't work. It results in confusing and boring the readers.

When you write for nonfiction readers, remember that your job is to capture the readers' attention and hold that attention throughout the work. Good titles and subheadings are excellent devices for getting attention. Holding it throughout every sentence isn't that easy. The only way it can be achieved is through careful editing and rewriting, ever keeping the readers in clear view and remembering that good authors are devoted servants.

Appendix D

Paragraphing Exercise Solution

The Party's Over—So What Is To Be Done?
By Richard Flacks

Two hundred years after the French revolution, when the division between Left and Right began to be used to map political alignments, it seems obvious to many that such clear-cut political differentiation has lost its meaning. Certainly, it is argued, the Left no longer can be said to have reality—with the collapse of international communism, the decomposition of the Soviet bloc, the abandonment of socialism by those living under its "actually existing" form, and the recent conservative drift of politics in many Western countries. I want to argue, however, that we still need "left" and "right" to signify certain essential political and cultural differences. I want to propose that what is dying is a particular type of political mobilization. It is, I want to suggest, the Left as Party which has come to an end.

The Left as a Tradition

The Left is, first of all, let us say, a tradition—a relatively distinct body of belief and action that began to have a coherent character at the time of the American and French revolutions. An enormous variety of ideological perspectives and a host of labels constitute that tradition: socialism, anarchism, communism, pacifism, radical democracy, feminism, certain variants of libertarianism; in the United States, instead of these relatively specific labels, leftists typically refer to themselves by using such ideologically euphemistic terms as progressive, liberal, populist, and radical.

Reprinted from *Social Research,* Vol. 60, No. 3 (Fall 1993) with permission.

Left ideological perspectives have often been propelled by organizations created to advance those perspectives. The proliferation of ideological perspectives, of variants within them, and of organizations representing these perspectives who are competing for support has meant that the tradition of the Left has been deeply structured by internecine struggle. Given the ideological divisions and warfare on the left, what warrants the assertion that there is nevertheless a shared tradition? What, if anything, do the Left fragments have in common?

One answer is that there is an essential idea that underlies these ideological differences. That idea, it seems to me, can be best captured by a statement like this: Society should be organized so that the people themselves make their own history. Here are some other ways of putting it: Social and economic life should be arranged so that every member of society has the chance to have some voice in shaping the conditions within which their lives are lived; socioeconomic arrangements in which a few can decide the lives of the many should be replaced by arrangements based on collective self-government; social life should be structured as much as possible on the basis of reasoned discourse among society's members, rather than by the exercise of power or by chance (or the working of impersonal markets).[1]

In short, the Left tradition is the cumulative struggle to envision and practice a fully realized democracy. Most of the ideological differences within the tradition of the Left have revolved around issues of power and strategy. Disputes over what kinds of power—economic, political, military, sexual—have primacy, and over the agencies, levers and processes of . . .

Appendix E

Sample Publication Guidelines

Guideline to Authors: *Psychological Review*

Psychological Review publishes articles that make important theoretical contributions to any area of scientific psychology. Preference is given to papers that advance theory rather than review it and to statements that are specifically theoretical rather than programmatic. Papers that point up critical flaws in existing theory or demonstrate the superiority of one theory over another will also be considered. Papers devoted primarily to surveys of the literature, problems of method and design, or reports of empirical findings are ordinarily not appropriate. Discussions of previously published articles will be considered for publication as Theoretical Notes on the basis of the scientific contribution represented.

Manuscripts: Effective in January 1994, the Incoming Editor is receiving all new submissions to the journal. Submissions that are accepted will be published beginning in the 1995 volume. Submit manuscripts to the Incoming Editor, Robert A. Bjork. Until January 1994, submit manuscripts to the Editor, Walter Kintsch. Refer to the Instructions to Authors published elsewhere in this issue for mailing addresses and more information (see the table of contents). The opinions and statements published are the responsibility of the authors, and such opinions and statements do not necessarily represent the policies of APA or the views of the Editor.

Copyright and Permission: Authors must secure from APA and the author of reproduced material written permission to reproduce a journal article in full or journal text of more than 500 words. APA normally grants permission contingent upon like permission of the author, inclusion of the APA copyright notice on the first page of reproduced material, and payment of a fee of $20 per page. Permission from APA and fees are waived for authors who wish to reproduce a single table or figure from a journal provided that the author's permission is obtained and full credit is given to APA as copyright holder and to the author through a complete citation. (Requestors requiring written permission for commercial use of a single table or figure will be assessed a $20 service fee.) Permission and fees are waived for authors who wish to reproduce their own material for personal use; fees only are waived for authors who wish to use more than a single table or figure of their own material commercially. Permission and fees are waived for the photocopying of isolated journal articles for nonprofit classroom or library reserve use by instructors and educational institutions. Access services may use unedited abstracts without the permission of APA or the author. Libraries are permitted to photocopy beyond the limits of U.S. copyright law: (1) post-1977 articles, provided the per-copy fee in the code for this journal (0033–295X/ 93/$3.00) is paid through the Copyright Clearance Center, 27 Congress Street, Salem, MA 01970: (2) pre-1978 articles, provided that the per-copy fee stated in the Publishers' Fee List is paid through the Copyright Clearance Center, 27 Congress Street, Salem, MA 01970. Address requests for reprint permission to the Permissions Office, American Psychological Association, 750 First Street, NE, Washington, DC 20002–4242.

Instructions to Authors

Authors should prepare manuscripts according to the *Publication Manual of the American Psychological Association* (3rd ed.). All manuscripts must include an abstract containing a maximum of 960 characters and spaces (which is approximately 120 words) typed on a separate sheet of paper. Typing instructions (all copy must be double-spaced) and instructions on preparing tables, figures, references, metrics, and abstracts appear in the *Manual.* Also, all manuscripts are subject to editing for sexist language.

APA policy prohibits an author from submitting the same manuscript for concurrent consideration by two or more publications. In addition, it is a violation of APA Ethical Principles to publish "as original data, data that have been previously published" (Standard 6.24). As this journal is a primary journal that publishes original material only, APA policy prohibits as well publication of any manuscript that has already been published in whole or substantial part elsewhere. Authors have an obligation to consult journal editors concerning prior publication of any data upon which their article depends. In addition, APA Ethical Principles specify that "after research results are published, psychologists do not withhold the data on which their conclusions are based from other competent professionals who seek to verify the substantive claims through reanalysis and who intend to use such data only for that purpose, provided that the confidentiality of the participants can be protected and unless legal rights concerning proprietary data preclude their release" (Standard 6.25). APA expects authors submitting to this journal to adhere to these standards. Specifically, authors of manuscripts submitted to APA journals are expected to have available their data throughout the editorial review process and for at least 5 years after the date of publication.

Authors will be required to state in writing that they have complied with APA ethical standards in the treatment of their sample, human or animal, or to describe the details of treatment. A copy of the APA Ethical Principles may be obtained by writing the APA Ethics Office, 750 First Street, NE, Washington, DC 20002–4242.

Masked reviews are optional, and authors who wish masked reviews must specifically request them when submitting their manuscripts. Each copy of a manuscript to be mask reviewed should include a separate title page with authors' names and affiliations, and these should not appear anywhere else on the manuscript. Footnotes that identify the authors should be typed on a separate page. Authors should make every effort to see that the manuscript itself contains no clues to their identities.

Manuscripts should be submitted in quadruplicate. All copies should be clear, readable, and on paper of good quality. A dot matrix or unusual typefaces acceptable only if it is clear and legible. Dittoed and mimeographed copies will not be considered. In addition to addresses and phone numbers, authors should supply electronic mail addresses and fax numbers, if available, for potential use by the editorial office and later by the production office. Authors should keep a copy of the manuscript to guard against loss. Effective in January 1994, the Incoming Editor is receiving all submissions to the journal. Submissions that are accepted will be published beginning in the 1995 volume. Mail manuscripts to the Incoming Editor, Robert A. Bjork, *Psychological Review,* Department of Psychology, University of California, Los Angeles, California 90024–1563, according to the instructions provided above. Until January 1994, mail manuscripts to the Editor, Walter Kintsch, *Psychological Review,* Department of Psychology, University of Colorado, Campus Box, 345, Boulder, Colorado 80309.

Notice to Contributors: *The American Historical Review*

Guidelines for Submission of Manuscripts

Manuscripts should be sent to the Editor, *American Historical Review,* 914 Atwater, Bloomington, Indiana 47401. Texts including quotations and footnotes, should be double-spaced with generous margins. Submissions sent from the North American continent should include four copies of the complete text (two copies if from abroad). Footnotes should be numbered consecutively throughout and should appear in a separate section at the end of the text. The editors prefer to work with manuscripts that are no more than 30 pages in length, not counting notes, tables, and charts. Especially helpful are submissions that are IBM compatible. These include word-processing programs on 5.25 or 3.5-inch diskettes supported by MS-DOS and, in particular, WordPerfect. To check if your disk is compatible, call our Production Manager at (812) 855–0024.

No manuscript will be considered for publication if it is concurrently under consideration by another journal or press or if it has been published or is soon to be published elsewhere. Both restrictions apply to the substance as well as to the exact wording of the manuscript. If the manuscript is accepted, the editors expect that its appearance in the *Review* will precede republication of the essay, or any significant part thereof, in another work.

Other guidelines for the preparation of manuscript for submission to and publication in the *AHR* will be sent upon request. Articles will be edited to conform to *AHR* style in matters of punctuation, capitalization, and the like. The editors may suggest other changes in the interest of clarity and economy of expression; such changes are not made without consultation with authors. The editors are the final arbiters of length, grammar, and usage.

Unsolicited book reviews are not accepted.

The *AHR* disclaims responsibility for statements, either of fact or opinion, made by contributors.

Action in Teacher Education
The Journal of the Association of Teacher Educators

The journal is seeking articles to fulfill its purpose of providing a forum for the exchange of information and ideas concerning the improvement of teaching and teacher education. Articles submitted should reflect this mission. Their focus should concern concepts, practices, or research that have practical dimensions, implications or applicability for practitioners involved with teaching.

Manuscripts are subject to review by members of the Professional Journal Committee and editorial consultants. Points of view and opinions are those of the individual authors and are not necessarily those of the Association. Permission to reproduce must be requested from the co-editors.

Manuscript Guidelines

- **Content:** Journal issues are either thematic or "open theme." Articles which address the themes should be submitted by the deadline for the thematic topic. Articles addressing concepts, practices, and practical dimensions or implications for practitioners are sought.
- **Length:** The manuscript, including all references, bibliographies, charts, figures, and tables, generally should not exceed 15 pages. Pages must be numbered.
- **Typing:** Double space all text with 1-1/2 inch margins all around.
- **Style:** For writing and editorial style, follow directions in the *Publication Manual of the American Psychological Association* (1983). References MUST follow the APA style. Authors are urged to avoid sexist language.
- **Cover Page:** Include the following information on a separate sheet at the beginning of the manuscript.

  1. Title of the manuscript.
  2. Thematic or open topic.
  3. Date of submission.
  4. Author's name, complete mailing address, business and home phone numbers; institutional affiliation and address.
  5. Brief biographical sketch, background, areas of specialization, major publications.
  6. If a computer is used, indicate IBM or Apple compatible. State compatibility and list word processing program used.

- **Abstract:** In 30 words or less, describe the essence of the manuscript. Place the abstract on a separate sheet at the beginning of the manuscript. Do not include your name or any other identifying information on the sheet.
- **Addendum:** Place tables, charts, figures, or illustrations at the end of the manuscript on separate pages.

Appendix F

Sample Call
for Manuscripts

The editors of *Educational Leadership* invite manuscripts on the following

Themes for 1991–92

Educating Today's Children and Youth (September 1991)
Values, goals, and interests of today's youth. Arrangements by schools to work with parents and community agencies.
Deadline: March 1, 1991

Curriculum Integration (October 1991)
Interdisciplinary programs, forms of literacy (scientific, musical, and so on) multiple intelligences.
Deadline: April 1, 1991

Teacher Education and Professional Development (November 1991)
Preservice and inservice teacher education. Career development and professionalization.
Deadline: May 1, 1991

Transforming Leadership (February 1992)
Shared leadership, teacher leadership, leader training.
Deadline: August 1, 1991

Schooling and Work (March 1992)
Vocational education, involvement of business and industry, tracking, proposals for national testing and certification.
Deadline: September 1, 1991

Beyond Effective Teaching (April 1992)
Current research on teaching and learning and its relation to practice.
Deadline: October 1, 1991

Whose Culture? (December 1991–
January 1992)
Multicultural education, culture-
centered programs, humanities.
Deadline: June 1, 1991

Assessment (May 1992)
Reports on current efforts to
develop measures more suitable
than multiple-choice tests by
which to evaluate students and
schools.
Deadline: November 1, 1991

What we look for . . .

The editors look for *brief* (1,500–2,000 words) manuscripts that are helpful to practicing K–12 educators. We are *not* looking for term papers or reviews of literature, and we rarely publish conventional research reports. We
prefer articles in which the writer speaks directly to thereader in an infor-
mal, conversational style and the treatment of the topic is interesting, insightful, and based on the writer's experience. We usually don't find query
letters helpful; we prefer to read the manuscript. Check each issue for an
expanded notice about a specific theme.

How to prepare your manuscript . . .

To prepare your manuscript, double space *all* copy; number *all* pages;
and show your name, address, phone number, and fax number on the cover
sheet only. On page one, just above the title, indicate the number of words
in the manuscript, including references, figures, and the like. Cite references
in the text like this (Jones 1978), and list them in bibliographic form at the
end of the article; or use citations in the form of numbered endnotes. See a
recent issue of *Educational Leadership* for examples of citations. For other
matters of style, refer to *The Chicago Manual of Style* and *Webster's Collegiate
Dictionary.*

How to submit your manuscript . . .

Send two copies, and include a self-addressed stamped 9 x 12 envelope
if you want them returned. It is not necessary to send unsolicited manuscripts by overnight mail—our deadlines are target dates, not factors in selection. You can expect to receive a postcard telling you that the manuscript
has arrived; a response from an editor should arrive within eight weeks. If
you discover a small error after mailing your manuscript, please do not
send a correction; small errors can be corrected in the editing process.

What happens next . . .

If your manuscript is accepted, even provisionally, we will ask you to
send a letter-quality original *or* an IBM-compatible diskette. Then your manuscript enters the pool of manuscripts on hand for a particular theme issue
(or for use in "Other Topics"). When the editors assemble a particular issue,
they review all manuscripts, both solicited and unsolicited, in order to make

selections for the table of contents. All unsolicited manuscript selections are tentative until we go to press.

How to survive the editing process . . .

If your manuscript becomes a contender for the final table of contents, it is assigned to a staff editor, who shepherds it through all the editing and layout processes. Once your manuscript is edited, you will receive an edited version for your review, correction, and approval. At this time you will have a chance to correct errors, answer our queries, and update any outdated information. The style requirements of *Educational Leadership* dictate heavy editing, and we appreciate collaboration with the authors at any time in the process.

About artwork and photographs . . .

The editors like to have photographs and artwork related to the manuscripts, but these do not influence editorial selection. We appreciate having the opportunity to see your artwork—photos (black and white are best for us), book covers, student papers, and the like. Send them when you are notified that your manuscript has been accepted or when we have begun the editing process.

Send manuscripts to:

Dr. Anne Meek, Managing Editor

Educational Leadership

ASCD

1250 N. Pitt St.

Alexandria, VA 22314–1403

Appendix G

Sample Announcement of Coming Themes and Requests for Manuscripts

March-April 1994:
Teacher Education and the Academic Disciplines

Criticism of the teaching of the core subjects in the nation's school is widespread. The remainder of the 1990s and the first decade of the 21st century will see continued discourse and debate about the teaching of the academic disciplines in the nation's secondary schools and perhaps in the upper levels of elementary schooling. Both thoughtful and ill-conceived solutions will appear in Sunday newspaper supplements, op ed pieces, and quasi-scholarly "reports."

The editors welcome substantive manuscripts that go beyond the conventional rhetoric often accompanying discussion of this highly charged topic. What is the role of teacher education in this matter? What does research in the teaching of the academic subjects tell us? How do we move from exhortations for improvement to demonstrably improved pedagogy in the subject matter domains? What are the implications of the current attempts to develop subject matter pedagogy? How can teacher education faculty function more effectively with colleagues in the academic disciplines? Are there extant, potent examples of teacher education and the academic discipline faculties working effectively on a long-term basis? If there are, what characterizes these efforts? Can they be replicated? Can teacher educators assist in bringing improvements in the teaching of the academic disciplines to those currently in the schools?

Manuscript submission deadline: June 1, 1993

May-June 1994:
The Changing Role of Teacher Educators
Economists forecast gloomy scenarios for the nation's economy; demographics continue to change dramatically; cries for accountability in higher education including teacher education abound; matters such as choice and site-based management promise an altered environment in the schools; partnerships between schools and industry, schools and business, schools and higher education grow. Teacher educators are in the midst of these and other far-reaching issues suggesting change in their roles.

The editors welcome both theory and practice manuscripts dealing with the complexities accompanying the changing environment. What are the policy implications of the reduced economy for teacher education in higher education? What changes in role are both explicit and implicit for teacher educators as local districts move more toward providing their own inservice programs? Can teacher education restructure itself to work more effectively with the schools? What does research suggest about these issues? What kind of leadership is needed in this changing world of higher education in which teacher education exists? What are the professional development issues for teacher education?
Manuscript submission deadline: August 1, 1993

September-October 1994:
Professional School reform and Public School Renewal
Reform movements in SCDEs and public schools frequently operate separately from one another with little shared dialogue or purpose. An SCDE faculty may, for example, make dramatic shifts in the preparation of teachers and administrators and never relate those changes to their work with the schools. Similarly, a school may dramatically alter its class schedule and its pupil placement practices without talking with the institutions which send them student teachers.

The editors are interested in manuscripts that take in-depth looks at the issues related to the linkage between professional school reform and public school renewal, including scholarly debunking of the whole process. We especially desire manuscripts exploring the research implications or, preferably, reporting on research dealing with the problem. Questions authors might consider include: What evidence is there that programs uniting professional school actions and public school efforts have value? What kind of value? Are more highly qualified teachers the result? Do children learn better? What implications are there for the preparation of teachers? In instances where such activities are ongoing, what are teacher education students reading and doing that is different from a "conventional" program? What are the research problems? What are the fiscal implications?
Manuscript submission deadline: October 1, 1993

November-December 1994:
Teacher Education Faculty in the 21st Century

SCDE faculty and teacher education faculty have been the subject of considerable writing and research in the past decade. The RATE studies and a work by numerous authors have described the work, demographics, productivity, and views and attitudes of the current faculty. The question of the type of faculty requisite for the next century is of interest in this theme.

The editors recognize that manuscripts addressing this issue will tend to be speculative and theoretical rather than heavily research-based, but they hope that authors will attend to social and technological trends, changes and constants as they develop their theses. They urge authors to consider the past as they project towards the future in this necessarily complex topic. Questions pertaining to this theme include: Do changes in schooling suggest necessary changes in teacher education faculty? How can a historically conservative body of individuals such as teacher education faculty change? Is change, in fact, necessary? What are teacher education faculty likely to be doing in the 21st century? What impact will projected advances in technology and media have on teacher education faculty? Will Dewey and other major figures still be relevant? If so, how are the teacher education faculty likely to present them and their ideas?

Manuscript submission deadline: December 1, 1993

Appendix H

Sample of Article Written Using Systematic Research Method

Application of Science Principles to Teaching
By Kenneth T. Henson

A Purpose for Principles

Science principles can be used by science teachers at all grade levels and in all areas of science to improve the clarity of the understanding developed in their classes. These results depend, however, on the approach used to present the principle to the science class.

A clear understanding of exactly what a science principle is must be possessed by both teacher and students. Scientists have always experienced difficulty in their attempt to fulfill the first and foremost objective of science—helping man understand his environment. The vast diversity of matter in our universe, and the many different ways in which it behaves, necessitate the development of techniques for simplifying our environment so that it can be analyzed and understood.

One method for simplifying the problem of diversity is to isolate each particle of matter for a thorough analysis of its characteristics. However, the scientist quickly recognizes that this technique has two limitations. First, it provides a descriptive study of still matter, and matter is rarely found in the static form. Secondly, as matter tends to remain in constant motion, it does not behave independently but acts in accordance with other matter in its environment which serve as stimuli. Therefore, to learn about the true

From *The Clearing House,* Vol. 46, November 1971, pp. 143–146. Reprinted with permission of the Helen Dwight Reid Educational Foundation. Published by Heldref Publications, 1319 18th Street, N.W., Washington, D.C. 20036–1802. Copyright 1971.

behavior of matter, the investigator must analyze matter in its natural environment. He must concentrate on the relative behavior of a number of objects simultaneously, at times focusing on a single object while constantly keeping his attention on the complete event. Because events recur in very similar patterns, essentially the same event can be observed and studied again and again until man can predict with great accuracy the sequence, rate, and degree of each separate action accompanying the event each time the event occurs.

The natural patterns of action which the scientist discovers are called principles. Each principle is the result of man's attempt to group events which are closely related. Because they are fewer in number than the many types of matter and the many events which occur, they are more manageable. Because they involve action, they provide an ideal method for studying about matter.

A Theory for Learning Science

What precisely is "thinking"? When at the reception of sense impressions, memory pictures emerge, that is not yet "thinking". And when such pictures form series, each member of which calls forth another, this too is not yet "thinking." When, however, a certain picture turns up in many series, then—precisely through such return—it becomes an ordering element for such series, in that it connects series which in themselves are unconnected. Such an element becomes an instrument, a concept. I think that the transition from free association or "dreaming" to thinking is characterized by the more or less dominating role which the "concept" plays in it.

In the preceding lines, Einstein tells us that the concept is the basis or the first step in thinking. Bruner's famous statement, "Anything can be taught to anyone at any age if properly structured," was based on the "concept" which he defined as a "rule for grouping." The contemporary learning theory specialists Tyson and Carroll view learning in the following way: "To conceptualize is to perceive a rule for grouping, to see a recurring pattern, to see the possibility of order" (Tyson, p. 26). When one notices a recurring pattern one begins to infer a sequential relationship between classes of events (Tyson, p. 36). This is what Tyson and Carroll call theorizing.

The learning of science also begins with concept formation. Once a recurring pattern is noted and concepts are formed these concepts can be seen to have sequential relationships. For example, someone sees a bright flash in the skies above. Again and again he sees similar flashes all similar in abruptness, all similar in intensity. He has formed a concept, which he has labeled "lightning." He hears a rumbling sound, again and again. Each time it sounds similar. He labels this concept "thunder." Now he is ready to notice a sequential relationship or a sequential pattern as it happens, always lightning—then thunder. He can now form a theory or principle. Lightning precedes thunder.

In science the principles are man's theories which describe how concepts are related in time. Once the principle is learned the student knows more than he knew when he only understood each isolated concept. The pattern may be: things-—concepts—principles. He can observe things (objects) without seeing a recurring pattern (concept). He may observe recurring patterns (concepts) without seeing a sequential relationship. But if sees a sequential relationship he understands more about his environment than if he only sees either unrelated things or concepts. The logical conclusion being, then, that the learning of science should be directed toward learning principles.

Instructional Theory for Science

For instructional theory in the sciences to be coherent with theories of learning, the science teacher who approaches teaching via principles should employ the following steps: (1) presentation through illustration, (2) examples and non-examples, (3) involvement through application or implementation.

(1) *Presentation through Illustration.* The science principle involves action. Because it involves action, it can be illustrated. Attempt should always be made to have the student see the events as they happen. The student should be trained to look for the sequential relationships. He should discover the principle for himself.

How should the principle be illustrated? In the most vivid way possible. If the events are too large to arrange, a scale model of them is desirable. If the natural process is too slow to see, a speeded-up model is desirable. If a model is not available, a motion film showing the process as it happens is desirable. If even this is not available, a series of still pictures should be used. The objective is to have the student "see" the principle in action . . . see the time relationships between natural concepts.

(2) *Examples and Non-examples.* Having identified a particular science principle, the student should be able to differentiate between examples and non-examples of the principle when presented with a list containing both. Finally, the teacher should require the student to provide additional examples of the principle.

(3) *Involvement Through Application and Implementation.* Student involvement allows the use of additional senses—touch, smell, sight, and taste. Students, therefore, should be involved in ways which will utilize as many of these senses as possible, to the greatest degree possible. Since emotional involvement increases both comprehension and memory, activities should be selected which are both enjoyable and exciting to the students. Most important of all, to avoid monotony a variety of activities should be used—constantly rotated from one to another. Clear directions and objectives must

accompany each activity. The teacher should always assign a task which requires use of knowledge of the principle just learned.

The science principle implies "wholeness." It is the action and the reaction, the cause and the effect. When presented to a class of students, it must be presented as a whole process. The principle often involves a series of steps which tends to complicate its comprehension. Once the complete principle has been introduced, the teacher must sort out the most important of its steps and present them simultaneously, showing their interrelations. When this is done, each step contributes to the understanding of other steps. Presenting all of the steps and showing their relationships serves to tie the steps together and enables the learner to grasp the complete principle. Two or more concepts are always involved in a science principle. Whether or not these concepts are events, their relationships should be seen.

Summary

Principles of science are actually man's interpretations of his environment. To utilize principles to develop understanding the learner must realize that the matter which surrounds him is in constant motion and that one event causes another or one series of events causes another. He must understand that nature behaves in certain patterns, enabling man to explain present and past events and even predict future events.

To actually use principles to develop understanding by others, the teacher must present the principle in the most natural form possible; that is, without simultaneously introducing information which is not essential to the understanding of the principle. While introducing the principle, the teacher must illustrate the principle—showing all of the action involved and letting the students identify the relationships among the concepts involved.

Following the introduction of the principle, the teacher should provide examples and non-examples of the principle and have the students differentiate among them—eventually requiring the students to provide other examples of the principle. Next, the student should be assigned a task which will require that he use the knowledge of the principle just learned.

Finally, the teacher should explain, ask the students to explain, or give tasks which show the relationships between the concepts involved in the principle.

BIBLIOGRAPHY

(1) Bruner, J. S., J. T. Goodnow, and George Austin. *A Study of Thinking*. New York: Science Editions, Inc., 1965, p. 45.
(2) Committee of Science Education in American Schools. "Science Education in American Schools," *Forty-sixth Yearbook of the National Society for the Study of Education, Part 1*. Chicago: The University of Chicago Press, 1947.

(3) Einstein, A. "Autobiographical Notes," *Albert Einstein: Philosopher-Scientist*, trans. P. A. Schilpp. the Library of Living Philosophers, VII, ed. P. A. Schilpp. New York: Tudor Publishing Co., 1957, p. 7.

(4) Henson, K. T. "The History and Status of the Science Principle," *Science Education*, Vol. 54, No. 4, December 1970, pp. 317–318.

(5) Henson, K. T. "Representation of Pertinent Earth Science Principles in Current Earth Science Textbooks," *School Science and Mathematics*, Vol. 70, No. 7, July, 1970, pp. 646–648.

(6) Johnson, P. G. "Emphasis of the Science Program Should be Based on Principles." *NEA Proceedings*, Vol. 1, 1933, pp. 535–537.

(7) Progressive Education Association, Commission on Secondary School Curriculum for Science in General Education. *Secondary School Curriculum for Science in General Education*. New York: Appleton-Century Company, 1938.

(8) Tyson, C. T. and M. A. Carroll. *Conceptual Tools for Teaching in Secondary Schools*. New York: Houghton Mifflin, 1970.

Ed. Note: Dr. Henson is presently a Fulbright Professor of Education at Battersea College of Education in London, England, for the 1971–72 school year.

Appendix I

Sample of Survey Questionnaire

The Status of the American Middle School Teacher

A. Your Professional Preparation

1. What is the *highest college degree* you hold?
   Do not report honorary degrees. Check ONE.
   [ ] Two-year college diploma, degree, or certificate
   [ ] Bachelor's degree
   [ ] Master's degree
   [ ] Professional diploma based on six years of college study
      (Specialist Degree)
   _____ Major field Bachelor's degree
   _____ Major field Master's degree
   _____ Major field Specialist degree
   _____ Major field Doctor's degree

2. In what *year* did you receive your highest college degree?
   _____ year

3. In what *type of institution* did you take the largest part of your years of college education? For each degree held, write in the number corresponding to the type of institution in which you took the largest part of your work. (Please answer in terms of the type of institution it was when you were graduated.)
   1 Public (tax-supported university or land-grant college)
   2 Public teachers college

3 Other public college
4 Nonpublic (privately supported) university
5 Nonpublic teachers college
6 Other nonpublic college
_____ Bachelor's degree
_____ Master's degree
_____ Professional diploma based on six years of college
_____ Doctor's degree

4. In terms of actual contribution to your success in teaching, how would you evaluate the amount and quality of your *undergraduate teacher preparation* program in the following areas? Check ONE space for EACH area.

PART I:

	Amount of preparation was		
	Too little	About right	Too much
a. Depth of knowledge in the subject fields in which you specialized	[ ]	[ ]	[ ]
b. General education—some knowledge in many fields	[ ]	[ ]	[ ]
c. Psychology of learning and teaching	[ ]	[ ]	[ ]
d. Human growth and development	[ ]	[ ]	[ ]
e. Teaching methods	[ ]	[ ]	[ ]
f. Classroom management, routines, discipline	[ ]	[ ]	[ ]
g. History and philosophy of education	[ ]	[ ]	[ ]
h. Use of audio-visual equipment and materials	[ ]	[ ]	[ ]

PART II:

	Quality of preparation was			
	No preparation	Satisfactory	Excellent	Poor
a. Depth of knowledge in the subject fields in which you specialized	[ ]	[ ]	[ ]	[ ]
b. General education— some knowledge in many fields	[ ]	[ ]	[ ]	[ ]

c. Psychology of learning
   and teaching   [ ]   [ ]   [ ]   [ ]
d. Human growth and
   development   [ ]   [ ]   [ ]   [ ]
e. Teaching methods   [ ]   [ ]   [ ]   [ ]
f. Classroom management,
   routines, discipline [ ]   [ ]   [ ]   [ ]
g. History and philosophy
   of education   [ ]   [ ]   [ ]   [ ]
h. Use of audio-visual
   equipment and material [ ]   [ ]   [ ]   [ ]

B. Your Teaching Experience

5. In what calendar year did you *begin* your first full-time teaching position?
   _____ year

6. How many years of full-time teaching experience have you completed, including the current year?
   _____ total years of experience
   _____ total years in present school system

7. Since you began teaching, in how many *different* public school systems have you taught full time? Count your present system as one.
   _____ system(s)

8. Has there been a break of as much as one year in your full-time teaching service? If so, how many such breaks? Disregard breaks of less than one full school year.
   _____ breaks in teaching service

9. If there has been a break of more than one full school year in your teaching service, what was your *primary reason* for temporarily leaving teaching? If there has been more than one break, answer for the most recent one. Check ONE.
   [ ] Marriage or full-time homemaking
   [ ] Maternity or child rearing
   [ ] Spouse's work took us to another community
   [ ] Further study
   [ ] Employment in a position out of education
   [ ] Employment in another educational position
   [ ] Military service
   [ ] Ill health
   [ ] Tired of teaching and wanted a rest

[ ] Dismissal or forced resignation from teaching
[ ] Other: (please write in) _____

C. Your Present Teaching Assignment

10. How many classroom teachers are there in your school? (Include your-self and all full-time persons half or more of whose work loads is class-room teaching.)
    _____ teachers

11. What grades are you teaching this year? Include any prekindergarten assignment under "PK". Circle *all* grades taught this year.

    PK   5   6   7   8   9

12. How is your present teaching assignment classified? Check ONE.
    [ ] Elementary teacher
    [ ] Junior high teacher
    [ ] Middle School—Junior high teacher
    [ ] Middle Junior—Senior high teacher
    [ ] Combination elementary-secondary teacher
    [ ] Other (please explain) _____

---

13. What percent of your total teaching time each week is spent in teaching grades or subjects that are *different from your major field of college prepara-tion?* Check ONE.
    [ ] None   [ ] 50–59%
    [ ] Some but less than 10%   [ ] 60–69%
    [ ] 10–19%   [ ] 70–79%
    [ ] 20–29%   [ ] 80–89%
    [ ] 30–39%   [ ] 90–99%
    [ ] 40–49%   [ ] 100%

14. Enrollment and contact time
    a. In what field (English, mathematics, etc.) are you currently teaching the *largest portion* of your time?
       _____

    b. What is the total number of *class periods* you teach *per week?* (Exclu-clude study halls and homeroom periods.)
       _____ class periods per week
    c. What is the average number of *pupils* you teach *per day?* (Exclude study halls and homeroom periods.)
       _____ pupils

d. What is the average *length of the class periods* in your school? (Include passing time.)

_____ minutes

e. How many unassigned (so-called "free" or planning) periods do you have in your own schedule each week?

_____ unassigned periods per week

f. How much time per day, on the average, are you *required* to be with pupils? (Include study halls, homeroom periods, scheduled conference periods, lunch periods if applicable.)

_____ hours and _____ minutes

15. What is the *exact length* of your required school day? (e.g., if you are required to be on duty by 8:15 A.M. and permitted to leave school at 3:30 P.M., the exact length of your required school days is 7 hours and 15 minutes.)

_____ hours and _____ minutes

16. On the average how many *hours per week* do you spend on noncompensated school related activities, such as lesson preparation, grading papers, making reports, extracurricular activities, meetings, etc.

_____ hours and _____ minutes

17. How many *days* will there be in your *school year* in 1984–1985?

_____ days of classroom teaching

_____ days of nonteaching duties before, during, or after the school year for pupils

18. Lunch period:

a. What is the average length of your lunch period?

_____ minutes

b. Do you usually eat lunch with your pupils (i.e., supervise their lunch period)?

[ ] Yes, all the time
[ ] Yes, on a rotating basis
[ ] No

c. If you answered Yes to "b" above, what is the reason?

[ ] My own preference
[ ] It is customary in my school
[ ] It is required in my school

19. How would you describe your *present teaching load?* Check ONE.

[ ] Reasonable
[ ] Heavy
[ ] Extremely heavy

20. How would you describe your feelings of *strain or tension* in your work? Check ONE.
    [ ] Little or no strain
    [ ] Moderate strain
    [ ] Considerable strain

D. Your Professional Growth Activities

21. Below are listed several types of *professional growth* activities. For those in which you have participated during the *past three years*, please check the extent to which you believe each activity contributed to improving the quality of your work in the classroom. Check ALL that apply.

Activity	Extent of contribution to professional growth		
	Great	Some	Little or no
Sabbatical leave: full-time college work	[ ]	[ ]	[ ]
Sabbatical leave: travel	[ ]	[ ]	[ ]
Other educational travel	[ ]	[ ]	[ ]
School system-sponsored workshops during regular school year	[ ]	[ ]	[ ]
School system-sponsored workshops during the summer	[ ]	[ ]	[ ]
Work on curriculum committee	[ ]	[ ]	[ ]
Committee work or special assignment *other than* curriculum	[ ]	[ ]	[ ]
Faculty meetings	[ ]	[ ]	[ ]
University extension courses	[ ]	[ ]	[ ]
College courses *in education* during regular school year	[ ]	[ ]	[ ]
College courses in subject-matter fields *other than education* during regular school year	[ ]	[ ]	[ ]
College courses in subject-matter fields *other than education* during regular school year	[ ]	[ ]	[ ]
College courses *in education* during the summer	[ ]	[ ]	[ ]
College courses in subject-matter fields *other than education* during the summer	[ ]	[ ]	[ ]
Professional growth activities sponsored by professional association(s)	[ ]	[ ]	[ ]

Professional reading done on my initiative	[ ]	[ ]	[ ]
Educational television programs	[ ]	[ ]	[ ]
Exchange teaching, domestic	[ ]	[ ]	[ ]
Exchange teaching, foreign	[ ]	[ ]	[ ]
Peace Corps	[ ]	[ ]	[ ]
Other (please specify)			
_____	[ ]	[ ]	[ ]
_____	[ ]	[ ]	[ ]

What single course, workshop, or other professional growth experience during the past three years *contributed most* to improving the quality of your work in the classroom?

_____

_____

22. Beginning with the summer of 1984 and ending with the close of the present school year in May or June 1984 *how much money* do you estimate that you will have spent from your own funds for *all professional growth activities* enumerated in Question 21? (Please EXCLUDE scholarship funds.)

Educational travel $ _____

All other activities $ _____

E. Your Economic Status

23. What is your *salary* as a classroom teacher for the school year 1984–85? (EXCLUDE any extra pay received for additional school duties.)

$ _____ for year

24. *Additional income.* Below are listed several possible sources of additional income for the full year *beginning with your summer vacation in 1984 and ending* with the last school month in May or June 1985. For each item that applies please indicate the *type of position held* and the *total amount of income received.* Check ALL items that apply.

a. Employment during summer 1984

[ ] *School work* (e.g., summer-school teaching curriculum work, school repair jobs, etc.) in your school system

Type of work _____

Total amount $ _____

[ ] *Outside work* (e.g., salesman, recreation director, camp counselor, teaching outside your own school system, etc.)

Type of work _____

Total amount $ _____

[ ] **Federal program** (e.g., NDEA or NSF institute or fellowship, Project Head-Start, Cooperative Research Grant, etc.)
Type of work _____
Total amount $ _____

b. Employment during school year 1984–85

[ ] **Extra pay for extra duties** (e.g., coaching, music, drama, counseling, publications work, etc. in your own school system)
Type of work _____
Total amount $ _____

[ ] **School work other than extra pay for extra cuties** (e.g., evening school, driving school bus, etc. in your own school system)
Type of work _____
Total amount $ _____

[ ] **Outside work** (e.g., salesperson, cab driver, tutoring, local college teaching, etc. outside your own school system)
Type of work _____
Total amount $ _____

c. Summer 1984 and school year 1984–85
Dividends, rents, interest, royalties, retirement annuity, other than current earnings
$ _____

25. How many persons, *excluding* yourself, your spouse, and your children, *depend* upon you for support, either wholly or partly? Include dependents living with you and those living elsewhere.
Number _____ dependents

26. Do you or your spouse own
a. Your own home? [ ] Yes [ ] No
b. A car? [ ] Yes [ ] No
How many cars? [ ] One [ ] Two [ ] Three or more

27. Have you taken a *vacation trip of at least two weeks* during the past three years (e.g., travel, camping, trip to lake or seashore)? Check ONE.
[ ] No
[ ] Yes, in one of the three years
[ ] Yes, in two of the three years
[ ] Yes, in all three years

F. You and Your Family

28. What is your *age?*
_____ years

29. What is your *sex?*
[ ] Male [ ] Female

30. What is your *marital status?*
   [ ] Single   [ ] Married
   [ ] Widowed   [ ] Divorced or separated
31. If you are married, is your husband or wife gainfully employed? Check ONE.
   [ ] Yes; employed full time
   [ ] Yes; employed part time
   [ ] No, but draws retirement pay
   [ ] Not, but is disabled and draws insurance or disability retirement benefits
   [ ] No, not gainfully employed at present
32. If you are married, and if your husband or wife is employed full time, is the employment in the teaching profession?
   [ ] Yes   [ ] No
   If Yes, is the employment in the same school system in which you teach?
   [ ] Yes   [ ] No
33. What are the ages of your children? Write in the *number* of children in each age group.
   _____ under 6 years of age
   _____ 6–11 years
   _____ 12–17 years
   _____ 18 years or older
   _____TOTAL NUMBER OF CHILDREN
   [ ] Have no children
34. If you have children below school age, who takes care of your children while you are teaching? Check ONE.
   [ ] Day care center, kindergarten, or nursery
   [ ] Relatives
   [ ] Friends
   [ ] Someone you hired in your home
   [ ] Someone you hired in their home
   [ ] Other, please specify
   _____
35. What was your main consideration in choosing *teaching* as a career? Please check ONE predominant reason.
   [ ] Opportunity for rendering important service
   [ ] Financial rewards
   [ ] Job security
   [ ] Stop-gap until marriage
   [ ] Example set by a favorite teacher
   [ ] Unsuccessful in another line of work
   [ ] Easiest preparation program in college

[ ] A tradition in my family
[ ] Desire to work with young people
[ ] Interest in subject-matter field
[ ] Other reason (please specify) _____

36. Have you ever served on *active duty* as a member of one of the Armed Forces of the United States?
[ ] Yes   [ ] No

G. You and the Community

37. Please check to indicate your *sense of identity* with the community (town, city, or other unit of population) where you live during the school year. Check ONE.
[ ] I am living in my home community where I have lived sincechildhood.
[ ] I came here as an adult and now feel that I belong.
[ ] I have been here for some time, but do not feel that I belong.
[ ] I have been here for too short a time to expect to feel that I belong.

38. Is your *residence* within the boundaries of the local system in which you teach?
[ ] Yes   [ ] No

39. Several types of religious, civic, professional, and social *organizations* are listed below. Please enter a number before each type that corresponds to one of the following statements, selecting the statement that represents your own relationship to the organization.
1 I am a member and very active worker.
2 I am a member and a fairly active worker.
3 I am a member but not an active worker.
4 I am not a member.
Write in—1, 2, 3, or 4—for each organization:
___ Church, or synagogue, or other formal religious group.
___ Youth-serving group—Y, Scouts, 4-H, etc.
___ Women's business, professional civic-social group—AAUW, B&PW, Quota, etc.
___ Men's service club—Rotary, Lions, etc.
___ Fraternal or auxiliary group (Knights of Columbus, Elks, Eastern Star, etc.)
___ Civil liberties group—ACLU, Urban League, NAACP, CORE, etc.
___ Veterans group
___ Political party organization
___ Parent-Teacher Association
___ Hobby Club—music, drama, gardening, etc.

___ National Education Association
___ State education association
___ Local education association
___ Subject-matter or professional special-interest association
___ American Federation of Teachers

40. How many hours *per month,* on the average, do you give during the school year to work for organizations such as those listed in Question 39? (Do not include time spent in school assigned activities or at services of religious worship.)
_____ hours per month

41. To what extent did you participate in the 1984 national elections? Check ALL items that apply.
[ ] Voted in the primary election
[ ] Voted in the general election
[ ] Contributed money to a political party
[ ] Contributed my services as a worker in behalf of a political party.
[ ] Did not participate in the 1984 national elections

42. While a teacher, have you ever been a *candidte* for election to a public office (local, county, state, or national)?
[ ] Yes   [ ] No

43. In your opinion, what level of prestige do teachers have in the community in which you teach?
[ ] High prestige
[ ] Medium prestige
[ ] Low prestige
[ ] Undecided

44. Do you feel that the community in which you teach places any personal pressures or restrictions on your activities outside school hours because you are a teacher?
[ ] No, not in any way
[ ] Yes, but not seriously
[ ] Yes, seriously
[ ] Undecided

H. Retrospect and Prospect

45. Suppose you could back to your college days and start over again; in view of your present knowledge, would you become a teacher? Check ONE.
[ ] *Certainly would* become a teacher
[ ] *Probably would* become a teacher
[ ] *Chances about even* for and against
[ ] *Probably would not* become a teacher
[ ] *Certainly would not* become a teacher

46. What were you doing during the 1984–84 school year (last year) and what do you expect to be doing during the 1985–86 school year (next year)? Please check ONE item in EACH column.

	1984–84 (last year)	1985–86 (next year)
a. Teaching full time in this school system	[ ]	[ ]
b. Teaching full time in another school system	[ ]	[ ]
c. Attending a college or university full time	[ ]	[ ]
d. In military service	[ ]	[ ]
e. Working in a nonteaching occupation	[ ]	[ ]
f. Homemaking and/or child rearing	[ ]	[ ]
g. Unemployed and seeking work	[ ]	[ ]
h. Retired	[ ]	[ ]
i. Other (please specify)	[ ]	[ ]

_____

_____

I. Your Professional Satisfactions and Problems

47. What elements in your present situation as a teacher *encourage and help you most* to render the best service of you you are capable?

_____

_____

_____

(use additional space on the back if desired)

48. What elements in your present situation as a teacher *discourage or hinder you most* in rendering the best service of which you are capable?

_____

_____

_____

(use additional space on the back if desired)

The Association is greatly indebted to you for the time you spent in completing this questionnaire. The information you have given will beheld in strictest confidence and tabulated with great care.

Should you wish to add your own comments, inspired or provoked by the questionnaire, we shall welcome them. Please use a separate sheet for this purpose. Again, THANK YOU!

Return to:
Early Childhood/Elementary Education
204 Graves Hall
P.O. Box R
The University of Alabama
College of Education
University, AL 35486
Phone: (205) 348-6070

This research project has been funded by the College of Education, The University of Alabama and constitutes a modified longitudinal study which was originated by the NEA Research Division.

Appendix J

Articles Based on Questionnaire: The Status of the U.S. American Middle School Teacher

1. Buttery, Thomas J., Henson, Kenneth T., and Chissom, Brad. (Summer, 1986). The Status of the Middle School Teacher: Professional Preparation. *American Middle School Education*, 9, (3), 26–31.
2. Buttery, Thomas J., Henson, Kenneth T., and Chissom, Brad. (Fall, 1986). The Status of the Middle School Teacher: Teaching Experience and Assignments. *American Middle School Education*, 9, (4): 34–39.
3. Chissom, Brad, Buttery, Thomas J., Chukabarah, Prince C., and Henson, Kenneth T. (Fall, 1987). A Qualitative Analysis of Variables Associated with Professional Satisfaction among Middle School Teachers. *Education*, 108, (1), 75–80.
4. Henson, Kenneth T., Buttery, Thomas J., and Chissom, Brad. (Spring, 1986). Improving Instruction in Middle Schools by Attending to Teachers' Needs. *American Middle School Education*, 9, 2–7.
5. Buttery, Thomas J., Henson, Kenneth T., and Chissom, Brad. (Summer, 1987). The Status of the Middle School Teacher: An Economic Perspective. *American Middle School Education*, 10, (2), 40–50.
6. Henson, Kenneth T., Buttery, Thomas J., and Chissom, Brad. (August, 1986). The Middle School Teacher: A Member of the Community. *The Middle School Journal*, 17, (4): 13–15.
7. Buttery, Thomas J., Henson, Kenneth T., and Chissom, Brad. (Spring, 1988). the Status of the Middle School Teacher: Personal Factors and Community Involvement. *American Middle School Education*, 11, (2): 55–65.
8. Henson, Kenneth T., Buttery, Thomas J., and Chissom, Brad. (November, 1986). The Middle School Teacher: As Perceived by Contemporary Teachers. *The Middle School Journal*, 18, (1), 22–23.

Appendix K

Attending Writing Workshops

By Kenneth T. Henson

I believe in attending workshops to learn how to improve your writing skills. While its true I might be just a little prejudiced since I give writing workshops, I also try to attend each one that comes to town. Others are as hooked as I am. One dedicated writer, a teacher who lives in Hollywood has driven her car to attend my workshops in Anaheim, Los Angeles, Las Vegas, and a week-long workshop in San Diego. I am telling you about her because she has taught me some things about attending workshops.

First, she sees the sacrifice of driving for a few hundred miles as acceptable because she perceives this expense as a professional investment. I think this is important because, when you invest in something, you expect a return—you plan a strategy to recoup your money. This participant arrives at each workshop with a list of questions. She doesn't dominate the workshop by asking all of them. Instead, she catches me during coffee breaks, and she joins my table at lunch. The topic of discussion is always "writing for publication," and she always gets in a few questions which she reads right off of her notepad.

Smart participants also sit up front and take notes. I once taught a course on radioactive fallout to a class of space scientists. As a young, college graduate, I was more than a little intimidated to begin this class. But because of their level of interest and learning strategies, it was the easiest workshop I had ever taught. Since then I have given my two-day writing for publication workshop to over 100 audiences and have always been pleased with the participants. Most of them arrive determined to get specific information, and they don't leave without it. Just remember, whether you bring questions and get them answered or just sit and take whatever comes your way, the cost is the same. Most speakers enjoy determined audiences because they are able to give their very best when the audience is actively pursuing their topics.

I always welcome participants to bring along a piece of their work. Some bring books they have written; others bring only a few sentences of a first draft on an article they hope to complete. The fact that they have something, however small, is a reminder that they are on their way toward a chosen destination. If nothing more, at least take a tentative topic or title or two. You may ditch these for better ones but only because these served as stepping stones enabling you to reach the preferred ones.

To recap these ideas, (thank goodness I no longer feel compelled to say recapitulate), here are some steps that I recommend you take before, during, and following your next writing workshop.

Before the workshop:

1. Write at least three or four questions that you want answered.
2. Jot down two or three possible topics.
3. Try to transform each topic into a tentative title.
4. Write down a goal or two that you hope to reach through writing for publication. These can be professional goals, private goals, or both.

During the writing workshop:

1. Ask at least one question during every segment of the workshop.
2. Arrive early and sit down front.
3. During each break, catch the speaker and ask one quick question.
4. If possible join the speaker for lunch, taking your written list of questions with you.

Following the writing workshop:

1. Review the answers you accumulated at the workshop and consider their implications for your writing program.
2. Review your goals and relate these to your workshop notes. What have you learned that can help you reach your goals?
3. Go home and write. Otherwise everything you have learned will gradually fade. Use the new information as if it were fresh vegetables that cost top dollar and will quickly spoil in the summer heat.
4. Give yourself a pat on the back. You have just done something for yourself that can help you grow.

Appendix L

University Presses

Columbia University Press, 562 W. 113th St., New York, NY 10025   Literature, philosophy, fine arts, Oriental studies, history, social sciences, science, and law.

Duquesne University Press, 600 Forbes Ave., Pittsburgh, PA 15282   Humanities, social sciences for academics, libraries, and college bookstores.

Fairleigh Dickenson University Press, 285 Madison Ave., Madison, NJ 07940   Art, business and economics, history, music, philosophy, politics, psychology, and sociology.

Howard University Press, 2900 Van Ness St., N.W., Washington, DC 20008   Americana, art, business and economics, health, history, music, philosophy, photography, politics, psychology, religion, sociology, sports, science, and literary criticism.

Indiana University Press, 10th and Morton Sts., Bloomington, IN 47405   Humanities, history, philosophy, translations, semiotics, public policy, film, music, linguistics, social sciences, regional materials, African studies, and women's studies.

Iowa State University Press, 2121 S. State Ave., Ames, IA 50010   Biography, history, scientific/technical textbooks, the arts and sciences, statistics and mathematics, and medical and veterinary sciences.

Johns Hopkins University Press, Baltimore, MD 21218   Biomedical sciences, history, literary theory and criticism, wildlife biology and management, psychology, political science, regional material, and economics.

Kent State University Press, Kent State University, Kent, OH 44242   History, regional Ohio, scholarly biographies, literary studies, archeological research, the arts, and general nonfiction.

Louisiana State University Press, Baton Rouge, LA 70803   Humanities, social sciences, Southern studies, French studies, political philosophy, and music.

New York University Press, Washington Square, New York, NY 10003   Art history, history, New York City regional history, philosophy, politics, and literary criticism.

Northern Illinois University Press, DeKalb, IL 60115   History, literary criticism.

Ohio State University Press, 150 Carmack Rd., Columbus, OH 43210   History, biography, science, philosophy, the arts, political science, law, literature, economics, education, sociology, anthropology, and geography.

Ohio University Press, Scott Quad, Ohio University, Athens, OH 45701   Nineteenth century literature and culture, history, social sciences, philosophy, business, and western regional works.

Oregon State University Press, 101 Waldo Hall, Corvallis, OR 97331   Americana, biography, economics, history, nature, philosophy, energy, and recreation, reference, scientific (biological sciences only), technical (energy), and American criticism.

Oxford University Press, 200 Madison Ave., New York, NY 10016   American history, music, political science, and reference.

The Pennsylvania State University Press, 215 Wagner Bldg., University Park, PA 16802   Agriculture, art, business, economics, history, medicine and psychology, music, nature, philosophy, politics, psychology, religion, science, sociology, technology, women's studies, and black studies.

Purdue University Press, South Campus Courts, Lafayette, IN 47907   Agriculture, Americana, art, biography, communication, economics, engineering, history, horticulture, literature, philosophy, political science, psychology, scientific, sociology, and literary criticism.

Rutgers University Press, 30 College Ave., New Brunswick, NJ 68903   History, literary criticism, anthropology, sociology, women's studies, and criminal justice.

Southern Illinois University Press, Box 3697, Carbondale, IL 62901   Humanities, social sciences, and contemporary material.

Stanford University Press, Stanford, CA 94305   European history, history of China and Japan, anthropology, psychology, taxonomy, literature, and Latin-American studies.

Syracuse University Press, 1600 Jamesville Ave., Syracuse, NY 13210   Education, all levels classroom practices, teacher training, special education, trends and issues, administration and supervision, curriculum, and sociology of education.

Teachers College Press, 1234 Amsterdam Ave., New York, NY 10027   Education, all levels classroom practices, teacher training, special education, trends and issues, administration and supervision, curriculum, and sociology of education.

Temple University Press, Broad and Oxford Sts., Philadelphia, PA 19122   American history, public policy and regional (Philadelphia area).

Texas A&M University Press, Drawer C, College Station, TX 77843   History, natural history, environmental history, economics, agriculture and regional studies.

Texas Christian University Press, Box 30783, Fort Worth, TX 76129   American studies, Texana, theology, and literature and criticism.

University of Alabama Press, Box 2877, University, AL 35486   Biography, business and economics, history, music, philosophy, politics, religion and sociology.

University of Alberta Press, 450 Athebasca Hall, Edmonton, Alberta T6G 2E8   Biography, how-to, reference, technical textbooks, and scholarly.

University of Arizona Press, 1615 E. Speedway, Tucson, AZ 85719   Regional Arizona, the Southwest, Mexico, anthropology, space sciences, Asian studies, Southeast Native Americans, and Mexico.

University of California Press, 2120 Berkeley Way, Berkeley, CA 94720   Art, literary studies, social sciences, and natural sciences.

University of Iowa Press, Graphic Services Building, Iowa City, IA 52242   Art, economics, history, music, philosophy, reference, and scientific books.

University of Massachusetts Press, Box 429, Amherst, MA 01004   Afro-American studies, art and architecture, biography, criticism, history, natural history, philosophy, poetry, psychology, public policy, sociology, and women's studies.

University of Michigan Press, 839 Green St., Ann Arbor, MI 48106   Americana, animals, art, biography, business/economics, health, history, music, nature, philosophy, photography, psychology, recreation, reference, religion, science, sociology, technical, textbooks, and travel.

University of Missouri Press, 200 Lewis Hall, Columbia, MO 65211   History, literary criticism, political science, social science, music, art history, and original poetry.

University of Nebraska Press, 901 N. 17th St., Lincoln, NE 68588–0520   Americana, biography, nature, photography, psychology, sports, literature, agriculture, and Native Americans.

University of Nevada Press, Reno, NV 89557   Regional history, natural history, anthropology, biographic, and Basque studies.

University of North Carolina Press, Box 2288, Chapel Hill, NC 27514   American and European history, Americana, classics, oral history, political science, urban studies, religious studies, psychology, dociology, nature books on Southeast.

University of Notre Dame Press, Notre Dame, IN 46556   Philosophy, theology, history, sociology, English literature, government, international relations, and Mexican-American studies.

University of Oklahoma Press, 1005 Asp Ave., Norman, OK 73019   North American Native American studies, Western history, Americana and art, Meso American studies, and Oklahoma.

University of Pittsburgh Press, 127 N. Bellefield Ave., Pittsburgh, PA 15260   Scholarly nonfiction. No textbooks.

University of Tennessee Press, 293 Communications Bldg., Knoxville, TN 37996   Regional: Tennessee, Appalachia, and the South. American history, political science, film studies, sports studies, literary criticism, anthropology, and folklore.

University of Texas Press, Box 7819, Austin, TX 78712   Astronomy, natural history, economics, Latin American and Middle East studies, native Americans, classics, films, medical, biology, health, sciences, international relations, linguistics, photography, twentieth-century and women's literature.

University of Utah Press, 101 University Services Bldg., Salt Lake City, UT 84112   Western history, philosophy, anthropology, Mesoamerican studies, folklore, and Middle Eastern studies.

University of Wisconsin Press, 114 N. Murray St., Madison, WI 53715   Regional: geographical and environmental emphasis.

University Press of Kansas, 303 Carruth, Lawrence, KS 66045   Biography, history, psychology, philosophy, politics, and regional subjects.

University Press of Kentucky, 102 Lafferty Hall, Lexington, KY 40506–0024   History, political science, literary criticism and history, politics, anthropology, law, philosophy, medical history, and nature.

University Press of Mississippi, 3825 Ridgewood Rd., Jackston, MS 39211   Americana, art, biography, business and economics, history, philosophy, politics, psychology, sociology, literary criticism, and folklore.

Utah State University Press, Logan, UT 84332   Biography, reference and textbooks on Americana, history, politics, and science.

Wayne State University Press, 5959 Woodward Ave., Detroit, MI 48202   Americana, biography, economics, history, law, medicine and psychiatry, music, philosophy, politics, psychology, and literature.

Appendix M

Sample Proposal
for Funding

Proposal to the State Department of Education
ECIA, Chapter 2
Mathematics and Science Improvement Program
Closing Date: February 15, 1985

NAME OF APPLICANT INSTITUTION		
The University of		

NAME AND ADDRESS OF OPERATING UNIT		

TITLE OF PROPOSED PROJECT	SUBJECT AREA	
Summer Institute for Precollege Teachers of Physics	Physics	

BUDGET TOTAL	DESIRED STARTING DATE	DURATION
$30,245.00	June 10, 1985	10 weeks

Certification and assurances:

The applicant institution has a State-approved teacher education program in the subject area of the proposed project. The person whose signature appears as project director is authorized by the applicant institution to make this proposal. If funded, the institute will be implemented as approved. The applicant institution will accept responsibility for complying with all applicable State and federal requirements including the resolution of any audit exceptions.

Endorsements for the applicant institution:

Signature _____
Name and Title _____

SECOND SIGNATURE, IF APPLICABLE:

Signature _____
Name and Title _____

Physics Teachers Summer Institute Proposal
Table of Contents

Proposal for Summer Institute
for Pre-College Teachers of Physics

II. PROJECT DESCRIPTION

A. Objectives

Physics is the study of the laws of nature at the most fundamental level. As a result, all of modern science and technology derives much of its success from physics. It is because of scientific discoveries and applications that we live in such a technologically advanced world. For decades the United States has been the world leader in science and technology, and as a result, it is the most economically and militarily powerful nation on earth. These past developments are strongly tied to the successful education of our citizenry, and education will continue to be the key in the development of our nation.

Education in the sciences and mathematics is not only important in terms of training future scientists, engineers, and technicians, it is equally important for those who opt for other careers. We live in a highly complex country in which the results of science and technology affect us on a daily basis. We benefit from advances in communications, entertainment, and medicine, and at the same time, we must contend with unwanted results such as pollution and the danger of nuclear annihilation. As consumers and as voting citizens, both scientists and nonscientists must be prepared to make intelligent decisions regarding science and technology.

Recent studies, such as *A Nation at Risk* by the National Commission on Excellence in Education, have shown that the United States has fallen behind many other industrialized countries in educating its citizens. In addressing the reasons for this decline, the Commission has pointed out a severe shortage of qualified science and mathematics teachers almost everywhere in the country. A recent survey of all the school superintendents in this state has documented the shortage of qualified physics teachers (see Attachment). While this study clearly identified secondary schools where inadequately prepared teachers are teaching physics, it did not include the many small, rural secondary schools throughout the state which do not offer physics at all because of the lack of a properly trained teacher. Both of these situations are of major concern.

Of the many alternatives which could prove to be effective solutions to this dilemma, the most immediate would seem to be to retrain secondary teachers who are already certified in other fields. It is for this reason that the university enthusiastically accepts the state department of education's call for proposals for summer physics institutes. The university proposes an institute which is planned to meet the following objectives. The program will provide 15 teachers from throughout the state opportunities to:

1. Develop the knowledge and understanding which is expected in basic university physics courses.
2. Develop the understandings and skills needed to effectively teach the most commonly used physics textbook in this state's schools at this time. An experienced secondary school physics teacher will provide specific training to help participants use this text in the classroom and in the laboratory.
3. Develop laboratory skills associated with basic physics courses, including the use of computers in the laboratory. Emphasis will be placed on designing low-cost experiments which can be used in all secondary schools, including those with the least facilities, equipment, and supplies.
4. Enable each participant to earn 12 semester hours of credit toward Class B certification in physics. It will be communicated, however, in the announcement of this program, that this benefit to the participants is secondary in significance, that the actual number of hours it will reduce certification attainment will vary among the participants, and that neither the university nor the state department of education will be obligated to provide further grants to those students to help them complete their certification requirements. Indeed, the participants, themselves, will be encouraged to assume this responsibility.

The program will provide for follow-up reinforcement and evaluation during the 1985–86 school year.

B. Participant Selection
1. Number of participants.

Fifteen participants will be provided total support. Up to three additional certified secondary teachers who wish to gain certification in the area of physics will be allowed to participate in the program without support. The university will provide tuition grants for these teachers.

2. Policy for admission.

Of particular concern is that some teachers are now teaching physics in the state's secondary schools without having been certified. Hence, the selection of participants for this institute will give first priority to non-certified teachers who are already teaching physics in our secondary schools.

Other secondary teachers who teach courses in other fields have been offered opportunities to teach physics as replacements for retiring teachers and non-certified teachers. These teachers who also have positions awaiting them next fall will receive secondary priority in the screening of applicants for this institute.

If there are other teachers who hold secondary teaching certificates who wish to achieve certification in the area of physics, they will receive the next priority in the selection process.

Candidates within each of these groups will be rated on the basis of letters from their employers, previous scholarships as evidenced by their academic records, and their personal commitment to teaching physics as expressed in a letter which they will be required to write. An attempt will be made to select applicants from small rural high schools over a broad geographic area.

3. Selection procedure.

a. All teachers holding temporary certification in physics will be identified through state department of education records. Each will receive a notice of this institute. All superintendents and curriculum supervisors will also receive a copy of the announcement. An announcement will also be sent to the state department of education with a request for inclusion in the state newsletter.

b. To be considered for this institute, applications must include a participant information form, a letter(s) of testimony from an appropriate school administrator(s) which specifies the candidates expected teaching assignment, an academic transcript, and, when available, test scores. Applications must be received by April 30, 1985.

c. The selection will be completed and notification will be sent by May 10. Participants will be asked to respond by May 22.

C. Program Content

The institute will begin on June 10, 1985 and run continuously until August 17, 1985. The three courses, tutorials, and seminars will require a total of 266 contact hours. The courses involved are as follows:

Course	Title	Credit (semester hours)	Contact Hours
PHYSICS 110*	Secondary Physics for teachers**	4	60
PHYSICS**	Physics Electives**	8	88
PHYSICS*	Integrated Physics Lab*	0	78
PHYSICS*	Seminar for Teachers*	0	10
PHYSICS	Tutorial*	0	30

*New Courses may be added specifically for summer institute.
**Participants may elect from the following:

PH 101–102 General Physics   4 semester hours
PH 105–106 General Physics with Calculus   4 semester hours
PH 253 Modern Physics   3 semester hours

The major components of this program are as follows:
1.   PHYSICS 110—Secondary School Physics for Teachers.

The most immediate impact the proposed program can have on the teaching of high school physics is to improve the effectiveness and confidence of the participating teachers in the use of a text and related materials in their classrooms in 1985–86. The most widely used of the state approved textbooks is *Modern Physics* (Holt, Rinehart and Winston, 1976). This text will be the focus of a four-credit-hour course meeting throughout the ten weeks of the institute (60 total contact hours). This course will concentrate mostly on the content of the text; laboratory work will be covered in a separate phase of the institute. Although all the institute staff will participate in this course in appropriate ways, the lead instructor will be an experienced high school teacher. The survey of the text will be intensive and detailed. The rationale for the course is that the most important prerequisite for effective use of the text is a teacher who has a thorough competence in all the subject matter of the text and confidence in his/her ability to explain that subject material to students. Each concept in the text will be examined and developed to whatever depth is necessary in order to achieve that competence on the part of all participants.

This course will also cover methods for supplementing the high school physics text. Demonstrations will be used as an aid in teaching the textbook material, with an emphasis on the use of low-cost demonstrations for high school courses. Computer-aided instruction will also be covered. Many high schools are acquiring microcomputers which can be used as a tool to help teach physics, if adequate software is available. A part of the course will emphasize selecting and using software for computer-aided physics instruction.

2.   Physics Electives

Each participant will select one appropriate undergraduate physics course during each session of the summer term. The courses that will be available are PH 101–102, General Physics; PHd 105–106, General Physics with Calculus, and PH 253, Modern Physics. The course selected by the participant will depend upon his/her prior experience. Participants who have not taken a physics course in recent years will be advised to enroll in PH 101. Because of the special needs of the participants, a special section of PH 101 will be offered during the first summer session which will be open only to the institute participants. Participants with a sufficiently strong background may choose instead to take PH 105 or PH 253, which are offered as regular classes during the summer session at the university. In addition to regular class attendance (44 contact hours), each participant will be scheduled for three hours per week (30 total hours) of tutorial meetings with the class instructor. The purpose of the tutorial meetings is to provide the extra in-depth explanations of course material that may be useful to participants who have been away from undergraduate study in the sciences for an extended period. Participants will be evaluated on their work in regular classroom activities as well as tutorial sessions.

3.   Integrated Laboratory for Physics Elective and for Physics 110.

Laboratory experiences are important both for the physics elective and the survey of a secondary school physics text. In the proposed program, these laboratory experiences will be integrated into a single laboratory organized for the institute participants. The laboratory will meet for thirteen three-hour sessions each term (78 total contact hours). Experiments will be selected from the regular lab of the physics elective and, wherever possible, will be conducted in parallel with similar experiments scaled for use in a high school laboratory. The purpose of this approach is to give participants two types of experiences. First, they need knowledge of the type of experiments currently conducted in undergraduate college level courses. More importantly, however, they need practical experience in setting up laboratory experiments appropriate for the high school physics laboratory (high school laboratories are more limited in time schedule and frequently in available equipment than college laboratories). The content of the integrated lab will be planned on an individual basis by the instructor of the physics elective and the consulting high school teacher. A graduate student will assist in the laboratory.

Some of the laboratory meetings will also be devoted to using micro-computers in the physics laboratory. Some experiments will be performed in which the computer is used to assist with taking and analyzing data.

4.   Seminar for Teachers.

In order that the separate components of the program may be brought together to form a more unified experience, a weekly seminar for participants in the institute will be held. The content of the seminar will, in part, be developed based on the perceived needs of participants. In part, however, the seminar will be directed toward supplemental material, such as articles from *Physics Today, Scientific American, Science Education, The Physics Teacher,* and other sources of information on topics of current interest, puzzles, and games that stimulate interest in physics.

D.   Additional Components

1.   Follow-Up Activities

During the second half of the fall semester the co-directors will make an on-site visit to each participant's school. This follow-up visit will serve two purposes: (1) it will provide an opportunity to assess the value of the institute and (2) it will provide each participant opportunities to clarify any misunderstandings and to fill in any knowledge gaps about the content or skills set forth in the objectives of this institute.

2. Evaluation

The proposed program will be subjected to two types of evaluation.

(a) *Evaluation by participants.* Participants will be asked to evaluate the program at two stages. The initial evaluation will be made by a questionnaire administered near the end of the summer session. The effectiveness of each component of the institute will be evaluated. A second evaluation will be conducted near the end of the 1985–86 school year after participants have had classroom experience in using skills developed in the institute.

(b) *Evaluation by an outside observer.* At an appropriate point in the institute an evaluation will be sought from one or more outside observers. For this evaluation an effort will be made to obtain the services of an individual with supervisory experience and special knowledge in secondary level science education, in a state school system, the state department of education, and/or another institution of higher education in the state.

III. STAFF

Professional staff for the proposed institute will be composed of one coordinator, two assistant coordinators, a consulting high school teacher, the instructors of the physics electives, and the lab instructor. Resumes of principal participating staff are included as an appendix.

A. The coordinator of the program will be Kenneth Henson, Head, Area of Curriculum Instruction, College of Education. Philip Coulter, Chairperson and Professor, Department of Physics and Astronomy, and J. W. Harrell, Associate Professor of Physics, will serve as assistant coordinators. Dr. Henson's responsibilities will include attaining publicity for the program, evaluating the program, and preparing an institute report. He will further provide assistance in announcing the program, selecting the participants, conducting the follow-up component, and participating in the weekly seminars. Dr. Harrell's responsibilities will include arranging the weekly seminars, correspondence related to selection and notification of participants, and paperwork associated with participant support. Dr. Coulter will coordinate the responsibilities of Physics faculty in the program, assist with the weekly seminars, and help with the paperwork associated with participant support.

B. Dr. Peggy Coulter, teacher of mathematics and physics at Central High School and Adjunct Associate Professor of Education, College of Education, is being asked to serve as lead instructor for PH 110 and as consultant for the integrated laboratory and the tutorial session for the physics electives. Dr. Harrell will assist in the instruction for PH 110 in the areas of computer-aided instruction and low-cost lecture demonstrations.

C. The instructors for the physics electives are as follows: PH 101—Professor J. W. Harrell; PH 105—Professor Chester Alexander; PH 102—Professor Richard Tipping; PH 253 and PH 106—Professor William Walker.

These individuals will participate as tutorial leaders for participants who are enrolled in their classes. They will also serve as consultants for PH 110, the integrated laboratory, and the seminar for teachers.

D. A physics graduate student with experience in physics laboratories will supervise the integrated laboratory. The content of the laboratory will be a joint responsibility of the consulting high school physics teacher and the instructors for the physics electives.

IV. FACILITIES
    A. Instructional Facilities.

Participants in the program will make use of facilities of the Physics Building of the university for work associated with the physics elective course, PH 110, the integrated laboratory, and tutorials. The computer laboratory in the College of Education will be available for use by the participants at specified times. This computer lab serves as the statewide depository for hardware and software. Participants will have the opportunity to duplicate any of the available programs that are in the public domain. The Seminar for Teachers will be scheduled at a lunch period and will make use of a private dining area in the Continuing Education Center.

    B. Housing Facilities.

Residential participants will be housed in _____
Hall, the Continuing Education Center of the university. Housing is available at the rate of $50 per week. Meal service is provided in the same building at the cost of $12.50 per day. Meal service is also available to commuting participants at the Continuing Education Center.

V. INSTITUTIONAL SUPPORT AND MANAGEMENT

The university is able to commit support to the proposed program in the following ways:

Released time for co-coordinators and secretarial staff (estimated in-kind contributions)

K. Henson	25% for 12 weeks	2,861.54
P. Coulter	15% for 12 weeks	1,759.50
Secretary	10% for 14 weeks	276.00

Supplies for curriculum development projects,
    correspondence, etc. (estimated cash contribution)   200.00
Travel for follow-up activities (estimated cash contribution)
    Per-diem for six days @ $40/day   240.00
Tuition grants will be provided by the university
    for up to three additional unsupported participants.
    3 participants @ $731.50   2,194.50

TOTAL IN-KIND CONTRIBUTION $7,531.54

VI. BUDGET

TUITION AND FEES:

Tuition	@	$552.00		
University Fees	@	104.50		
Lab Fees 3 @ 25.00		75.00		
		731.50 x 15 =		10,972.50

FIRST-TIME APPLICANTS:	6 @	15.00	=	120.00

PARTICIPANT SUPPORT:

Commuters (4)
Mileage
(3000 @ .22)   660.00
Meals
(50 @ $4.25)   212.50
Lab kits/materials   40.00
Textbooks   25.00
                              ———————
                               937.50
                                 x 4 = 3,750.00

Residents (11)
Room
(10 weeks @ $50)   500.00
Mileage   60.00
Meals*   577.50
Lab kids/materials   40.00
Textbooks   25.00
                             ————————
                             1,202.50
                                 x 11 = 13,227.50

TOTAL PARTICIPANT SUPPORT	16,977.50
TRAVEL FOR FOLLOW-UP ACTIVITIES	400.00
INDIRECT COST REIMBURSEMENT (16% of $11,072.50)	1,775.00
PROJECT BUDGET TOTAL for 15	30,245.00

Appendix N

Sample Proposal Rating Form

ECIA, Chapter 2
Mathematics and Science Improvement Program
Closing Date: **February 15, 1985**

INSTRUCTIONS TO THE REVIEWER: Study entire proposal before beginning the rating process because information relevant to a single rating criterion may be found in several sections of the proposal. Respond to each item on the rating form by (1) commenting on the strengths or weaknesses of the proposed project and (2) indicating the earned point-value on the scale, 0 through 5. The highest composite scores will identify the meritorious proposals. It may be helpful to note in your comments where in the proposal you found the significant data.

Indicate the total number of points awarded to the proposal at the bottom of page 3. On page 4 suggest any revisions that would better meet the overall objective of improving statewide teacher qualification in mathematics, chemistry, and physics.

Complete the reviewer identification section below. Send two copies of each review, one signed and one unsigned, to _____

Reviewer Name: _____
Address: _____

Office
Telephone: _____ Hours: _____ Home Telephone: _____

Reviewer Signature: _____

Date Signed: _____

A. Are the objectives to be achieved in the institute precisely stated and reasonable?
   Comment(s): _____

   _____

   Points earned: ____ ____ ____ ____ ____ ____
                 (0)   (1)   (2)   (3)   (4)   (5)

B. Are the recruiting and selection procedures appropriate?
   Comment(s): _____

   _____

   Points earned: ____ ____ ____ ____ ____ ____
                 (0)   (1)   (2)   (3)   (4)   (5)

C. Do the proposed courses give reasonable assurance of achieving the objectives of the institute?
   Comment(s): _____
   Points earned: ____ ____ ____ ____ ____ ____
                 (0)   (1)   (2)   (3)   (4)   (5)

D. Is the instructional staff apapropriate to the successful implementation of the institute?
   Comment(s): _____
   Points earned: ____ ____ ____ ____ ____ ____
                 (0)   (1)   (2)   (3)   (4)   (5)

E. Have adequate provisions been made for management and support personnel?
   Comment(s): _____
   Points Earned: ____ ____ ____ ____ ____ ____
                 (0)   (1)   (2)   (3)   (4)   (5)

F. Are sound evaluation procedures included that will assure obtaining usable information about the degree of attainment of project objectives?
   Comment(s): _____
   Points Earned: ____ ____ ____ ____ ____ ____
                 (0)   (1)   (2)   (3)   (4)   (5)

G. Has the sponsoring institution committed the necessary facilities, including instructional equipment, to the institute?
   Comment(s): _____
   Points earned: ____ ____ ____ ____ ____ ____
                 (0)   (1)   (2)   (3)   (4)   (5)

H. Does the proposal indicate an adequate level of fiscal and in-kind sup-
port from the sponsoring institution?
Comment(s): _____
Points earned: _____ _____ _____ _____ _____ _____
     (0) (1) (2) (3) (4) (5)

I. Is the proposed budget consistent with the size and scope of the pro-
posed institute?
Comment(s): _____
Points earned: _____ _____ _____ _____ _____ _____
     (0) (1) (2) (3) (4) (5)

TOTAL POINTS AWARDED_____

Glossary

Advance   Money a writer receives prior to publication to help cover the expense associated with preparing a manuscript. These expenses are usually deducted from the first royalty check.

Agent, Literary   Writers' assistants who help get contracts, more pay, and more rights and who help improve manuscripts.

Agent's Commission   Fee agents charge for services. Usually 15 percent.

American Society of Journalists and Authors (ASJA)   A national association of over 600 nonfiction writers which works to enhance the quality of writing. Publishes a newsletter and holds conferences. Located at 1501 Broadway, Suite 1907, New York, NY 10036.

Anecdote   A brief account of an incident, often humorous and often used to illustrate a principle.

Annotation   A note that explains a text.

Anthology   A collection of writings by the same or different authors.

A.P.A. Style   American Psychological Association's guidelines and rules for referencing.

Assignment, writing   Commissioned work usually with either a set guaranteed pay or a set kill fee.

Author's Guidelines   Instructions printed in a journal to help prospective contributors prepare article manuscripts for that journal.

Author's Page   A page that lists the author's name and institutional affiliation.

Book Clubs   A club that buys large numbers of books at a grossly discounted price. Author's royalty rate is also usually significantly reduced.

Book Contract   A written agreement that spells out the responsibilities and rights of the author and the publisher.

Book Index   A list of major topics in a book. The author can either make up the index or have the publisher hire someone in-house or outside to make the index whereupon the publisher deducts the indexer's fee from the author's first royalties.

Book Review A written assessment of a book, intended to help a prospective consumer quickly determine if the book is worth buying or reading.

Bottom Line Writing A style of writing that is brief and to the point.

Call for Manuscripts A journal's advertisement written to solicit article manuscripts.

Chunking Breaking complex numbers or other information into small parts to facilitate its comprehension or recall.

Chicago Style A set of referencing guidelines contained in *A Manual of Style* published by the University of Chicago Press. Also called the Taurabian style.

Cliche An overused phrase. Authors are often advised to avoid their use because they are more damaging than helpful.

Collaboration Two or more writers working on the same writing piece.

Content Comparison Chart A matrix designed to facilitate the comparison of similar documents.

Copyedited Manuscript A manuscript that has been edited to remove errors and improve its communications.

Copyright Legal protection against unfair use of an author's work.

Copy Editor A publishing company employee who edits a book or article manuscript, correcting errors in punctuation, spelling, and syntax.

Cover Letter (Also called a covering letter). A letter that accompanies a manuscript. Correctly designed, the cover letter reminds the editor of his or her expressed interest in the work, and reestablishes the author's credibility and the manuscript's currency.

Credibility, Author Assurance that an author has the expertise required to write whatever that author is writing for publication.

Credit Line The author's name and affiliation and sometimes information to capture the reader's interest.

Data Base A collection of related information stored in a computer.

Deadline A specified time by which the author promises to submit a complete manuscript to the editor.

Editing Reading the manuscript and making improvements by changing the content and syntax or removing errors and excessive words.

Editor, Acquisitions An editor who seeks authors and manuscripts that match the company's publishing needs. Often working through agents, the acquisitions editor designs contracts.

Fair Use The amount of copyrighted material that can be used without breaking copyright law.

Filler A short manuscript used to "fill out" a journal issue.

Finishing Out Locating a short manuscript or other material needed to complete an issue of a journal.

Fog Index A formula for determining a writing's level of reading difficulty.

Freelance Writer A writer who sells work to more than one client.

Galley Proof   A manuscript set into print type.

Genre   A category of writings (for example, self-help, how-to, or mystery books).

Glossary   A list of definitions belonging to the same subject.

Guest Editor   A professional outside the journal's staff who is invited or permitted to plan and construct an issue of that journal.

How-to Books   A genre of books designed to explain how to accomplish particular tasks.

Kill Fee   Compensation paid to an author for working on a project that is later canceled.

Lead Sentence   The first sentence in a paragraph.

Model Release   A written document granting permission to use someone's photograph in a publication.

On Speculation   (Also called "on spec"). Non-obligatory agreement to consider a manuscript.

Proactive business writing   A style of writing that empowers businessmen and business women.

Professional Book   A book written to enable individual professionals to improve their professional skills.

Proofreading   Reading a manuscript to remove errors.

Prospectus, Book   A package of material an author designs to convince an acquisitions editor to offer a contract for a new book. Usually includes a acknowledgements, preface, contents, and sample chapters.

Pseudonym   A fictitious name for an author used to protect the author's identity.

Query Letter   (Also called a query). A letter to an editor that precedes the sending of the manuscript. Query letters are used to get the editor's interest in a manuscript.

Quotations, books of   Collections of quotations often used by writers.

Rating Scale   Guidelines supplied by a journal for referees to use when evaluating a manuscript's potential for publication.

Refereed Article   An article judged acceptable by selected professionals who use a rating scale and examine a manuscript anonymously.

Reference Books   Books that writers use when writing.

RFP   Request for proposals, usually containing specific instructions on the desired content and format of proposals, deadline for submission of proposals, and other requirements.

Rejection Slip   A notification from an editor rejecting a manuscript.

SASE   Self-addressed stamped envelope which editors expect author's to provide for the possible return of their manuscripts.

Self-help Books   A genre of books written to help individuals improve their lives.

Self-publishing   An author's publishing his or her own manuscripts.

Support Group   A group of writers who meet regularly to improve their writing skills.

Theme Issue   An issue of a journal having all or most articles written on the same theme.

Trade Book   Fiction and nonfiction books written to be sold to a mass market.

Turnaround Time   The time an editor requires to reach a publishing decision.

University Press   A book publisher associated with and usually belonging to a university. Most university presses specialize in a narrow subject range.

Vanity Publisher   A publishing company that requires authors to pay part of the publishing expenses.

Writer's Market   A comprehensive reference book for authors produced annually by the Writer's Digest.

Writer's Workshops   Workshops designed to help novice writers and experienced writers improve their writing skills.

Name Index

Subject Index

DATE DUE

NOV 4 1998			